Acclaim for
Share My Insanity **and Francesca De Grandis**

"Like all good humorists, Francesca De Grandis has a radical and subversive agenda."   —Peter Coyote, actor and writer

"[A] group studying the writings of Francesca De Grandis or Thomas Merton could provide a wonderful and vibrant community."   —*The Aspiring Mystic*, Carl McColman

"While protesting at the Wisconsin Capitol, I was also in the middle of my own personal upheavals. I sat inside the capitol building, reading a preview copy of *Share My Insanity*. The book helped me to make sense of all the inner and outer turmoil, how it fits into my life, and pointed a way to finding balance again."   —Kat Anderson

"If you're tired of thinking no one understands you, read *Share My Insanity*. You're not alone. And Francesca shows that it's safe to be you and to grow. Here's freedom from putting yourself down and isolation. Freedom to soar."
—MaryColleen MacDougall, President Emeritus
Interfaith Council of Franklin Co Massachusetts

"*Share My Insanity* helps entrepreneurs, potential entrepreneurs, artists, and people from many other walks of life achieve major goals with serenity, joy, and self-love."
—Beverly Macy, Author of *The Power of Real-Time Social Media Marketing*

"[Francesca] is not intimidated by the ignorance, bigotry, and small-mindedness of other people, and she teaches her readers the same supreme self-confidence with wisdom, compassion, and a great deal of humor."
—Oberon Zell-Ravenheart, Author of
Grimoire for the Apprentice Wizard

"Francesca De Grandis made numerous breakthroughs . . . her insightful research in anthropology led to her innovative work in the modalities of healing."
—S.S. Kush, Professor of Anthropology

"She has the trustworthy ethics of a Buddhist priest [and] psychologically sound respect for the complexity of human process . . . The techniques Francesca teaches for spiritual growth and healing of psyche, soma, and soul are creative and powerful."
—Adrienne Amundsen, Ph.D., and clinical psychologist

"Everyone is crazy. We all have our struggles. We all need this book. This includes people with mental disabilities, their caretakers, and loved ones."
—Angela Terhune, Para Educator, Severe Mental
Handicap Classroom, Middle School

"If someone doesn't know the subculture in which people with mental disabilities live, he might condescendingly rush to defend us from *Share My Insanity*. Francesca's work has contributed to my mental health like nothing else has. Nothing replaces therapy and meds, but she helped save my butt, and my therapist approves."

—Tyler Gray, diagnosed with Bipolar Type I, and Panic Disorder

"Francesca, you have something very special to offer to the world. [Housebound with physical disabilities,] your home is the center—but not the boundary—of your love. You certainly reach out great distances to touch many people."

—Steve Aschmann, Unitarian Universalist minister

"I could draw stars and rainbows all over this book. I've been spiritually alienated by books that espouse one right way of being. But Francesca's different. She doesn't try to force a square peg into a round hole. *Share My Insanity* gives me a sense of connection and contentment, and snaps me back to myself, my body, and my needs. It's real—it's an intimate conversation with Francesca. Maybe that's why I felt at home and accepted."

—Ljot Lokadis, gender performer

"Francesca sees the world through the eyes of a wise spiritual master, a sadhu, a shaman. And she writes in the voice of a renegade, a wild woman, a trickster, a sacred clown. The resulting combination of her profound sensibility and wacky lunacy is irresistible and transformative."

—Donna Henes, Author *The Queen of My Self*

Share My Insanity

Other Books by Francesca De Grandis

Her Winged Silence: A Shaman's Notebook

Be a Goddess!: A Guide to Celtic Spells and Wisdom for Self-Healing, Prosperity, and Great Sex

Goddess Initiation: A Practical Celtic Program for Soul-Healing, Self-Fulfillment, and Wild Wisdom

The Modern Goddess' Guide to Life: How to Be Absolutely Divine on a Daily Basis

Be a Teen Goddess!: Magical Charms, Spells, and Wiccan Wisdom for the Wild Ride of Life

The Ecstatic Goddess!: Wild Meditations, Lyrical Rituals, and Earth Sexuality for the Pagan Heart

Bardic Alchemy: Enchanted Tales about the Quest for God/dess and Self

Share My Insanity

Insanity

It Improves Everything

Francesca De Grandis

White River Press
Amherst, Massachusetts

Share My Insanity: It Improves Everything

Material in this book has appeared, perhaps in different form, in: The Third Road training material; Another Step training material; Writing Magic training material; www.outlawbunny.com; and in presentations—live, and on radio and television—throughout the United States and Britain.

Cover art by outlaw bunny. Cover design by Dave Gilham. Layout by Kathi Somers.

First published 2011

White River Press
PO Box 3561
Amherst, MA 01004

www.whiteriverpress.com

ISBN: 978-1-935052-53-1

Library of Congress Cataloging-in-Publication Data

De Grandis, Francesca.
  Share my insanity : it improves everything / Francesca De Grandis.
     p. cm.
  ISBN 978-1-935052-53-1 (pbk. : alk. paper)
  1. Self-help--Humor. 2. Life--Humor. I. Title.
  BF632.D4 2012
  158.102'07--dc23
                                    2011029120

Dedicated to my community

Contents

Chapter Four
Cock-eyed, Out of Your Mind, and Having Taken Leave of Your Senses   102

Chapter Five
Lovers Like the Full Moon, It Turns Them into Werewolves   141

Chapter Six
Parenting, Potato Chips, and Postal Carriers   173

Chapter Seven
Spiritual Fun—Making Wreaths with Bottle Caps 214

Share My Insanity

Chapter One
Maybe You're Not Crazy Enough

Perhaps you're a dreamer whose family says, "Get *real!* You'll never find a life that's up to *your* expectations." Or maybe you believe in Faeries—I mean *really* believe. Or you think world peace is possible and devote yourself to it 24/7. Then again, you might get hunches so accurate that they creep out your friends. There are innumerable ways to be lusciously "odd"—I couldn't name them all.

The world is full of marvelous oddballs; we who are oddballs are blessed indeed. This book is for us; it's for original thinkers—people who want to soar past the confines of limiting definitions, stifling mindsets, and self-defeat mechanisms.

Don't you dare think, "Well, I don't fit into her examples of innovative, so this book isn't for me." Just trust your own definition of innovative. Originality can be an inclusive—not *exclusive*—concept. For example, your uniqueness might express itself in the way you manage the family's household budget, get the kids to school on time, and raise happy children. "Us plain folk" have *plenty* of our own special ways.

1

If life isn't going the way you want, your creative efforts lack oomph, or you're too afraid of living life all the way, maybe you're not crazy enough. Maybe you need a complete lunatic—like me—to help you get utterly loony.

There Are a Hundred Types of Useful Insanity—I Have Them All

Consider the following highly respectable list: Sane. Sober. Rational. Balanced. Logical. Acceptable. The well-researched option. The decision based in hard evidence. The reasonable risk. The prudently pondered plan.

It's a great list, a useful, absolutely necessary one. However, I've learned that there's also enormous merit in: The crackpot opinion. Doing something crazy because the other option is even crazier. Illusions of grandeur. The wildest, most impossible and unreasonable goals. A hope that's utterly ridiculous and totally luscious. There are a hundred types of useful insanities. I seem to have every one of them, and I wrote this book so you could borrow as many as you'd like. They have been pivotal to effectiveness, originality, and success in everything I do. They also make me whole.

My twenty-plus years as a pastoral counselor and spiritual teacher have focused on helping people find both personal fulfillment and the power to make a difference in their communities. By *personal fulfillment*, I don't mean the "I'm so holy" version, but the yummy, good food, good sex, "I love my feet" rendition. My pastoral counseling is what you could call *renegade style*. This interfaith ministry has taught me that I'm hardly the only one who can benefit from my off-the-wall theories and methods.

Positive feedback from my students and counseling clients made me realize I should commit my insanity to paper. Crazy times call for healthy madness!

Share My Insanity. It Improves Everything

I have paid many bills over the years by writing books. Before doing that, my *sole* bread and butter for ten years was working as a spiritual counselor/teacher. A wacky mindset does not leave one bereft of practicality, discipline, or a work ethic (which are all required to be self-employed, let alone earn your living as a spiritual teacher outside organized religion, which is next to impossible to do.).

Folks get real solutions from my sane insanity. Inner peace, personal growth, sensitivity to loved ones, career advancement, social change, and recovery from trauma can demand a shift from the placid, mental middle ground reminiscent of being in a chain store until the bland aesthetic and visual boredom stupefies the senses and the soul. Healthy madness is the way to go!

This book will always give down-to-earth perspectives and methods that help you get what you want from life and have the maximum power to make the world a better place for everyone. And I suggest solutions a person can actually manage to *accomplish*.

Madness knows no bounds. My insanity improves *everything*. We're going to take on everything from New Age dogma to effective prayer to political activism to the fine art of flirting to urban pretenses to rural eccentricities to parenting.

(Um, I *am* a New Age, praying, political, flirting, pretentious, eccentric, formerly urban, now rural parent. I make fun of myself. After all, if I don't, who will?) I treasure a letter from a member of the U.S. armed forces stationed in Iraq, who told me that one of my books helped her stay together during her tour of duty.

People recovering from trauma, or who wish to further an already happy life, or who are doing *both* have found my approach immensely useful. Ditto straight-ahead fun lovers who want to get the most out of life and be everything they can, inside and out. But wait, there's more! Sharing my insanity has also profited those who want to: improve their spiritual life; enhance self-confidence; create self-fulfillment (including sexually); or be more effective agents of change through volunteer, political, or other community service, or with their own families and friends.

I invite readers from all religions and people who are fine 'n' dandy without one. I'm focusing not on religion but on a spiritual sensibility. Folks who don't know me well sometimes expect all my close friends to be overtly spiritual people [shamans, New Agers, priest(esse)s, etc.]. Nah! A lot of people who don't *consider* themselves spiritual are among the most spiritual people I meet. It's about how you treat others, not about what you think or say. It's about loving *action* and being of service, not rhetoric or insistently preaching at someone about how your way of understanding the cosmos is best, and will solve her or his problems. Just as my close pals are often not "spiritual," many atheist and agnostic readers tell me that my rants (um, I mean *ideas*) affirm their own thoughts and choices, and help them in their efforts to be kind, compassionate, and helpful to others.

Regarding my personal stories: I hope the enclosed moments from my life bring you some of the power, healing, and insights they represent to me. In sharing the risks I have taken in thought, word, and deed, I encourage you to love and draw on your own healthy madness. After all, insanity's very nature is the privilege to have your own special form of nuttiness.

Another advantage is the inability to recognize any topic as off-limits. Thus, you will say something when others don't dare. This is a way to take on matters that *matter*. Speak your crazy mind. Our eccentricities, off-the-wall perspectives, and human peculiarities are often the urges, visions, and acts out of which we can make heroic lives.

Rants, Revelations, and Recipes

People constantly raise their eyebrows at my remarks and choices. So I started making up names for what I think and do, as a way to explain and honor it. (Or at least to make it seem cool.) Hence, the following list of terms will sufficiently arm you against those who are perhaps too sane for their own good (they are *definitely* too sane for mine): Wacky wisdom. Illuminated lunacy. Healthy madness. Crazy Sage teachings. Insanely-fresh-perspectives-that-measure-up-to-today's-modern-challenges. Highly technical terms, aren't they? In this book, I use these and similar expressions as synonyms.

Sometimes wacky wisdom is expressed through a revelation, a great big "ah-ha" that only the insanity of the starry-eyed mystic creates—or trusts. Wacky wisdom might instead be expressed when one is so fed up that the boundaries of propriety are forgotten, and one starts waving one's arms up and down while loudly declaring everything one has always needed to say but left unspoken. There are many means whereby healthy madness expresses itself.

Therefore, this book consists of rants, revelations, and recipes—yes, yummy food recipes that you can mix up in your kitchen—as well as memoirs, anecdotes, wisecracks, methods, and musings. These are all ways to share my insanity.

If my writing doesn't seem insane to you, great! I actually think I'm perfectly clear-headed. The point isn't for me to jump up and down, pointing to myself, as I yell, "Hey, look at me! Ain't I *so* wacky?" Garg. *That* is not wacky wisdom. I just want to share.

The other point is humor. Divinely dizzy ditziness—let's keep coining terms to show insanity in a positive light—is well expressed through wit, even if it's the witless variety. We're talking anything from the roll-on-the-floor-howling-with-laughter-that-embarrasses-you, to the wee smirk that you cover with a hand because the joke's just *too* wicked, to the sigh of both exasperation and relief brought on by the blackest humor, to the slight lift of the corner of your mouth because you're quietly, but truly, amused. Suddenly, we can escape the boundaries of our oh-too-sensible-society.

That only begins a long list of humor's benefits. Laughing in the worst of times may be crazy, but those of us who have weathered those times know that anything even mildly amusing can keep you going.

I'm not being callous or cruel when I crack jokes about sensitive subjects; it's important to be able to laugh about the most serious issues. I'm a person with disabilities—wheelchair and all. You *bet* I make cripple jokes. The more scary or dire a human concern—and the more pain and tragedy involved—the more it may require a seemingly ruthless humor to cope (and perhaps even triumph). It is yet another privilege of the insane to employ such boldness. Please, do.

Sharing my insanity with others is a form of traditional spiritual healing (more about that later) that can heal both their souls and mine. It is also practical, helping folks be highly effective in their mundane endeavors.

Before going any further, it is vital to address some specific issues.

The suffering of my fellow humans is one of the main things that motivate my work. The concept of healthy madness is not meant to trivialize the hell of mental illness. The exact opposite is true. I know that the anguish of some people with mental disabilities is so enormous that it can be beyond description. And I believe that a *healthy* madness can help you avoid—and even heal—the psychological damage that society inflicts.

But a spiritual approach is no substitute for a competent psychiatrist or therapist. It is an erroneous—though all-too-common—belief that clear intentions and spiritual development can completely explain or fully repair the torment of severe mental or emotional disorders and pain. Medications and psychological treatment can make the difference between life and death for someone who suffers from schizophrenia, depression, bipolar disorder, or other psychiatric problems. And if anything I say in this book feels triggering or unhelpful to you, please, by all means, put the book down or ignore what doesn't work for you.

Our society's definition of what is healthy does cause immense suffering, and invalidates some of our most important traits. Spirituality is an approach—as is a deep embrace of viewpoints that are too often dismissed as "crazy"—that can be immensely helpful to people confronting all *kinds* of challenges and difficulties. Just don't use either tool as a substitute for other types of work. Please don't!

Every chapter after this one focuses on an arena of life, such as romance, community service, or potato chips. Nevertheless, feel free to skip from a piece in one chapter to a piece in another. Indulge your penchant for flitting about. It'll be a relief! Furthermore, maybe you'll find—or affirm—the wisdom innate in your meandering.

I will repeat myself, because we learn not only through repetition but by hearing the same things in a variety of contexts, each revealing a new facet of the topic in question.

Sometimes this book will fly from one topic to another in a way that may make no obvious sense. That's when you let go of logic. Go along for the ride. And don't squelch the ridiculous thoughts or feelings that come up—they might be your wacky wisdom connecting the dots for you: The universe is like a connect-the-dots picture except each dot connects with all the other dots, making a picture that only the mad see. That picture can inspire and empower, can provide experiences so profound or loving that you're flying. Share my insanity, and if you don't see the picture at first, you will in time.

Yes, I'm asking you to trust a crazy person. It can take some real insanity to shake up your life enough to open you to greater joy and possibility. This book ain't standardized white-bread self-help-101, but ecstatically-unhinged-earthy-grungy-ancient-wonder. *Your* goals, challenges, and dreams have immense value. They're worth more than me writing—or you using—the same ol' material. It never managed to take you *all the way* to what you long for, deserve, and are capable of achieving. You just need the right kind of help.

Chapter Two
Confidently Coping with Chaos

Each piece in this chapter presents wacky ways to overcome the typical challenges that are just part of everyone's daily life yet feel monumental and overwhelming. For example, credit card bills.

Okay, credit card bills often *are* monumental problems. (I know mine are!) This chapter will also look at ordinary and not-so-ordinary daily problems that constitute major life crises.

As you read, you'll see that the Crazy Sage often speaks "sanely," seriously, and logically; if it was *all* "nonsense," naysayers wouldn't be threatened and consequently quick to discount it as nuts. Besides, Crazy Sage teachings, to truly convey wisdom, have to be part of a larger teaching that is sober and linear. Or you might say the reverse: that the serious, logical material is *part* of wacky wisdom. It's a matter of perspective. The point is, we don't have to choose between the two. It's not an either/or proposition. Insanity defies such limits. We can have it *all*, and *must* in order to be true to ourselves.

It will spare you confusion if you know that I use *subchapter*, *essay*, and *piece* as synonyms. Enough explanations. Let's move on, to the first piece about confidently coping with chaos.

The Surgeon General Has Declared, "Living May Be Hazardous to Your Health."

The Surgeon General declared, "Living may be hazardous to your health." That's just like the government, to back off with a half-truth. There's no doubt about it—living *is* bad for you. Fatal, in fact. No matter what you do, life will get you. Not only at the end of your days, but also in the meantime. You are constantly ill, depressed, or suffering any number of other problems. And it doesn't matter *how* you live—when it comes to diet, exercise, stress-reduction, and so on—because as long as you're alive, you'll eventually die.

I even suspect life itself is a carcinogen. I know that sounds crazy, but you *have* seen the title of this book, right? Besides, I relentlessly pursue validation of my crackpot theories: I called Domenick Casuccio of The American Cancer Society, and he agreed that my premise has validity. He also said you can link cancer to just about anything and concurred that, nowadays, unless you're the-boy-in-the-bubble, you're subjected to *something*.

So when it comes to doing a good job of coping with whatever comes our way, it's not about avoiding unpleasantries. Even breathing eventually wears out the lungs. We need to live well *while* life is doing its dastardly deed of fatally deteriorating us. We need to find serenity amidst chaos. More, we need to find meaning in chaos. Because what I understand to be God (Goddess, Nameless Creator, Flow of Goodness in the Universe, Great Eagle, Process, God/dess Within, or Whatever You Choose to Call It) has an enormous intelligence. It's so big *all* things are comprehended by it. Therefore, I think chaos, randomness, and inexplicable events are not in fact chaotic, random, or inexplicable. God (or Whatever You Call It) has a perfectly understandable plan. However, you'd have to be a deity, with that omniscient brainpower, to understand it.

And my job, as a finite human, is to understand what bits I can, and make peace with *all* of it. Part of the latter is plugging into the whole shebang, so that it can carry me toward my ideal life. Pulling off these things demands wacky wisdom.

Before we go further, here's an aside about God: Depending on the moment, my personal god ranges from The Old Man—wearing a long beard and sitting on a cloud—who protects me with all His mighty might, to the compassionate Mother who holds me tenderly, safely, every second of the day. Those are only two members of what I call "my God committee." Put the whole committee together, and I have everything I need in a Divinity.

Spirituality is a complex, personal thing. You may have your own definition of God. Is your God a tree? A genderbender? There are infinite ways to define the Divine. Not all include deity. Do you see the Divine not as Deity but as the Cosmic Song? Dance? The power of love? Henceforth, I'll do two things:

1) For simplicity's sake, I'll use the word *God* or *Goddess*, and *He* or *She*. Whenever you see either, please adapt it to suit your own belief system.

2) I'll randomly alternate God's gender, before the

attempt to do otherwise makes you and me crazy. In fact, deities aside, I'll randomly alternate *all* gender pronouns (e.g., *he, she, her, his*) to alleviate our language's gender bias. I know no pronoun usage that truly addresses gender issues. For example, alternating pronouns may not represent the gender identification of someone who feels like neither man nor woman, nor even like a combination of both, but like a third gender. Gender can be just as complex and personal as spirituality. It is great when a person finds pronoun usage that works for them as an *individual*, but I know no boilerplate that works for all readers. I trust your brain and heart: I hope you will adapt my pronouns if you need to, because I want you here, with me.

Back to our topic: Everything I've said so far in this piece is a *core* wacky wisdom—a primary jumping off point, philosophy, or perspective from which one can do well by oneself (and for one's community). Here's a personal example.

Like many people, I am perpetually tired. Try as I might, there's never enough rest. I meditate on rest, pray for rest, lay down to rest, take herbs to rest, discuss rest, and ask Goddess why I'm resisting rest.

If I finally manage to sleep longer at night, I work too hard the next day. I learn to nap, then can't sleep at night. This is serious—I'm so exhausted that I have terrible health problems.

I keep giving this problem to God and He doesn't fix it. So, I try harder and worry more.

Then today I realized it doesn't matter whether I get the sleep I need, because life's a carcinogen anyhow—or at least causes *some* kind of fatal condition, as well as problems throughout your days. The point is not whether I sleep enough. I supposedly put that problem in God's hands. Sure, God's not gonna let me sit back and stop trying. She's only gonna help me if I help myself. But, more important than sleep *is how I deal with the lack thereof.*

As I said, I gave that lack of sleep to Goddess, told Her, "Please take care of this. It's beyond *me. You've* got all that omnipotence, so I trust you're up to the challenge." Therefore, *I can stop worrying now and make the best of my sleepy days.* I can keep trying to sleep but not brood about it, since I know God is covering my back.

I suspect that this will help me sleep better.

By the way, the Surgeon General never issued the statement attributed above. The fictitious quote was a joke. I hope that's clear, so that there's no reason for men in black suits to show up at my door.

All **Times**
4/03

The following can be used as a prayer or affirmation. The quick and dirty explanation of affirmations: An affirmation *affirms* a belief or set of beliefs, an action or set of actions, an emotional sensibility, or a specific spiritual mode of being. Saying an affirmation, silently or out loud, is kind of a positive reinforcement. It helps you be whatever it is you are reciting.

If you don't believe the words are true, that's ok—
sometimes, the point of saying them is to change your beliefs
or feelings. In these cases, reciting the words is not dishonest.
It is an experiment: After you've used an affirmation for a
while, see if it has started to shift you, opened you to a better
way of being.

You can say an affirmation just once, but some people
find value in reciting it over and over for a minute or two.
You can also repeat it once a day for a while, or several
times a day for awhile. Some folks find it useful to slowly
say an affirmation by reciting one small bit, then taking a
silent moment to be with the bit you've said, then reciting the
next bit, being with *that* a moment, one bit at a time until
the affirmation's end. Throughout this book are action steps:
affirmations, exercises, and other practices and acts that
further help you *embody* wacky wisdom.

Sleep.

Not worry about sleep.

Sleep.

After prayer for sleep.

Rest.

After prayer for rest.

Acceptance

and no worry

when there's neither rest nor sleep.

Because Holy Mother and Father—Divine Parents—watch over

not only our sleeping nights

but our sleepless times.

They take care of us

fully and well,

at *all* times.

Mother and Father—

not worry, but

Mother and Father.

In Praise of Chaos

To sum up the last essay: A reconciliation with, and
constructive use of, life's innate chaos—and with what *seems*
like poor planning by God concerning humankind's lot—
demands healthy madness. A lot of this book's stories and
suggestions come down to exactly that, in one way or another.
(Thank God for insanity!)

So let's look *at* chaos. Most people think of it as a bad
thing. In fantasy movies, the villains worship a god of chaos,
who strives to overthrow all that is sane and good. But a chaos
god would probably try to triumph over all that is sane and
ridiculous. Sanity's not always the best measure of our needs
or morality.

Of course, chaos is like everything else—it can be
really good, really bad, or anywhere in between. However,
we've all been indoctrinated with the idea that chaos is bad,

bad, bad. Therefore, let's look at the *other* side to balance things. There is no way this explanation can be entirely linear. Believe me, I tried. Finally, after throwing the manuscript across the room in frustration, I had to laugh. The papers sat in a jumbled heap, in a beautiful chaos. And I, someone who *never* becomes that frustrated writing, understood that I had been attempting the ridiculous: to organize chaos.

What a fool! Too sane. Instead, let's go along for Mr. Toad's Wild Ride—one of my favorite parts of Disneyland— not worrying if we careen about a bit, and trusting that in the end, things will not only come out fabulously, but also make sense (well, a mad and *useful* sense).

There are those who may discount my personal tales, musings, and opinions—which is what you'll find herein—with, "Aw, you're *nuts!*" (They're not reading this book, probably.) Then there are the individuals who either agree I'm crazy but consider that a compliment, or don't consider me the least bit odd. Perhaps they *celebrate* the uncontrollable chaos that is life. They have enough madness to understand—even if it's subconsciously—that the orderly universe perceived by most of the populace is actually an illusion. Society, emotions, atoms, and—let's be thorough and accurate—life itself, in all its parts, are actually glorious and *beneficent* jumbles. Existence is an every-which-way rhapsody—that's the *real* norm.

Now add the following to the mix, as the ride takes a sharp curve. (Hang in with me for a bit.) Ancient shamans knew, and modern physicists understand, that the entire cosmos is like the connect-the-dots painting mentioned earlier, in which all the dots connect to all the other dots. You sneeze, and a pizza burns in Chicago.

Some people have a profound grasp of this. They may not be able to boil it down into a theoretical explanation, but they apply it all the time. A person might, for example, bring up her feelings about work at a corporate board meeting. Discounted by another board member who insists, "Emotions don't belong here. This is *business*," our wholly holistic friend might aptly respond, "I bring *all* of me to work." Some people think she's rambling on, but she's perceiving the impact caused by the relationship between things. Dots! What "things" do I mean? In the case of our emotive board member: When you bring your feelings (dots) to work, you are more likely to tailor the business's products or services (dots) to customers' needs (dots), instead of selfishly focusing on financial gain. If *all* of you (lotsa dots!) is functioning, you can be a hero *and* make bucks.

When people connect dots that seem even more unrelated, they're *really* gonna be called nuts. The mystic who feels the union of *all* things is a perfect example of someone discounted as out-of-his-mind. Funny thing is: he *is*. But in the best possible way! He's traveling beyond the limits of his own brain and body, dancing on the high wires between the stars, and having adventures in the spaces between atoms.

As such, he might tap into that connect-the-dots picture. From the perspective that everything is isolated in its own separate, labeled box, where it sits static, controllable, and utterly knowable, that connect-the-dots picture appears as chaos—endless random connections between dots. But with a mind askew? It's love. It's God. It's life and bounty and opportunity. It's the Divine Blueprint. And this brings us full circle 'round: crazy people and chaos go hand in hand; insanity can help us see the connections, construct the full picture, and thus tap into chaos's gifts.

If you have a shred of common sense, you are thinking, "Um, Francesca? Does this have any *practical* use? Is this at all relevant to my life? WILL THIS HELP ME?"

You betcha. Since chaos underpins our daily goings-on, we can control our lives if, paradoxically, we surrender to chaos and trust its *goodness*. (I am *not* suggesting we surrender to the evil deterioration of either society's necessary order or of your mental and moral health.) And, once again, a lot of healthy madness comes down to exactly that—ways to benefit from chaos. Here's a way right now: Remember all the dots in you *also* connect to all the other dots in the universe. In addition, you *are* a universe, a vast wealth of different aspects (dots!), all of them connected, whether you know it or not. You work as a whole.

Of course, you often need to draw on just a part of yourself: If a friend's mom has died, you're likely to put your party self aside to be less carefree and more sensitive to what your grieving, vulnerable friend needs. That's healthy and appropriate. Nevertheless, we too often compartmentalize ourselves. Some of the most brilliant mathematicians of our time will tell you they use intuition to reach their conclusions. If hunches can be useful in *math*, which is supposedly a left-brain linear process, that tells us that a lot of dots in us profitably connect to all *sorts* of situations.

What I've learned working with clients, however, is

that we tend to ruthlessly filter the constant ideas, hunches, and emotions that rise to the surface of our awareness. In other words, I've watched my clients ignore all sorts of useful information they're giving themselves.

The following counter-method, called *Removing the Filter*, helps them. I suggest not reading about it before you try it, or you might defeat its purpose. And don't stop reading just because you think you need time to prepare. Removing the filter is an easy technique. Simply keep on reading, and follow the instructions as they come up.

I'm going to ask a question. Please answer it without pause. Don't even pause for one-tenth of a second. It doesn't matter if your answer is incorrect, dishonest, gibberish, or otherwise "wrong."

Your specific response is unimportant, because the point of the exercise is to recognize and remove the filter that causes us to automatically discount half the input we give ourselves, often so quickly that we don't even realize it. Once the filter is *off*, new wisdoms and self-knowledge flow. We notice a marvelous abundance of ideas, intuitions, motivations, feelings, etc. You do have to sort through them to find the useful and accurate stuff, but with the filter in place, we don't get the chance to sort wheat from chaff.

Even if you're in touch with yourself, please do this exercise. My clients include the most self-aware people possible; they still profit from removing their filters. They often filter enough to miss *some* awareness and personal truths necessary to live as fully as they dream of, or even to be on top of the minutiae of daily life.

Again, as soon as you read the question, don't read ahead *past* it, just answer. Respond even if the question makes no sense to you. Here's the question: **What do you need to tell yourself right this second?**

Did you hesitate even for a fraction of a second? If so, good chance your filter was on and kept out a part of you (a dot) that wanted to join in the conversation. If you're like most people, you paused, however briefly.

Though I say that removing the filter is the important thing, as opposed to what you answer, half the time what you declare *is* remarkably pertinent to your current situation— information that'll help you bunches. (Dots connecting!)

Removing the filter completely might take one-on-one guidance from someone suitable. But the sheer attempt to remove the filter—by doing the above exercise—loosens it. Wisdom, in the form of thoughts, feelings, or hunches, starts to slip by your guard. You also are more likely to notice your filter is on, and listen to yourself better.

I'm not suggesting you're dishonest or otherwise screwed up. Perhaps you *usually* hesitate just to gather your thoughts. That's an ideal thing to do in society. However if you do it during this exercise, it is likely a self-defeating avoidance of *some* of those thoughts, and happening so quickly you don't realize it. Draw on *all* your wisdom.

We don't just filter our thoughts, but also emotions, physical sensations, hunches, etc. They're all connected dots. Throughout your day, note what you discard as irrelevant (or otherwise unworthy).

Not that you should mindlessly act on whatever pops up. But take a second to see if it has worth, find out if it's relevant to the immediate moment at hand. Do this enough and, well, consider it lunacy training: You'll more and more find how *lots* of the dots in you connect to your activities in life-changing ways. In addition, removal of the filter is an innate result of just reading this book and taking its recommended action steps. The text also gives other suggestions to help you draw on all your inner resources. For now: Believe in yourself—exactly who you are right this minute, with your seemingly random ideas, urges, etc.

Realize that when your mind takes confusing mental leaps or reaches conclusions that seem to represent an absurd muddle, it might instead be the wisdom of your inner Crazy Sage emerging. In that vein:

As with my explanation of chaos, many lessons that I give seem to leap about illogically in a random connection of all the dots. If you want to understand the true nature of those connections—and the deeper logic that's operating—a step-by-step linear explanation won't help. Instead, go along for the ride—Toad's Wild Ride!—and read this book for the *experience*, which will convey hidden wisdoms and powers. Now, let's move onto one of my favorite Chaos Gods—Bugs Bunny.

Bugs Bunny: Spiritual Role Model

I absolutely worship Bugs Bunny and suspect my response to him is hardly unique: If I'm bogged down, his antics change all that. I end up with a grin so huge that it opens up my chest, my spirit, my outlook, and the world. I feel big and capable, a giant of productive, optimistic well-being.

As he does for many people, Bugs tickles my heart and makes me giggle with delight. I think a lot of people identify with his mischief and outrageous boldness. They want to take the sort of crazy risks and perpetuate the same manic plots that he gets away with. Maybe they don't literally want to do this, but his escapades symbolically embody something we long for—not to actually hurt people the way the Warner rabbit does, but to enjoy his mad freedom and fun. Here's how I discovered he's a great spiritual role model:

I was working on a publishing project with an extraordinarily controlling person. She would manipulate, wheedle, and lie to have her way, ignoring my legal and artistic right to codetermine the project's parameters. I was letting this drive me crazy—not in a good way.

She was engaged in war, and I finally decided that I would neither stop her nor engage in her fight. I let her continue on—all on her own. She could have her battle all by herself! I don't mean I went belly up; I held firm about the project.

I laughed with a friend at the absurdity of it, then he added, "It's like the Bugs Bunny cartoon—he's sword fighting, but actually he just holds the sword while reading a book, or doing his nails, while his opponent fights away and gets exhausted." Cartoon Taoism.

Let's jump from Taoism to totems. A totem is a spiritual tool used in many native cultures; it is an animal that has powers one tries to emulate. And/or a totem is an animal you identify with, or even identify *as* in some way; its strengths, weaknesses, and wisdoms are within you. Common totems are wolf, eagle, owl, hawk, fox, deer, bear, coyote, and spider— all very magnificent, impressive animals. While my totem is rabbit. (Yup, a wee, hopping ball of fur and nervousness.) In addition, I fancy myself a spiritual outlaw (my website is www. outlawbunny.com). So I of course identify with and want to be like Bugs. Since my friend's quip, Bugs has become an additional totem for me, in the sense of a role model.

My friend's fabulous analogy also reminded me to draw on, let's call Her, the Great Trickster. I prayed, "Let me be like Bugs and not go nuts from this *impossible* woman." Voilà—I managed to avoid being drawn into her "battle," kept the partial control needed for the project to be high quality, and stayed relatively relaxed. Adapt my prayer for yourself. It works.

I believe there's a Goddess of Chaos, The Ultimate Trickster, and from Her fingers pour currents of events that necessarily disrupt our lives. This flurry of seemingly meaningless problems, roadblocks, and maybe even insanity ends up being exactly what we need to become happier. This Divine Fool also helps me emulate Bugs Bunny—for example, by placidly polishing my nails mid-attack.

Bugs is the modern embodiment of the ancient trickster (a spiritual guide whose antics conveyed life lessons. More on that later.). Nobody does it better. By following his example, we can coast through life's ups and downs. Therefore, your spiritual homework, boys and girls, is to watch a Bugs Bunny cartoon. Plain 'n' simple: So do *not* try to analyze it, grimly setting your jaw and clouding your mind with anxious focus. Instead, relax and simply enjoy the show. Remember what I said earlier: All the dots in you connect, in the sense that every bit of you is connected to every other bit. When you sit down to watch the cartoon, don't even try to recall why you're doing so. Part of you will remember, even if it's subconscious. As you watch, that part will offer up a lesson with no effort on your part; you'll see a practical way to cope with your day. Or a week later something will pop into your head along the same line.

You'll also acquire more trust of your aforementioned inner chaos—because you watched the cartoon without being hyper-organized. You let a lesson "randomly" emerge in your consciousness. If you want, try to apply the filter work from "In Praise of Chaos:" Watch the cartoon and don't edit any lessons you extrapolate as bad or good; don't discount one without first looking at it to see if it has any value.

Here's a lesson that emerged for me, a way that the big gray bunny uses wacky wisdom to cope with daily problems. I call it the *Crazy Side-Step*, a little dance he does that we can all use: My all-time favorite Cwazy Wabbit moment is when a monster is chasing him through an old, musty castle. Suddenly our hero stops, a beauty shop set-up appears, and Bugs Bunny gives the ragged-clawed beast a manicure. Bugs did the Crazy Side-Step; the chase stops.

Don't we wish we could so easily side-step the "monsters" that pursue *us*? I think we can. At least, there's *one* monster who is easily mastered with a little shuffle-ball-change. It's the "Logic Will Drive You into the Ground and Utterly

Suppress You" monster. Don't let it get you! Here's how. Give up trying to argue logically against a well-reasoned statement or social norm that restricts you. Just step sideways *illogically* around it—that beautician routine in the cartoon doesn't make *any* sense—and proceed as you will. The Crazy Side-Step dance is a way to take advantage of insanity.

Example: Al's boss insisted that Al's new product idea would never fly. The boss's argument was cogent, comprehensive, and informed. But Al did the Crazy Side-Step: He decided that, despite sound logical evidence, he had to give his invention a chance.

So he met with a marketing consultant, and discovered he had simply hit on a market that his employer hadn't recognized. Despite the best of intentions, Al's boss had just missed the mark. Al now has his *own* business manufacturing his product.

People have all sorts of reasons they try to dissuade us from going along with our feelings, dreams, insights, plans, and intuitions. And thank God they do. If I'm gonna do something self-destructive, let's hope a friend argues me out of it. Crazy Sage wisdom isn't about doing away with logic. It's about not worshiping it as the overriding end all and be all.

This means that even if someone's intentions are the best, you may need to do your Warner cartoon dance around them and go along your own merry way. Hey, make that your Merry *Melody* way.

Other reasons people may *wrongly* naysay you: They are being overprotective; they are trying to sabotage you; they don't have the optimism, hope, skills, or perseverance needed to pull off your project, and therefore think it is impossible. Nevertheless, their motivation doesn't matter. Get out your manicure kit! Or, if that's too overt, side step more politely and subtly: Simply say, "Thank you. I know you're concerned. This is something I need to do anyway."

It's a moment when you embrace chaos with all its potential. Like Bugs, you do the ridiculous. And we all know that, in his wacky way, he knows how to get what he wants.

Bugs is not only a fine totem but also a great representation of that Chaos Deity I mentioned earlier. I have a Bugs Bunny Pez dispenser attached to the outside of my back door. It's my way of saying, "Chaos God, you are honored in this home. I want your blessings. I love you." (It's also my way of covering up a nail the house's previous owner hammered into the door, and that kept scratching me as I passed it.)

I mentioned earlier that I worship Bugs. In my way, I *do*. Crazy? It's a good life. I also said that watching his cartoons helps make my spirit whole when I'm bogged down and feeling low. That makes TV viewing a religious service of sorts. Yes, I'm stretching things, but some of us draw on God's Divine Blessings in ways other than those prescribed by organized religion; it's important to validate our own ways of touching God. It's hard to connect with, and draw on the power of, a Deity amidst life's daily pressures. Any means you have, you should use. What's *your* "odd" way of letting the Divine fill you? Validate it. Use it. If a Pez dispenser works for me, why should you doubt anything *you* wanna employ?

Listen To Wind

Instead of focusing on the chaos of our *internal* landscapes, the following tale illustrates more about drawing on the beneficial jumble, tumble, and bumble of events *outside* you.

Recently, at about 11 p.m., I decided to proofread some typing. Ganesh, my cat, started meowing—that awful, loud, and insistent yowling that cats *know* drives you to distraction. Sure enough, I couldn't concentrate. I chased him off repeatedly, to no avail.

Finally, I said to my older cat, Teenie—Ganesh is, let's say, college freshman age—"Would you please take care of him for a while so I can work?" (Ignore the fact that I talk to cats.) Teenie came over to my table and—oh, lawd—promptly settled down onto the document I was trying to correct, completely covering it.

I looked at her and thought, *Okay, I surrender!*

I should've known better than to try to work when one of my cats was interfering. They do it for my own good when I need a break but am workaholically plugging away.

A friend expressed it perfectly when I called to tell her this true-life parable: We need to listen to our betters.

Sometimes, those superior beings are pets, but myriads of other forms can manifest. For example, the wind may whip a hat off because it looks silly, thus sparing you a fashion gaffe. A superior being might also be the god within you, who's telling you to do something *other* than what you are engaged in right then.

Whatever those helpful entities and traits are, to

repeat earlier thoughts in a new context, they're often part of the chaos that we resist, thinking we need to cling to some everything's-in-its-right-place-and-time plan, and/or some "appropriate" *order* we imagine to be the underpinning of happiness and even of life itself. Sometimes, of course, it is good to cling to order, and there *is* an orderliness to the cosmos that guides us, nurtures us, and sets us free. However, chaos is another of life's underpinnings, and not always a bad one. Often it acts like my cats, lovingly guiding us to the happiest possible conditions. Besides, chaos is simply part of the order that we can't see the logic to. Doesn't mean it's not there. When life's chaos interferes with our plans, it reflects a *truer* plan, one in accord with our real—but possibly ignored or even unknown—needs and longings. Nanao Sakaki, the renowned poet, said, "Listen to wind." I'll also listen to cats. An odd form of Divine guidance? Odd is good.

I Wanna Live in Mayberry!

Since we're validating our weirdness as positive, insightful, and a touchstone for what's important in life, I want to share another personal story:

I wanted to live where the air was clean, the pace was slower, and the backyards were visited by deer—a small town like the ones in old Jimmy Stewart films. However, the dream didn't stop there. I wanted to live just outside of that town, in the woods where I'd grow herbs and boil them up into medicines. I'd feel utterly tuned into the subtleties of these natural gifts, these plants with all their life force and healing power. Heck, I would be so enamored of life and self that

I'd dance alone amidst the trees, thinking the forest the most important audience in the world. A beautiful dance!

Finally, I had to try it. No matter how crazy it was to try to become the archetypal wild woman of the forest, I felt that if I didn't, I might never meet a crucial part of myself. Nevertheless, I still worried: What if my longing to move from big-hopping-noisy city to way-in-the-middle-of-nowhere country was no more than escapism? What if the grass wasn't greener once I arrived?

Then I met Sandra when I was researching Meadville, Pennsylvania, a town I considered for my dream home. I spoke with a lot of strangers during that period, trying to learn about everything from property prices to local pollution to the political climate. Sandra was one of those strangers.

She was also, I believe, Goddess-sent. I don't even remember why she brought it up, but she told me that she had been sick of city life, and had virtually stuck a pin in a map. It landed on Meadville, so she called a realtor there.

Once on the phone, she suddenly found herself sobbing to the realtor, and, in a passionate outburst, exclaiming to him, "I wanna live in Mayberry!"

Sandra told me she hadn't been disappointed. And that meant I wasn't the only one. I wasn't a deluded escapist! Shortly thereafter, I had the thought that, nevertheless, maybe *my* move was wrongly-motivated. There was a lot to consider, but, finally, the only way I was going to be sure was to try for that greener grass.

It's a few years later and, my dear readers, I do not regret the move. My expectations have been fulfilled. Pipe dreams like that of being the herb-woman dancing in the forest can be the basis of important change. The return to nature scenario, as crazy as it seemed, is bit by bit coming true.

When we share our useful lunacies with each other, we're empowered by a collective madness. I hope *you* share about how your insanity works for you. Or go even further, to create an *immense* tribal celebration of life's true potential: We drive home the validity of our wacky wisdom when we share with others how it plays out *long-term* in our lives. For one thing, you'll provide anecdotal support for so-called "dubious" premises that you and others like you may hold. This can make them feel validated.

So, throughout these pages, I'll talk about my transition from city to rural life, showing a bit of how it developed over time. In fact, the rest of this chapter's pieces further chronicle my attempt to follow the "crazy" dream of "returning to nature." Then, a handful of pieces scattered through the book continue the tale.

For now, though, I'll end by saying that my solitary dance in the woods hasn't happened yet. I'm disabled, and the wild physical expression that I envisioned is beyond me. But maybe that doesn't matter. Because one starlit night, when the ground was blanketed with snow, and the air was frosty, I hobbled outside. With my headset blasting *South Park's* raucous, irreverent, and *marvelous* "Merry F___ing Christmas," I swayed and rocked and felt like the world and I were both spinning deliriously amidst the rural darkness. What a dance!

Crazy People Go Nowhere—It's Where Everything Happens

An aside: This chapter is about coping with daily life. For the healthily mad, your hopes and visions aren't *separate* from that daily existence; they can't be if you're to face the day with any equanimity, let alone joy. The above piece was about the risks connected with changing your whole life in order to live a myth. Can't get more day-to-day about what'll happen than that. And this piece is about living *nowhere*—that'll affect your daily activities, for sure.

Any thoughts about living your visions affect the moment to moment beingness that makes up your existence. My aside ends.

Those dubbed crazy—mystics, shamans, saints, artists, dreamers, social innovators, and other original thinkers—go "nowhere." It's where everything happens. These magical beings seek, and *live* in, places that other people say don't exist—in other words, in the realms of imagination, hope, and fruitful solitude. I insist these are viable places to exist. If I can imagine something, it can preserve my spirit. If I can hope, I know that my efforts as one small person can make a difference. In quiet solitude, I start revolutions. I can also find my integrity and courage, which protect me from a miserly existence. I choose to live nowhere!

To return to an earlier point, I don't mean *original thinker* in any way that leaves you out. We are all, each and every one of us, a cosmos. When you're sitting on a bus, your mind filled with ideas—or fatigue—and your spirit soaring because of a new romance or sagging over a breakup, the people on the bus might seem like the backdrop. You see their surface. But they only see yours, in kind. There's a bus full of cosmoses, who don't recognize each other as such. Bit by bit, this text will discuss how to change this and draw on people whose wondrousness we hadn't noticed. This will provide untold power to change the world and our personal lives (not to mention have bunches of fun). For example, we won't feel so alone with our unusual ideas, or be without the support to keep on thinking them.

For now, though, the important point is to at least *theoretically* recognize the people on the bus. The bus is life. And you're on it with me. I know there is a cosmos in you, and that only *you* think, act, and feel the way *you* do. I may have no idea what your cosmos is actually like, but I know it's amazing. So don't cut yourself out of what's happening in this book by feeling excluded when I discuss original thinkers or the likes. Find a way to feel included: play around with my words, change their meaning, add your own, or do whatever else is needed to profit from Crazy Sage moi. The biggest lone wolfs/outsiders/rebels/etc. have used these tools and ideas with amazing results.

Perhaps you think I only mean the overt lunatics, the *obvious* ones. However, many people are almost invisible when it comes to their "oddness." They seem "normal" unless you're up close. *Then* you get to see the creative ways they raise their kids or handle enormous—but typical—difficulties. These folks are also living "nowhere," off in their amazing, quiet worlds, being their *own* type of dreamer, mystic, rebel, innovator . . .

And this brings me back to the main point of this subchapter: Be a shaman, saint, artist, or other crazy person— go "nowhere." I beg you, follow your dreams.

I followed mine, to move across the country to live in the middle of "nowhere"—Pennsylvania's Meadville is a *flyover's* flyover. This isolated, small, blue-collar, farming community has a short growing season, long cold winters, and warm, welcoming, big-hearted people. The land, the community, and the spirits there called me. It's not the middle of nowhere in *truth*, but a place that was in my imagination and hope, where I knew I'd find a mystic's gentle solitude— which I needed to be at spiritual peace so that I could continue to make a difference in the world.

In the 11th century, the longhouse people migrated from the Great Lakes area to New York, passing through where I now live. According to anthropologist Steven S. Kushner: They built ritual mounds, which made the area a powerful spiritual reservoir; they were, according to their beliefs, "using the earth to think into the heavens;" in other words, they joined with both heaven and earth to bring the two into a conjunction. In simpler terms? Meadville is where heaven and earth meet; the sky touches humanity here. So, when I need to travel* from my peaceful Meadville "cave"—with its adjacent vegetable garden—in order to do the parts of my work that

---

*Travel is no longer the right word, not in the usual sense. When I wrote this piece (reminder: I'm using *piece*, *subchapter*, and *essay* as synonyms), I didn't know if my illness would continue. Years later, my health still keeps me basically housebound. Nevertheless, the paragraph holds true: I constantly travel in *spirit* to do work—e.g., teach classes through group phone calls.

can't be done *here*, I will do so knowing that, having been in the middle of nowhere, I've in fact had my finger on the pulse of the cosmos.

I like to think that Merlin did as I'm doing, and that's why he was so crucial in shaping King Arthur's rule: I imagine Merlin off in his cave, masterminding his plans for England and creating their potent underpinnings. After he picked the burrs from his hair and got all clean and spiffy, and then went to Arthur's court to do the more overtly influential work, it was effective because of the immense solitary labors already accomplished.

I like my myth. Being "in the mix" in the ordinary sense has never been a myth that I believed in. Being influential is another matter entirely. So is utterly, effectively, and *completely* changing the world. For example, some folks assume that because my first book went into thirteen printings and is in three languages that I am constantly running about networking and sitting on committees. Nope. Instead, I do what I can to help people. It's that simple: I've learned helping others is what it takes to effectively be of service *and* network, *and* be pivotally influential whether you're talking local, national, or international arenas. So:

Go for it. Bravely go nowhere!

Remarks at the bottom of pages, marked by asterisks or other symbols (see bottom of previous page), are not inconsequential notations. They're fully part of whatever topic is at hand. When you're having a great talk with a close friend, conversation can go twenty directions, all of them relevant. That's because you're talking about your *real* lives in a *real* way. Outpourings! Discussing the wild dance that is life, we can't always narrow it down to strict regulated speech. We make asides, interrupting *ourselves*, which can make it hard to fit everything in on paper. So when there's no other place to insert a relevant thought, I put it at the bottom of the page.

Sometimes You Have To Do Something Crazy Because the Alternative Is Even Crazier

Okay, let's wrap up this chapter by carrying weirdness to the nth.

When we've been pushed to the wall, and there's no escape, we *have* to find ways to both cope and impact the situation. At these times we also need to express ourselves, not only for the sake of survival, but also because our souls demand to be heard; otherwise, our spiritual wholeness is lost.

A relevant tale: As previously stated, I moved to Pennsylvania to follow a dream. Nevertheless, life's rarely that simple; I also relocated out of necessity. In 2001, I became radically disabled. This incurred major expenses as well as limited my ability to earn. On top of that, 9/11 caused a string of events that hit me financially, as it did many Americans. San Francisco, as a result, was too expensive a place to remain.

I had a fabulous apartment with ten years' rent control. Everyone thought it was a great deal. In San Francisco, it truly was. Nevertheless, its rent was twice what I pay to own a house in Pennsylvania. And now I live on seven-tenths of a partially wooded acre, where I watch deer and bunnies from my porch.

I had to face awful facts: I needed to leave the apartment because its mold problem was exacerbating my medical condition; if I paid the same rent—remember, I would no longer have rent control—it would put me in a slum.

Even if I stayed in the apartment, its cost, plus that of living in San Francisco, was too high. Because I've been so active in community service, there were international fundraisers to help me with medical costs. In addition, friends, acquaintances, and even strangers came over to wash dishes and take care of other chores that are now beyond me. Everyone selflessly contributed time and money to help me through that awful patch. But they could only do so much, and—another of the awful facts I had to face up to—I was going down the tubes financially.

Don't think I'm exaggerating. It might be hard to understand that an influential woman whose healing material is used throughout the world, and who is widely published, could be in a serious financial bind. It's not uncommon, though.

So, there I was, too poor to stay unless I moved into a slum; even then I didn't think I could pay all my bills because my health limited my work. I continued to teach one-hour teleseminars (classes-by-phone), but the three-hour and weekend-long classes that were a large portion of my income became too physically demanding to do as often.

How was I to survive? Just as important, how was I to maintain my quality of life?

When I heard about the little town of Meadville, something in my gut said, "That's your home." However I was too sick to make the trip across country, let alone *remain* in Pennsylvania without my caretakers. I couldn't wash dishes, use the computer, or even lift a heavy book—they were doing it all for me. The books I've published, since the disability happened, were only possible because volunteers typed my handwritten versions, taking dictation when I couldn't physically manage to write, and so on. How could I manage to move a household? How would I survive without my community's help in Pennsylvania? And could my heart *bear* to leave my beloved friends; could life be so unfair that I would need to leave a community I'd spent 25 years building?

I discussed all this with my most down-to-earth pals, and what we came up with was that it was crazy to move. We also agreed that it was even crazier to stay. Simple as that.

Not that I didn't do everything possible to make this move work, best it could. I researched Meadville up, down, and backwards, regarding each and every detail related to my health, finances, and happiness. I jumped through hoops to create the support I'd need to survive as a disabled person in my new home. For example, I made sure I could have groceries delivered. A small thing to some but, for me, it's delivery or starvation. I needed to be certain I wasn't leaving my support system for a place in the middle of the woods where I'd have no food.

Sometimes you have to do something crazy because the alternative is even crazier. It's not just the even-crazier-ness of solving financial duress and surviving. Going off into the woods, off into that isolation, with all my physical problems and the risks involved, is less crazy than *not* risking it, simply in terms of my happiness. As I said a few pages back, in times of maximum difficulty, survival is not the only important thing. We also need spiritual wholeness and self-expression to maintain the *strength* to survive. And besides, our souls, our souls, our souls, *demand* the freedom to follow bliss.

There can come a time when insane risk is the only choice that allows us not only to cope, but also to triumph, with joy, and in celebration of life's possibilities. As to that medically naysayed trip from California to Pennsylvania—I'll tell you about it further on—it was the fabulous ride of a lifetime.

Chapter Three
Self-Help, Advice from a Cat,
and Fabulous Makeup

This chapter focuses on personal growth. Yes, *most* of the book does so; methods for inner change are often more successful when intertwined with real life—intertwined with *all* parts of real life. So, a self-help chapter in a book that is already a self-help book. What can I say?

But the following pieces *will* indicate a self-help approach that's zany. Ever hear the expression *crazy-like-a-fox*?

However, nothing in this chapter weighs more than pieces in other chapters when it comes to defining my self-help approach. That definition is large and complex. As such, it is spread through my books, my oral teachings, and parts of my notes (and my brain) that I've not shared yet.

I can't explain *every* reason I put certain pieces in this chapter or why a self-help chapter at all. I remember a few reasons; none were to define my self-help approach. Some pieces are here because they seemed to want their own chapter, or more overtly address the self-help paradigm, or might be fun for you to have here, or . . . I no longer remember. I'm a painstaking writer; thus far, this book has taken six years to write. Downside: I occasionally forget something, despite copious notes and detailed outline.

What I do know is: The thoughts in this chapter could have been in other chapters—and vice versa. Also, now that we're past the book's initial pages, there will be no visible overall scheme that develops step by step. Let go, do chaos. By *do chaos*, I mean that the moments of reading this book are in themselves doing chaos.

I teach this way in my classes. Students say their lives change for the immense better. So please try it: As you read, continue to bear with me, let go, do chaos. Be in the moment with me. The book provides a specific experience that cannot be developed in a way that appears logical on paper. In fact, trying to parse an underpinning theory or structure as you read may block that experience, as much as it might were you parsing a sunset instead of letting its beauty thrill your heart. *Sometimes* analysis is part of enjoying beauty or otherwise being tuned into the moment, but not during the specific experience herein. At least not if we do what our culture would have us: Think our way through each moment to *such* a degree that we experience nothing else in that moment.

I'm not advocating a swing from the dominance of the intellect to the other extreme of ignoring your brain altogether. If you have studied music theory, you know Bach's music is math; each piece has its logic, but not a typical logic. You just listen, letting yourself hear, be touched, be present. In that process, the atypical logic might even present itself, but in an organic manner, happening on its own. If you dig for it like a frenzied mole, you may miss it and everything else. Instead, let your fine mind relax: Then intellectual dissection and appreciation will integrate into the larger whole of your experience, naturally and to good purpose.* And with that:

My Inner Nag (Resisting Personal Growth)

I've made the acquaintance of my inner nag. This is how she works.

I say, "I think I'll make meatballs for dinner. I would really enjoy that."

She responds, "Hamburgers are faster, and need less clean-up afterwards."

Or, I work out for an hour. She comments, "It would be better if you did fifteen more minutes."

I try to change some behavior, let's say my never slowing down to take a few deep breaths (let alone a nap). She points out, repeatedly, all day long, "You're doing it again, you're doing it again. You're overworking. You have to stop this!"

Now, you might think it's good that she keeps me mindful of my failure to improve, and offers other well-meant feedback. But I'm beginning to suspect that nags have the same result whether they're a protective loved one or part of your internal self.

Said loved one has your best interests in mind. And

---

* I don't believe the ultimate solution to a problematic extreme is to polarize against it. As they say, opposites are flip sides of the same coin.

However, on the way to that definitive solution, we may need to swing to extremes as a temporary fix. That's part of how humans manage to reject what doesn't work and find the most successful approach possible. It's not a process accomplished in one simple step.

So be in that process: For now, if your head gets in the way of this book, cut it off (says the Red Queen!).

likely is stocked with a great deal of truthful, useful info that theoretically should motivate you. For example, she tells you, "Smoking takes X number of years off your life. You should quit *now*." Or, "If you don't stop overeating soon, you'll be diabetic . . . It's not too late. You should really make an effort to eat sensibly while you're still okay . . . Do you know you can lose your eyesight to diabetes?" On and on.

The problem is not with the information per se, nor the intentions. Constant pressure is the problem. So you resist, and nothing is solved.

I wonder if the same goes for my inner nag. I mean well, barraging myself all day long with ideas about how I could do better, or about what crisis is going to befall me if I don't change such 'n' such behavior. But I don't always change.

So, from now on, when my inner nag starts in, I'm going to kindly thank her for her thoughts, and then think of something nice about the matter at hand. "Isn't it great that I work out more than most people!" "Meatballs are yummy! I'll enjoy them."

I won't argue with myself. For example, when she insists I forgo preparing one of my favorite dishes, and instead cook something quick 'n' easy, I shall *not* respond, "Meatballs are *worth* the time and clean-up." Nags only get worse when you answer back. I'll just, as I said, focus on something nice about the matter at hand.

I'm discovering the inner cheerleader. She is optimistic and knows better than to enter into debate with a wet blanket. She simply says, "Rah, rah, rah!" As the smiley sort who comments on the positive aspect of things, hopefully she will motivate me to—guess what!—change for the better.

Rah, rah, rah!

Self-Help Glitter

I love cosmetics. Don't think I've fallen for the notion that they're needed to bring a person's appearance up to snuff; they don't have to be used with a focus on correction. Humans are gorgeous, and that's all there is to it. But adornment— another matter entirely. I played a lot of dress-up as a kid.

I'm not ignoring serious injuries and other compelling conditions which one might reasonably cover or otherwise cope with. However, most women think their perfectly normal attributes are defective when in fact they're lovely. Skin too pale, too dark, nose too big, too small, mouth wrong size—I simply don't buy it (nor the products that are pitched with that message!). I prefer a Land of Oz approach to makeup; half the time I look like a character in a fantasy movie. Red powdered rouge pressed into service as eye shadow; lots of glitter (maybe pink on eyelids, red on lips); a tiny, pink, faceted crystal placed strategically, perhaps high on a cheekbone. And, in addition, eight pigtails. This is all way more fun than thinking I have to *fix* something supposedly wrong with my face.

Mind you, if I'm getting ready for a business meeting or television appearance, I try to look like someone who's not crazy. The Ozland aesthetic goes out the window. (That *can* backfire. One of my readers saw a show I was on and, when she met me for the first time, told me she had been disappointed that I had looked so *normal* on TV.) But a lot of the rest of the time? Glitter!

I use it because I love it, end of sentence. However, I really suggest you try it if you're down on your looks. Glitter is the makeup that helps you feel gorgeous instead of desperately painted over.

First of all, you'll never see an article refer to glitter as a way to correct your bad skin, unfashionable cheeks, incorrect lips, improper nose, or unlawful eyes. Therefore, when you approach the mirror, glitter in hand, you won't be preprogrammed to watch for flaws to fix, and end up standing there becoming more and more demoralized. Look for defects, you'll find 'em. Eck! Instead, you'll be there to *play*.

BTW, I am not excluding men. If you guys enjoy make-up, please have fun with cosmetic glitters, not only as a way to celebrate yourselves and life, but also to stop thinking you need to fix physical "defects," and instead appreciate the gorgeousness that is a man!

If you have the cash, please buy *lots* of different glitters. They're not all the same, and you want to be sure you find ones that suit you. Some will look good on you, some awful, and some—absolutely magical. Also, if you really get into it, you'll discover many you like, all for different effects! (Glitter comes not just in lotsa different colors but also in a whole world of splendid effects.) See *Resources for Illuminated Lunatics*, at book's end, for the only source of sufficient variety I know.

A lot of glitter used cosmetically is labeled, "Don't use near eyes." Heed this warning. Most glitter will send you to the hospital with a nasty eye injury should it get *in* your eye. Again, see *Resources for Illuminated Lunatics* for where to purchase glitter specifically made for safe use around eyes. Thank the Goddess! There are days when pink glitter on my lids is the only thing that cheers me up, the one thing that delights me.

Extrapolate my "self-help glitter" to the self-help movement's focus on fixing what is wrong—instead of celebrating what is fabulously right—and the way that can make us feel we are very damaged when we are not.

The self-help movement's focus on fixing what's wrong is not always good. Sometimes, it reinforces the message that hurt us so much in the first place: "There's something terrible about me." Mind you, as a self-help teacher, I realize we *do* have to face our faults, fears, and *all* the things inside that keep us from living the way we want. We also hope to be rid of these inner blocks. Fact is, the hard work involved is often a focus of my teaching and counseling; so I'm not suggesting that folks wiggle out of a truly difficult process. (Sorry.) But it can't be the sole focus, or you lose self-confidence. Instead, *celebrate* yourself and life. You'll learn how great—and capable—you already are. One way to do this is to glitter yourself, shamelessly and often. It's the kind of fun that calls forth the wide-eyed child you still are, the mystical being who's in awe of the universe, self, and glitter. The power you shall then wield—enjoy it. And use it to create your dream job, ideal romance, *etc.*

Know Your Beauty—*All* Your Beauty

I suggest you not skip over any of this book's discussions of a personal issue on the grounds that you've overcome, or never had, the problem in question. For example, if I discuss a self-esteem issue, don't pass over it thinking, "I've got good self-esteem." If I suggest you honor diversity, don't assume, "I don't need to read what comes next, because I already respect people unlike myself."

Despite their intent, people who have or strive for self-awareness fall easily into the trap of disavowing their need to work on whatever problematic trait is on the table.

They might say, "I don't have that problem" or "I don't have it any more." However, when I ask you to examine yourself for a specific inner block—let's say low self-esteem—I'm not implying that you have no self-esteem at *all*. I know you might really value yourself. Instead, I'm asking you to see how you can grow *more* self-esteem. (It's kinda like growing a garden of pretty flowers that love you. Ok, that may be a weird image. But it's still a marvelous picture of self-worth: Flowers beaming at me, their smiles reinforcing the joy I take in being me—or helping me find that joy for the first time—like a mother's smile makes her children feel good about themselves. It's so much better than those nasty flowers in Wonderland who scolded Alice. Yes, let's have *lots* of nice, beaming flowers.) I want you to know *all* your beauty.

Or, to continue the example of self-esteem, you might recognize your worth *fully* in your mind, but not realize it *deep* in your gut yet. Then, the belief of self-worth may not translate into action, in the sense of your taking great care of you. (A lot of this book, mostly without saying so, helps you *fully* embody your cherished beliefs.)

We who do a lot of work on ourselves resist further growth. Hey, I just thought of something. If your response to that sentence was, "I don't do that. I'm always trying to grow," or "Nope, I'm trying hard," you may have done exactly what I'm cautioning against. Even those who *always* put shoulder to the wheel of inner change and spiritual development have ways they avoid the very improvements they seek.

Humans have simultaneous contradictions within them, constantly. When I'm addressing one of them, by suggesting you look at a possible negative trait, I'm not naysaying the other more positive ones.

Here's another common way folks resist growth: We can blind ourselves to one of our negative traits by looking *solely* at ways it does *not* operate. A proclivity to see one's strengths as obviating the need to build on those strengths is typical of strong, self-aware, independent thinkers.

You also may reject suggestions about self-improvement if you mishear them as implying you're innately bad, you're not trying to be the best you can, or you should feel shame about your efforts or errors. Shame does not heal. We're innately good. I believe we all try our best; if someone's not trying at all, I figure that's the best they can do at the moment. Mind you, I also believe it's vital to have the highest standards we can envision, and do our utmost to move toward them. But we'll never be perfect. (Or at all close to it, if I'm someone to judge by!) Punishing ourselves about what we do, or don't do, is not helpful. What is helpful is ideas that facilitate our creative expression, peace of mind, connection to the Divine, unique viewpoints, effectiveness in our careers, ability to serve others, and other happiness-inducing concerns. I point out possible inner blocks to these—not to make you shrink, but to help you expand.

A few times, this book reminds you to watch for resistance to change. Watch your response to not just my but also *other* people's ideas.

When those closest to you give input about how you might grow, it's easy to automatically refute them. This knee-jerk reaction is just human. When you do it, don't think you're atypical.

I want you to know your beauty. More, I want to provide support that helps you know *all* your beauty.

Ragamuffin Manicure a Go-Go

Give me the Nobel! I've solved one of women's major challenges—chipped nail polish. (And, à la the above glitter piece: If you're a guy who likes paint as part of your manicure, read on.)

A manicure is doomed to a blemished state within perhaps minutes of its completion. Nail polish immediately chips off. So I started filling in the places where the polish chips with a different color. I call it "Ragamuffin Manicure a Go-Go." Every time a piece flakes off, I add another color in its place. My hands display a colorful patchwork, a crazy-quilt exuberant combination. Day by day, new colors and shapes come into play, and my ever-evolving work of art entertains me.

You can take it further: Start with three to four colors to begin with, painting a few nails one color, a few another, a few others *yet* another. Add a nail decal here and there. Then, wait for the chipping to start, at which point your manicure goes *ultra*-ragamuffin, the patched-up bits a medley of whatever colors appeal to you. Voilà—crazy quilt nails to the *extreme*!

Next day, more chips? Paint away. When the nail grows out and reveals itself bare at the base, it's another opportunity for creativity. Fill it in with glitter polish or whatever else appeals.

The longer you play with this, the more possibilities you discover. For example, my manicure was getting too old, ragamuffin look notwithstanding. Or so I thought. Then I realized I could strip just two of the worst nails and repaint. The other two really bad ones were chipped in a way and of such a color that a layer of glitter polish over the whole nail disguised the problem. La!

Glitter polish lasts forever. In fact, here's another option for longer lasting nail polish. It is a French Manicure with a twist. Apply silver glitter at the nails' tips, colored glitter the rest of each nail. (And when it chips, start making your crazy quilt.)

Now, if I could only find a substitute for the under-wire bra. It is so uplifting but *so* uncomfortable.

In the meantime, damned if I'm gonna forego self-adornment play-time just because nail polish is supposed to be "perfect," "right," or "just so," or because a typical manicure is short-lived, quickly past the point of no return. You have to strip off the whole polish job pretty soon after you first put it on. I forsake the "proper" nail job that can only be retouched just so much, and that maintaining for its short life is such a hassle that it's enough to make you not bother doing your nails in the first place. I forsake the touch-up that has to be done fastidiously for it to work, which is annoyingly painstaking.

I doubt I'm the only woman who feels frustrated by the upkeep that fashion dictates. I can't be the sole female who hates to go to all the exact same trouble over and over and over and over. So I offer my crazy quilt nails that allow a manicure to last way longer. And is entertaining to boot, as you choose the new colors to add and watch the whole "picture" evolve.

Do you have your counterpart of my ragamuffin manicure, a problem solver with your hair or clothes or make-up that is not "proper" fashion? Self-express! Define fashion *yourself*. Then share the trick with friends. Challenge fashion standards that insist on fastidiousness, perfectionism, and an absurd amount of time and worry.

Humor as Healing

Some self-help approaches are psychologically-based. Some are spiritually-based. I am definitely no psychologist. And nowadays, maintaining a sense of humor may be as important as practicing a spiritual way of life. Even better is having both! In fact, maybe you can't be spiritual *without* a sense of humor. As far as self-help goes, humor adds so much buoyancy to the spirit that we can rise above prosaic views and, renewed, see entirely different perspectives that help us grow and find more inner strength.

As I said earlier, the advantages of comedy and the like are innumerable. The ancient Hopi priest never led a ceremony without a trickster as a partner. This disruptor of the procedure, this sacred clown performing antics and tomfoolery during *holy* rites, was so important that he was given a large portion of the fee the priest earned. The Sacred Fools with all their jokes—these are time-tested guides and actual healers of the soul. Though I've coined lots of terms for what I try to do in these pages, it already has a name and an ancient tradition. The terms *Sacred Fool* and *Holy Clown* are well known.

Humor is a powerful healer. For example, sometimes a joke can confront a taboo subject, and then make us laugh and relax while the jest merrily slips past our barriers to honesty about our shortcomings and mistakes, sorrows and regrets. That same joke might bring joy that hard times have banished, an elation that helps reconnect us to the larger flow of humanity, and even hook us up to the larger flow of God and an immense cosmos rich with the ecstatic. This connectivity allows immense healing forces to flow through us, shifting our tense molecules into happier, healthier, loose 'n' slipping 'n' sliding ones. For example, this song of the cosmos may be just the right song to thaw a long-frozen heart, a heart that was made stone through too many disappointments.

Some of the Holy Clown's jests are no more than absurdities that offer neither meaning nor insight. Just a bit of goofiness can add levity, liveliness, a wee smile, or distraction, which are not only needed but also teach us a happy, spontaneous spirit. A lot of the material in this book doesn't necessarily belong here because it's insane per se, but because it's silly or funny. Maybe not always ha-ha-out-loud funny, but perhaps causing the internal li'l laugh. High jinx, applied even in the most sacred moments and most desperate times, are definitely part of a healthy insanity. They belong here!

Through its above-mentioned merits, humor can successfully address the concerns and challenges that many original thinkers have. We are people able to laugh at ourselves, and who want the honest self-assessment that a jest can so easily provide sans the sting of harsh judgment.

A joking barb that shames or embarrasses us for our typical human foibles is awful. But a *truly* good-natured joke about our faults can be an appreciation of our *whole* self, a celebration even of our shortcomings. God wants me to do my best to change my faults, but She also loves every bit of me, which gives me permission to do the same. Laughing at my faults is part of that, part of the self-love and compassion for self that *help* me change.

Later, we'll look more at the Sacred Fool and how the fun of the Crazy Sage Tradition helps create personal power and spiritual health. But for now, realize that many pieces herein *embody* this—they don't describe crazy wisdom, they *apply* it, by using wit (I *hope* it is wit) to provide insight, empowerment, and wholeness. I don't mean the idea of wholeness, but the actual thing itself. For example, the aforementioned cosmic tune helps make us whole.

On a related note: This fool spent years creating her tomfooleries. I'm my own style of Sacred Trickster, yaya. I developed this book's teachings and methods. They are part of a larger, more sober, body of theories and methodologies I created, called *Another Step*. More about all this later.

For now, I'll add: Like everyone, the past informs me. When I honor that, as I did above by talking about a *tradition* of sacred tricksters, it often makes people assume I'm not the originator of what I teach. For example, some people may not pause to consider that there is such a thing as a spiritual innovator. Other people assume a woman's teachings were learned from a man.

It would be wrong for me not to honor my innovations: My originality is a gift I am lucky to have been given by the Divine; I give thanks for gifts from God by recognizing them, instead of adopting false humility. *Real* humility means knowing that whatever I offer community exists only because Goddess has bestowed it on me. In one sense, I can take no credit for it. But I live in paradox: I both give thanks *and* pat myself on the back for what I accomplish. I also let others know what I'm capable of, so that they can take full advantage of it. God gave me certain gifts so I can serve others with them. I cannot serve if no one knows what services I have to offer. False humility can actually be selfish if it keeps, for example, an incest survivor, who wants support in a healing process, from knowing that many people find me an effective tool for healing.

This aside may be helpful to you, because the sense of self I'm delineating, combined with this paradoxical realization that ultimately God is the one bestowing that which each of us gives to others, is part of achieving the *total* self-expression and effectiveness I discuss in the next piece. Going the last nine yards to your goals—and to being *fully* yourself—can require a balance between humility and healthy pride.

The Modern Renaissance Person

Applying *all* your talents helps you overcome problems and create your ideal life.

Wacky wisdom breaks through the inner restraints to total self-expression and effectiveness in achieving goals. Note the word *total*; many people who have learned to really be themselves aren't sure how to go the last nine yards. In other words, they darn well should be proud of how hip and free they are, and perhaps have had to *fight* to become. But they're still unable to write their great American novel, so to speak. There's something stopping them from *actualizing* some of their dreams. So whether you're like that, or only now just beginning to become yourself, Crazy Sage teachings can provide the missing steps.

For certain individuals, the missing step is seeing oneself as a modern renaissance person. It can take *all* your resources to get through the day, to be brave, to be original, to fulfill your daring fantasies, to be *unstoppable*.

Everyone is multifaceted, with many useful skills, fabulously disparate traits, and shifting personalities. The latter is not to suggest that each and every human is a multiple personality . . . Well, actually, I guess I *am* saying that. In a *good* way: No one is just a parent. Or just a Christian. Or just a mystic or artist or Buddhist or pagan or grade-school teacher. Someone is more likely to be a grade-school

teacher who's also a mystic and artist. Or someone might be
a mystical artist and truck-driving father of four. Or a Taoist
who works as an ad executive yet owns a tattoo parlor on
the side because body art constitutes a piece of spirituality
missing from his Taoist practices. And someone *else* might be
a mystical artist, *former* grade-school teacher, who's driving
a truck now that her four children have grown, while she's
studying to become an ad executive *and* tattoo artist. Oh, and
she's flirting with both paganism and Buddhism.

Some people will not be contained by one definition,
one role in life, one personality. They shift and transmute
constantly. A woman might one moment dazzle everyone with
her brilliant mind, the next moment be a boring but necessary
work horse, and the next a vulnerable sex kitten. And that's
all in a two-hour time span. The rest of the day may be just
as far-ranging. Our various aspects may seem a contradiction
but, hell, insane people not only ignore such things, they also
realize that none of these disparate aspects are fake. They're
all real as rocks!

I want to use myself as an example of something that
can go wrong regarding all this. Thom Fowler called me
"one of those multi-hyphenated types." There are plenty of
the aforementioned "contradictions:" I'm a humorist, mystic,
spiritual counselor, public figure, semi-recluse, musician, poet,
author, teacher, gardener, religious leader, and a Buffy the
Vampire Slayer fan to such an extreme that there's no other
word for me but *geek*. And I'm hardly unique. But when
I used to think otherwise, I was isolated, thought no one
could understand me, and therefore didn't open enough to

completely benefit from the immense power, effectiveness, love, and camaraderie of group efforts. So it was harder to go *all* the way to my dreams.

It's vital that we multiple personalities don't think we're too special in our specialness. We can have great lives—not to mention change the world—if we learn to perceive, develop, and support the genius of *every* living, and supposedly nonliving, being. Ditto, if we appreciate the multifaceted gem each person, the planet, and society constitutes. Express all your talents, respect all your aspects, honor diversity, and help others do all these things as well. (And make lotsa jokes—which, of course, are some of the sparkly facets on those aforementioned gems of life.)

This book helps you celebrate your *inner* diversity. For example, earlier lessons about tapping into the chaos within help you draw on parts of yourself you might not otherwise.

In Mary Shelley's *Frankenstein*, the young scientist, Frankenstein (yes, that was originally the name of the monster's creator, not the monster himself), studies the works of Agrippa, Paracelsus, and Albertus Magnus, authors invalidated by the scientists of the time in which the novel is set. Commenting on this and his subsequent university education, Frankenstein says, "I was required to exchange chimeras of boundless grandeur for realities of little worth." While I do not find modern science worthless, and I totally believe in "boundless grandeur," I loved his remark anyway. Despite its overt meaning, it implied the importance of dreaming as big as you want. Greatness needn't be impractical delusions. Be big! Use every part of you! How else can you meet the challenges you inevitably confront just in the course of going about your business, let alone hang in until you succeed at your dreams?

Let's twist Shelley's concept and words around, and bend them not to their opposite meaning but to a different one altogether: Ignore people's didactic, small-minded realities. These "facts" have little worth. Their sole power is their smothering "proof" that we should drop our wild, heartfelt wisdoms of boundless grandeur, knowledge that is *not* chimera but the doorway into a serene daily life and the achievement of our wildest goals, goals that spring from our passion for living and that feed that passion, keeping it alive.

Let's focus on methods that help you take advantage of all your *talents*, both your innate and developed skills. So, you are a modern Renaissance (wo)man. Yes, you. Even if you know that, you may have abilities you don't see. Here are stories about people who had skills they didn't realize. The process that helped them spot these unseen resources might be useful to you. Adapt as needed.

The first story is about my friend Jami. I don't have the bucks for big promotional campaigns, but I'm a grassroots girl and find my own funky ways to let people know about my books or services. It always shocks me that it works, but it does. For one thing, people are very kind, supportive, and generous when it comes to lending a hand.

One day, I needed help getting word out about a new book I had written. I asked Jami to go online, find web sites related to the book's topic, and then enlist those sites' owners in helping us.

She said that she didn't know how to do that, adding that she knew nothing about promotion. I insisted that she actually *did* have the knowledge and just didn't realize it, then started the following dialog to prove that to her.

I said, "What are we gonna ask these site-owners to do?"

Response: "To promote your book."
Me: "But what does that actually mean?"
Jami: "That they publicize it?"
Me: "But what does that, again, actually mean?"
Jami: "That they tell people about the book?"
Me: "Yup! And how could a site-owner do that?"
Jami: "By reviewing the book on their site?"
Me: "Bingo! How else?"
Jami: "By interviewing you on the site?"
Me: "You got it!"

She now knew what to ask for: reviews and interviews! Sure, I could've just told her. But I wanted her to figure it out herself, so that she would better appreciate her fine mind, and not let promotion—such a *scary* word—intimidate her so that she forgot her mental prowess. Promotional know-how is one of an endless number of skills that people can have an instinct for but not realize it. However, Jami's and my dialog helped her think things through; when you logically pick something apart like that, step by step, you can often figure out how to pull off the most mysterious, intimidating things. Trust yourself.

My one talk with Jami hardly made her a marketing guru. There was plenty to learn yet. But, here's the thing: She'd figured out enough to realize she could figure out *more* about something that had been too intimidating only minutes before. Sure, I had to give her additional instructions to what we'd discussed. But so what! Skill and intelligence don't obviate the need for input! Run your ideas by folks who have expertise in what you're trying to learn. You should do that in any case; get a mentor.

If you don't know someone with the talents in question, talk with a person whose abilities are somewhat related. For example, as I said, I'm a grassroots girl. So navigating mass media as a writer took some doing in the early days; publishing is a corporate world. I called up an old friend who's a high-powered corporate executive in the *computer* biz, and she mentored me about how to navigate in big business.

Another method for trusting yourself is to see the ways you're self-educated and exactly how you went about it, then apply those methods to arenas that have you *stymied*. Example: I counseled a woman, Georgia, who wanted to start a business but was completely stumped by the prospect. (Some people don't see why a *spiritual* counseling session would involve coaching someone regarding business skills. Again, all the parts of you connect to all the other parts. Besides, it's *spiritual* to help someone see their assets and help them succeed with the practical things in life.) So we looked at how she could conquer all the components of becoming an entrepreneur; I started by asking if she had ever learned to do anything on her own. First, she insisted that she hadn't done anything of worth. So I walked back through her life with her until she realized that she had taught herself how to quilt, raise a family, and cook, as well as how to make fabulous cosmetics for herself: eyeliner, lipstick, you name it.

The quality of the cosmetics far surpassed what you could purchase unless you were a Hollywood star linked into the most expensive, exclusive products. Georgia had figured out how to make them by reading, researching on the web, and experimenting. I convinced her that she could use the same methods to determine how to run a business. She'd just been intimidated by the *concept* of business, whereas cosmetics had seemed less threatening.

They were, in fact, the product she wanted to go into business with, but she had had no commercial ambitions regarding cosmetics when she was first making them, so they hadn't been a scary proposition. She had felt safe to learn. But once she decided to make them to *sell*, she froze. Had she at that point decided to learn to make the cosmetics, she'd probably have been overwhelmed and never learned.

Use the steps I brought Georgia through:

1) What have *you* taught yourself to do? Knit? Make cosmetics? Fix a car engine? Do psychic readings? Bake éclairs? Make herbal medicinal tinctures?

2) What methods did you use to learn? Did you experiment? Follow instructions in a book or website? Jump in and figure out your own kooky methods? Make a gazillion mistakes but not worry about it? Learn a tiny bit at a time? Or . . .? Think back; once you remember your approach, you know what works for you and can use it to teach yourself other stuff.

3) Use your specific methods to learn other things! It'll boost your confidence. You have many innate talents. Give them a chance to shine.

Teaching yourself is a *skill*. If you can figure out on your own how to, let's say, garden (I use that as an example because it's a relatively unthreatening activity for most folks), you have the ability to do the same with things that seem shrouded and impenetrable to you.

The specific field of endeavor that feels unapproachable changes from person to person. What's easy for one person might be scary for another. But here are additional ones that at least *some* folks fear: writing a book, woodworking, and selling your art. Oddly enough, any of the activities I listed in item number 1, as ones you might have confidently learned, may be difficult for someone else.

Here's another story about someone with unrecognized skills: Alison was a stripper who came to me for spiritual counseling. She wanted to leave the sex industry but felt she lacked the necessary experience in business. I had her break down everything she did at work and helped her see she had acquired many marketable skills. Examples:

◊   She was a high-earner because of her tips. This meant, I explained, that she knew how, to put it in the most straight-ahead terms, to get money from people. However, because her earnings came from strip clubs, she discounted her ability to earn. Wrong! Earning is earning. Period.

◊   Getting this money involved the exact people skills

needed to succeed in any business. Again, she had discounted those skills in *herself* because of the sexual context. The way many people look down on sex industry workers had made her do the same; she had been unable to see a lot of the talents her job required.

◊ When her stage show ended each night, her job entailed approaching customers and offering table dances. That's where the real money was. It takes initiative to walk over to someone to get the cash out of their wallet. She was amazing!

A lot of women fail in big-money careers because they don't have sufficient initiative. And Alison showed even more than that: She had developed a *method*, including a sales pitch. In other words, in a million years, I couldn't figure out how to walk up to a table of guys and know what to say and do that would make them agree to pay me for a table dance— it's an actual "routine" that needs to be effective. Alison had developed an approach that worked. Which meant she was capable of developing approaches for all *sorts* of business interactions. However, not until I was able to help her see that; Alison was discounting herself because the transaction was sexy. She could only imagine herself selling a sexy product or service, through a sexy "pitch." She couldn't see the innate, straight-ahead, pure salesmanship involved in her work. Humans often write off what they know, thinking that if *they* know it, it must be without value; she wasn't unusual!

Alison is now a successful realtor, applying her people skills, initiative, and know-how about approaching folks and pitching to them. (The sales pitches she developed to promote table dances involved a lot of the same skills as selling a house.)

By the way, I'm not anti sex-industry. I just help people enter the field they most want. Many women would probably find more self-esteem—and cash—as a stripper than as a secretary! I'm also not against a sexy sales pitch, if it's fun and not manipulative or otherwise creepy. But you might miss the point of my story if you think that the sales skills I say Alison used as an erotic dancer were *all* sexual enticement or otherwise sexy. She used the same basic sales methods that any successful sales person in the U.S. eventually learns. And *this* is what she was invalidating and not realizing she could take into another business arena.

The three examples in this subchapter are about women and business. Though the topic at hand applies to *all* parts of our lives, I'm focusing on career and women for two reasons. First, it's an arena where I've watched many a competent woman's confidence in herself vanish. Second, the examples'll convey more through the cumulative effect of being all about one area. But my three tales address things relevant to any arena of life, for women *and* men. Applying all your talents not only gives you a degree of mastery over daily challenges—both large and small—but also helps you create the ideal life.

In this book, you'll find other tools that will help you understand that you're innately a modern Renaissance person so that you *draw* on all your talents. Some of the tools will be obvious but, fact is, a lot of lessons herein help do the trick though they may not seem directly related. Remember: Every part of you is connected to every other part.

There are many other ways that this book focuses on madness setting you utterly free. Wacky wisdom continually helps you break through the internal barriers to being free, seeing your beauty, and fulfilling your most daring dreams. For one thing, the text addresses hard-wired inner limits, self-defeat mechanisms that the hippest, most free souls often have without even being aware of it.

No matter how much we're told to "Be sensible"—translate that as "Give up!"—the human spirit will be free. We're beings that by our very nature will eventually escape the bonds of dogmatic restrictions, tunnel vision, or peer pressure. All of you longs to express itself, and *will* express itself. That process might unfold slowly; perhaps you only express yourself a bit, then a bit more, and then a bit more yet again—over and over. But you're flying—trust me—even if it doesn't feel like it yet.

Cooking is one of *my* skills that I use to cope with life. Aren't I a good role model? Indeedy. And the more you gain for yourself, the more power you have to help others; so in learning to use all my assets to live well, I'm then able to use them to help others do the same: I hope the following recipe and the musings that accompany it add a bit to *your* life. Indeedy.

Afterthoughts: Using all your talents doesn't mean you're doomed to becoming "a jack of all trades, master of none." You can develop expertise in one (or more) area, and still pursue a wide range of other activities. Example: I concentrate on building the skills needed to do community shamanic work—e.g., the curriculums I develop, and the counseling sessions I give—including its combined poetry of word, act, and being. All this is my primary art form. (I've broad definitions of art and poetry. Perhaps *your* art/ poetry is raising a family or creating an effective structure for a community service org.) But I will not deny myself the domestic arts, even if Martha Stewart would be horrified by the pillowcases I made for my sofa. They cheer me up.

Also, using all your talents is not trying to be all things to all people. Unless we focus, we're so mentally scattered and our efforts so diffused that we get little or nothing accomplished. I make music, but I back away from it when I need to give my full attention elsewhere.

Use your whole self to improve the world and your life, by drawing on each of your talents to an *appropriate* degree, instead of bowing to the societal norm that you stick to one or two talents, or ignore them altogether! My music serves community—in the sense that some people enjoy it—even though I don't spend as much time on it as I do on teaching. Music also entails a creative process unlike that of teaching. So playing music informs my creative process as a teacher.

Over or underestimating any of your talents helps no one. In fact, evaluating your work's worth is—in *some* ways—not your job. Your job is to offer all of you, and let others decide what—if any—they want. I'm not suggesting you should lack standards or make sloppy efforts. I do my best. In that sense, it *is* my job to evaluate my work while *creating* it.

As is not offering anything I think harmful. But we can't always see the value of what we produce.

When we have a low opinion of something we make, it can be selfish to not share it anyway. The only way to serve others is by offering ourselves to them. All we have to offer *is* ourselves. I learned a big lesson about this: I hated an early painting of mine—I thought it was trash. It was one of my first paintings. I'm not sure why I tried to sell it. Maybe I just wanted it out of the house. I was shocked: People praised the painting, and it was the first picture I sold! I didn't understand, and I *still* don't see its worth (and I don't have to. It's not hanging in *my* home). I realized I don't have to be as good as Picasso for my painting to contribute something. The visual arts I indulge in don't turn out as well as my other creative endeavors. But who am I to judge? Someone else might like them better than anything else I do.

The pursuit of visual arts has also been an inner journey, spiritually speaking. It has helped me come home to myself the past few years. Each pursuit you choose has its use and its place.

I'm a Genius Gelatin
Seasonal Desserts

This is the first of the book's recipes. Used the right way, delicious food and the preparation thereof are effective self-help modalities.

I'm Italian, from a family of chefs and cooks. Food and its preparation are so much a part of my being that cuisine is sacred to me, and cooking is one of life's mysteries. When I'm chopping, stirring, compiling recipes, thinking up new ones, adapting old ones, I'm peaceful and—honest to Goddess— feel one with all things. This is one of the ways I cope with my problems.

I love to cook for friends. It's a great pleasure to share such a powerful joy.

My culinary attitude is à la Crazy Sage teachings: Earlier, this chapter told us that life isn't divided up into narrow categories created by linear logic, but is instead a blend in which *everything* connects so that *anything* might be relevant. Cooking and food can surely be relevant to spiritual wholeness, inner change, and coping with life.

Every recipe in this book—or the telling of the recipe— is a formula to change your life. Think of them as self-help recipes (seasoned with a healthy dash of even healthier madness). You can whip up concoctions that'll please the palate as well as tickle the soul.

Or call the pieces herein with recipes *exercises in spiritual growth* or *rituals* (or whatever other term works for you). They're all accurate. If life is beyond exact definitions, you needn't use one that makes you feel these recipes aren't for *you*. Don't restrict yourself that way.

We focus far too much on names. If these recipes are exercises in spiritual growth, call me a *healer*. Rites, then call me *shaman*. Ceremonies? Call me *priestess*. Healings— minister or witch. Or call me *Christian*, or *Buddhist*, or *Taoist*, or *homemaker*.

You have a variety of *accurate* choices to make you feel secure. Healthy insanity lets me claim all the universe offers, know they're valid, and use their power. If you want to feel loved and supported, and participate in community, call me— and everyone else!—something that makes you feel akin. It's really hard to deal with daily life when you feel alone.

Otherwise, names become a means for shadow-projections, accusations. Someone calls me something that he *isn't* as a way to feel better than me. Or, without realizing it, to end up feeling different, alone.

Healthy madness is about ending *isolation* and the celebration that is all of life's parts in *union*. And, to circle 'round to cooking, here's a recipe that helps create that unifying celebration. It's called **I'm a Genius Gelatin**:

One way I celebrate life is being in touch with the natural world. Food (and cooking it) is an easy way to tune into nature. In that sense of being connected to other dots in the cosmos, you can enjoy yourself—*that* helps keep you from getting bogged down by daily problems.

Ingredients

◊ one 11.5 oz can of Welch's frozen white grape juice concentrate (Examine carefully: Their various grape juice *cocktail* labels look a lot like their *juice* labels.)

◊ water

◊ 3½ envelopes Knox® Unflavored Gelatin

◊ fresh rose-geranium leaves (If you can't get these, adaptations are below.)

1. Pour the juice concentrate into a sauce pan. Then pour in a can and a half of water.

2. Add the gelatin to the juice. After stirring, let it sit ten minutes.

3. Add three very loose, small handfuls of fresh rose-geranium leaves and bring to a boil.

4. Quickly reduce heat and simmer on low for ten minutes.

5. Cool, then taste to decide whether the liquid needs to be diluted further. Do you like desserts that are more flavorful than sweet? You might want to add more water. Do you prefer what others might consider icky-sweet (like cotton candy)? When you sample the brew you might think it's fine as is.

6. Pour this concoction into a transparent pretty bowl—the dessert will look like a clear white wine with leaves gracefully held in it, and will taste like a gourmet treat for Gods—elegant to the eye and palate.

7. Refrigerate until it sets.

I'm a Genius Gelatin is an elegant champagne-colored gelatin dessert with a rose geranium flavor. I prepare it every summer because it helps me enjoy that season, tune into it as I said. I like food that helps me feel connected to nature *as the season turns*. Each recipe below draws on seasonal plants a bit, as well as celebrates what my taste buds want that time of year.

I made up I'm a Genius Gelatin because my rose geranium plant said, "Hey! C'mon. Play with me. Let's do something." We had fun. (And the recipe proves my genius because it's a *fabulous* dessert.)

When I served I'm a Genius Gelatin to friends, one said it was like eating jellied honey! Since I'm always making up new made-from-scratch gelatin desserts, they suggested some. I only had versions for spring and summer, and needed ideas for fall and winter. One idea was Persimmon "Jello." Another was creating an apple juice, cinnamon, orange slice beverage and jelling it.

The geranium dessert, as I said, is for summer. As for spring recipes that prove my genius, my favorite is to use the white grape juice and steep fresh mint in it with a few organic rose petals for visual effect. (Any fairies you have in your house will think it's pretty. Keep them entertained in ways like that, and they'll bless your home. *That*'ll help with your day-to-day coping, for sure.) Or forget the roses. With a bit of green food coloring, it's perfect summer ambrosia. (Fairies like bright green, so they'll still think you're cool and help out.) Replace the roses with coconut and bananas for another spring dish.

To make any of these concoctions, simply adapt the first recipe. And then, enjoy.

I love creating gelatin dessert recipes, and am happy that my idea to make them with juice concentrate worked. I love their taste, and it satisfies my sweet tooth without resorting to white sugar. (Don't knock it! Good health makes for a better sex drive!)

Inner Growth—Not a Commodity

While we're in the kitchen: Have you noticed how, sitting in the kitchen drinking tea or coffee with a friend, you talk about all sorts of things, from puzzling beaus to the seemingly unattainable nature of world peace? It's tea time! Grab a cup, which will give me a chance to rant to you about a new, completely non-culinary topic. Here goes:

We live in a commodity culture, and it impacts how we view personal change: "I took the workshop, I grew, now I *have* growth." Inner growth, whether spiritual or emotional, is not an object, a *thing* one owns. It is a state of being one achieves, which has to be maintained, or it is lost. There is no "I found peace, now I *have* peace." No "I found ways to be more kind, now I have kindness." No "I achieved <u>fill in the blank</u>, now I have <u>fill in the blank the same way</u>."

I've noticed people doing really well when taking a year-long personal-growth seminar with me. Or when they work hard on themselves in Alcoholics Anonymous or another twelve-step program. Or when they otherwise put their shoulder to the wheel of inner transformation. Then they stop their efforts and wonder why their newly found creativity, or forward momentum, or peace of mind, or zest for life *stops*.

I do not think poorly of them. People do the best they can. In a culture that is based in capitalism, the most anti-establishment of us can fall for a subtle consumer spiritual mentality.

I hope no one thinks that I'm implying my methods are ineffective. Time has shown that I do not put temporary band-aids on deep soul wounds. I see my students years later, and the work "took." But the best methods are useless unless we maintain the gifts they give us.

Self realization is not something you achieve quickly. Or even slowly. And it's *never* achieved in the sense of "You did it. Now you're done." There is always the downhill slope, waiting. I do not mean that in a doom and gloom sense reminiscent of preacher-talk about the Devil's gonna getcha— talk that makes you never feel good about your headway, but instead always feel bad about who you are.

Instead, I'm talking about human process: We exist in whatever day we're in, so spiritual practices are required *that* day to meet its challenges and opportunities. Examples: We need exercises that help us have determination, serenity, a connection to our God that nourishes us while the boss yells, and a good intuitive grasp about what to do when our kids scrape knees and the rest of the play-by-play of the passing hours. (A *personal* example: I'm the sort of person who wakes up angry and ready to ruin the day in a million ways. Daily spiritual practices keep me more balanced and better able to live according to my beliefs.) There is also long-term work that needs to be done consistently; its results ripple through *all* our days. (In a bit, I'll talk about programs that fulfill everything described in this paragraph.)

As far as that message that makes you never feel good about your headway: Fact is, after strenuously pushing toward a spiritual breakthrough *and* then getting through to the other side of it, we may need a break from demanding inner work. This gives us the strength needed to return to yet more growth,

and to do what's needed to hold onto our gains. (It is a lot
of work to maintain one's gains.) Taking a rest may *constitute*
growth for someone who drives themselves too hard, or is a
perfectionist who thinks nothing they do is ever good enough.
Working toward our ideals *and* taking breaks are both ways
to affirm our goodness.

A minor detour: It is important to have the highest ideal
you can envision and vigorously strive toward it. It is equally
important to know you will never achieve it. And to not beat
yourself up for your inability to do so, or for your oh-so-human
lack of working as hard toward your ideal as you think you
should. After all, the degree of effort that you envision as ideal
is, well, yet another *ideal.*

Okay, back to the commodity style of self-improvement.
As I said, it takes a lot to keep your gains. So most of my
books—and classes—consist of practices (also call them
exercises, meditations, and the like) I've developed that help
people find and maintain inner strength (e.g., confidence,
self-knowledge, commitment to their true path). I tend to
teach a coherent body of ongoing practices that maintain the
benefits one obtained when one first does the book's or class's
program. The practices as a whole create a firm sustaining
daily path under one's feet as one wanders the wondrous yet
difficult road of life. This book adds significant aspects to the
published body of practices I've developed. One book cannot
provide all the practices, so this book alone will not fulfill the
program described in this paragraph.

My point *here* is that it feels imperative to confront
the terrible message that so many of us have been given in

this commodity culture: "You *got* it, you're done." I hate how much pain this belief causes people, when it can be avoided with the knowledge that inner gems like peace, confidence, generosity, self-love, and assertiveness need to be nourished or they weaken. We lose our gains.

Advice from a Cat
How to Eat, Sleep, and Purr Your Way Through Life, Love, and Success

Speaking of books, I had a bad dream. In it, I was browsing in a book store, and a volume fell off the shelf. I picked it up and read its back cover:

"When self-help writer, Francesca De Grandis, found out that her cat, Teenie, had managed to sell a book of kitty wisdom, Francesca was put out, to say the least.

"After all, *she* was supposed to be the expert in the field, not her house pet. Teenie pointed out that Francesca had mentioned in two books what a saint her cat is. At which point Francesca conceded her point, and even offered to help Teenie write the book.

"Their combined efforts resulted in *How to Eat, Sleep, and Purr Your Way Through Life, Love, and Success*, an 80-page text filled with whimsy and down-to-earth advice about everything from serving a dinner party to serious life issues, such as divorce."

I woke up sweating. The dream had ended with the book becoming a best seller. And Teenie giving all the profits to her favorite charity. What a repulsive idea! Don't get me wrong, I truly believe Teenie was Buddha in a former life. So, I guess I shouldn't be upset. But I work so *hard* as a writer. And then to be bettered in sales by a *cat*?

When I cooled down, it made sense, though. In addition to Teenie's almost-divine wisdom, cats are great. Look at the record. The ancient Egyptians worshiped cats as deities, witches keep cats as familiars (magical helpers), feisty women live with feline companions, and children can't resist kittens. Why? Because deep down, we all instinctively know that cats have been keeping the secrets of life from us all these years. And now my black, short-hair domestic has decided to share this long-hidden knowledge. We should all learn how a cat stays serene, elegant, and content no matter what comes her way. Maybe I'll write the book with her: Its back cover will say, "Discover how Teenie stays poised and still can:

◊ cope with difficult roommates
◊ maintain an exercise program
◊ keep her weight down
◊ attract the dream lover
◊ be an inspiring force to those she loves
◊ have someone wait on her hand and foot
◊ find self-expression
◊ be worshiped by those who visit her home
◊ and have endless fun with nothing more than fur, tongue, and a body-length piece of string."

Robert A. Heinlein said, "Women and cats will do as they please, and men and dogs should relax and get used to the idea." But in my particular situation, I'm in the same boat as the men. So, hey, I look forward to the royalty checks!

Full-Tilt Living—It's Not Just Bungee-Jumping

A publishing colleague and I were playing with words, trying to title this book. I suggested that the phrase "full-tilt living" be included. She countered, "That won't work in the title, because you're not a full-tilt living type."

I objected. "Hey, my entire life is constant risk. I just moved across the country so disabled that, medically speaking, I wasn't supposed to make the trip. But I was following a dream. I'm also out of the broom closet as a pagan, big time. I'm self-employed doing lunatic things that don't always pay the bills. I live my life fully—c'mon!"

However, she explained that she wasn't speaking personally but in publishing short-hand: As far as most people go, a book title with "full-tilt living" in it denotes bungee-jumping.

Yeah, bungee-jumping, and club-hopping til 4 A.M., and irresponsible sex. As well as defiance that adds up to little more than change of dress and mannerisms. Not to mention truths that, though hip, deep, and concerned, become dogma invalidating other truths that are hip, deep, and concerned.

And how about the "You can't mess with me, dude!" mentality? It seems to be a necessary step in moving away from dominant paradigms that hurt us—whether dominant in society as a whole or only in personal spheres, such as family—but *staying* the rebel-without-a-cause constitutes having moved from the original painful cage to yet another.

Real full-tilt living is not necessarily visible. And when it is, it might be because the person showing it is doing so at risk of life and limb, like Martin Luther King Jr. His walks were full-tilt living.

The attempt for wild self-expression is often waylaid by, to repeat my above examples, club-hopping, irresponsible sex, immature defiance, and a penchant for hip dogma, all of which often don't deliver the sense of being fully alive and free that's expected. Let a new definition of full-tilt living emerge: the invisible *inner* adventure of following your dreams. (And when you do *that*, you can end up with *truly* free, fun, and oh-wow-I-can't-believe-how-good-that-felt sex.)

If my talk about false freedom makes you think of people who are exactly what I've described, that's fine. But it's easy to see how people other than oneself fail in the search for selfhood. Harder, and more important, is asking oneself, "What false freedom have I fallen prey to? How is rebelliousness making me do something other than what would *really* constitute freedom? What need I do instead?"

Just as important is examining yourself regarding the following problem, which I see hurt and alienate almost every free-thinker I meet. Let's say a lot of people made fun of your unusual ideas, invalidated them in other ways, or otherwise rejected you for your non-conformity. They preferred oppressive beliefs and values that restricted you. But then you fully claimed your own notions about life. This empowerment was hard-won. There was a lot of pain and battle beforehand. If, after claiming your freeing insights as good and appropriate, you have not *fully* resolved the inner turmoil and hurt from being "different," it can keep you from bonding with any like-minded people.

How so? Asking yourself the following questions, and variations thereof, will show you: Do I hear *any* disagreement with my free thinking as an attack? If someone agrees with almost every point of my hard won, beloved, important ideas, but they don't see eye to eye on one detail, do I have a knee-jerk reaction of "They don't understand me *at all* and are *trying to get me to revert to the old ways that suppressed me?*"

Even if you've learned to be proud of who you are and what you think, *some* insecurities can remain from having been pummeled by mainstream hurtful opinions. If so, anxiety, even if subconscious, can make you cling to your new improved realizations too tightly. And this is key: We must allow our freeing ideas to be challenged without thinking that the challenger is trying to get us to revert to the old ways and ideas that once restricted us. Because no matter how much we have grown, and *how hard* we worked to become freer, *we'll lose that freedom unless we see it as just one more step along the road toward greater wholeness of self.*

Example: Colin overcomes the nasty little idea that sex is sinful. Great! So he is no longer ashamed of his sexual longings. Great! Then his best friend Jonathan says, "It is a bad idea to be coming onto Andrea right now. She's very vulnerable, since her father just died, and you are taking advantage of her fragile state." Instead of hearing what Jonathan means, Colin answers, "Hey, there is nothing wrong or bad about sex." In doing away with the sin idea, Colin threw the baby out with the bathwater, deciding that *any* sexual behavior is acceptable, and that to challenge *anything* he does sexually is to insist that he go back to his shameful ways.

I often criticize the alternative community and will do it plenty herein, but I do it as a member of that community. And as someone who adores that community. In fact, I believe its members are powerful and caring enough to keep growing, no matter how hard it may have been to get to where we already are. We have the strength to not rest on our laurels. We have the fine minds needed to make gentle distinctions. We have the intellect to keep making the sort of distinctions that allow us to grow past any "all or nothing" positions that may subtly infiltrate our thoughts. (One theme in this book, viewed through the lens of wacky wisdom, is the flaws in the counterculture that keep it from being more powerful, more effective, and more caring for its members.)

So when someone questions your behavior or beliefs, ask yourself, "Are they possibly trying to get me to *build* on those beliefs and improve them, instead of asking me to reject my beliefs and go back to the old hurtful ways? Do I feel like I must battle with someone who disagrees even if that person is really on my side?" I'm gonna ask *myself* all these questions. Again and again.

Afterthoughts: So, being free is hard work, and it doesn't stop. People who refute hurtful mainstream religious or societal beliefs—with all the bravery and hard work it entails—still may not live as happily as they had hoped. Sometimes, the reason is that, *without realizing it*, these folks may not be acting according to their new principles yet. For example, my student Georgette rejected unhealthy hierarchy, wanting freedom. Despite this huge leap, she still felt dominated—by vague inner forces. But she overcame them when I gave her new ways of looking at—and dealing with—them. In the same way, I try herein to provide experiences and ideas that help one's hard won doctrines bear fruit as a way of life, instead of remaining mere concepts.

There are *many* ways that people get stuck, when first trying to change for the better, because they don't know the exact step(s) needed for the point they're at. There are also many times that people *embrace* real change yet remain unable to achieve their goals because there's an additional step (or steps) needed. This book shows many of the missing steps.

The following exercise is one of them. Don't mistake any part of it as denigrating the amazing advances that leaders in self-help and new consciousness create. It's about taking things yet another step, all the way home to your goals, whether you're new to inner transformation or an old hand at it.

The exercise is to consider methods for change you're thinking about possibly using or have used. (I'm not talking about mainstream modalities, like organized religion. Look at unusual or alternative methods, because that is needed for this specific exercise.) Find one method—just one—that isn't effective, whether you know this through experience or just common sense. (It's valuable to look at why mainstream approaches don't work. Do so if that helps you, but not for this exercise.)

After you've chosen one item, be a step past the cutting edge: Take the item apart, whether it's a pseudo-meaningful trend, current hip pose, or counter-culture dogma that's the same old nonsense with new verbiage. In other words, explain to yourself why it doesn't work. One reason is plenty.

Examples: Perhaps a trend or viewpoint offers a certain benefit, but you notice it also gives a subtle message negating that benefit.

Or perhaps you worked hard using a self-help, spiritual, or political body of work, and it left you without any of the joys, powers, or freedoms that all your efforts were geared toward. Or it left you with ridiculously few. Ask yourself why.

Or maybe you're new to self-analysis and inner growth, but your instinct is telling you to back away from a teacher even though she's offering classes that sound just right. When you hesitate to enroll, she pressures you by saying that you're just afraid to grow. That's a sure sign the class won't be effective enough. (And don't let anyone pressure you.)

Or a curriculum might propose that you be yourself and be uninhibited, but it's framed in a shaming way, making you feel "less than" its teacher—that's the same old hierarchical nonsense the curriculum is supposedly helping you overcome. It does the exact opposite, *stifling* your freedom and self-expression. Insights into how we might improve can be coupled with warmth and compassion. We needn't be ruthless with ourselves or others as we try to find sound, mature approaches to personal and social change.

My need for full-tilt living challenges me to move past any headway I've already gained. Whatever inner transformation I've achieved, I want to grow more, into yet greater personal fulfillment and community responsibility. If this is true for you, if you want to live according to your ideals, trust your unique value, and otherwise stick to your guns despite self-doubt caused by changing social mores, economic hardship, or other awful, insistent pressure, and despite *any* other road blocks, we'll keep on growing *together*.

Food for the Fairy Folk: Everyone Can Eat It!

I eat breakfast in my garden as often as I can. Being self-employed plugs you into the rat-race in extremes that only the self-employed understand. It's not that I believe I have things more difficult than people who work for a boss. However, if you use a measure-the-degree-of-on-the-job-misery meter, the needle can go all the way to the far end of the scale even if you're your *own* boss. And the extremity of the problem has its own style.

For example, rolling out of bed and immediately into one's home office on a daily basis easily reduces one to a miserable automaton whose life is not life, but an endless, gray and drab set of mechanized jobs. You can get on a bad track from the get-go, first thing in the morning.

So I try to roll out of bed and into the garden, breakfast in hand. When I start out that way, my day unfolds somewhat sanely, perhaps even beautifully, and with dignity and grace. (I use the word "sanely" in its best sense. Crazy folks are allowed to do that.) Otherwise, I'm prone to spend the day in a miserable, frustrated, frenzied state of workaholic angst.

On my days off, I have more time to spend preparing meals. So the garden breakfast is like a fairy tale!

Today, I had to work. Nevertheless, I still lived in my fairy tale with this simple menu: goat cheese mixed with raisins, pumpkin seeds, almonds, macadamia nuts, walnuts, and some primrose seed oil. This blend, after I sprinkled gobs of delicious bee pollen on it, went in the middle of a plate with orange slices and strawberries all around the edge. I felt like I was preparing a repast for a hobbit! Or fairy, or wood nymph, or other wondrous forest-dwelling being.

And with that in mind, I relished my garden fare, declaring it absolutely yummy. My simple culinary concoction fed my heart beauty, and set my spirit singing.

Later, I mentioned my cheese dish to a friend, who said, "Sounds healthy." Yeah, but if I think of *that*, I won't enjoy such a meal half as much. If I think "hobbit food," however, I'll open to the food's fresh tastes, special subtleties, and vibrant energy = I end up feeling magic in my tummy and spirit.

Even before my friend had made her comment, I had started to think of my meals—I eat wholesome, organic food—as hobbit delights. Relish the bites, enjoy the Tolkien-like wonder and enchantment of the way the dishes sound—"goat cheese, primrose seed oil, bee pollen"—and all and all paint a much nicer experience for myself than "a healthy meal." Who wants to eat while feeling like a responsible drudge? Playing at being a hobbit chef actually lets the healthy meal do its healthy thing to my body; the wholesomeness of the ingredients dances a rumba through my being, making it ring with delight, the very cells tickled and giggling.

Hobbit food, garden breakfast—these are among my little tricks that keep me sane and happy. I hope sharing them here encourages you to find your own, or use ones you already have more often. My vivid fantasies at breakfast create peace—instead of workaholism—for the day ahead. So don't naysay *your* ideas just because they're weird 'n' crazy.

It's easy to forget to let go and enjoy riding the chaos. I'll remind you a few times: There seems a chaos to some of my essays—the following one included—but in fact we travel through a coherent landscape; we cannot find wisdom by ideas alone, but by journeying together along life's paths, which spin and swirl.

There Is Always Someone Home

I want to move toward the chapter's end on a serious note. Sometimes, people with serious psychiatric problems are subjected to a view of insanity summed up by "You're nuts, there's no one home upstairs." This might keep them from recovering. Instead, they must be viewed as still being "real" people. And in some cases, telling clinically insane people that the inner hell they live in is *real* can validate them sufficiently to be a means to healing. The constructs of "no one home" and "your hell is not real" are part and parcel of the same roadblock to mental healing that is a main thrust of this essay.

In other words, I don't believe insanity exists, at least not in some of the ways it is defined.* We all live in worlds of our own internal designs, and all the cosmos mirrors each person's mind, uniquely, and becomes engulfed within each person's psyche.

---

* Note that I wrote, "*some* of the ways it is defined." There are definitely types of mental illness that are not the focus of this essay.

These landscapes are cultivated by storm and sun, balmy rains, and random winds that blow the seeds of fortune onto soil, soil that is fertile, claylike, or sandy to begin with.

Sometimes a healer helps by moving into someone's so-called insane world. If at those times, instead, the healer decides, "You're nuts, there's no one home," they cannot be a guide within the hellish realm who points to the exit. And a world denied means no landscape; no landscape means there is no point in a road map showing a route through and out.

The healer descends into the person's nightmares, torments, hopes, all the time saying, "Yes, this is the real world. Let's talk here, work here, celebrate here."

Here is my point, and it is not *necessarily* about dealing with someone who is mentally ill: There are reasons other than mental illness that might cause us to think "There's no one home." We might, perhaps subconsciously, consider someone not quite real because they lack formal education. Or because they're bigoted or bad tempered or have opinions unlike our own. Or lack "social graces." Or do not appreciate something we hold precious, such as ballet, hand-crafted items, the environment, our religion, or our innovative approach to life. Or they might have such immense artistry or have accomplished so much that we assume they're not subject to all the usual fear, inner turmoil, and other foibles the rest of us have—in other words, they are not fully human. E.g., I once found myself thinking that someone who'd succeeded in filmmaking could only have done so because he didn't have the artistic depth of concerns that I do. Egad! Yes, I actually assumed he lacked substance, just because he'd done well in Hollywood! There's always someone home. And when I think otherwise about someone, I've exempted that person from the human race. Think of the implications: For one thing, if someone is not home, we are allowed to treat them badly; there is no point in honoring their human rights! Or in being sensitive to their vulnerabilities—I mean the emotional vulnerabilities that *all* humans have. I also mean vulnerabilities to mundane problems; for example, if we think a successful artist is innately immune to others, we might say and do things without realizing that it can destroy that person's family or life's work.

Even if mental illness is not involved, all us humans need to have—and be—companions, wherever we're mentally residing on any given day. And we all need guides. Maybe we don't need help navigating the passage out of a nightmare caused by a psychiatric problem. But there are lesser territories in the dark recesses of *anyone's* mind, and these are places we don't like to stay long. And no one can be a companion or guide unless they can convey in word *and* deed, "I see you I see you I see you. And I see where you are I see where you are I see where you are. I live there with you right this minute. And *this* minute too. And *this* minute."

Mind you, we don't have to know each others' *exact* minds, we don't have to know each others' exact fears, but we must never think so poorly of a person that they do not quite exist to us as fully human or that the world they live in is too farfetched. Whenever I have hit such a point, I am not quite human *myself*.

To build the best possible alternative community for

yourself, know that there is always someone home. Seeing that others fully exist will not only help them, will not only build community, it will also empower you in ways I can't explain, you have to experience it. All I can say is: The more real and full others seem to you, the more real and full you will seem to yourself, the more compassionate you will become to yourself, the more valid you will seem to yourself. The more home *you* will be. Come home, come home, come home to yourself, come home to yourself *fully*.

I Love My Community

In this essay, I have to say good things about my work. To be able to do so has taken a lot of inner change. I had to move through mega-fear. No, not fear. Terror. But as I said earlier, I came to learn that when fear keeps me from letting someone know I have skills that might help them, it is not modest; it is selfish. But it still terrifies me sometimes, because it draws fire. And with that:

At the beginning of *Share My Insanity*, I said what I hoped to accomplish for you. It's time to add to that overview.

1) I try to show exactly how advances in alternative living aren't delivering everything we'd hoped. Example: Alternative tools help people embrace the importance of celebrating their uniqueness and following their dreams. But they still might not be able to achieve all their heartfelt goals. They may not understand the discrepancy and *why* they are not more successful. I provide explanations and solutions. My students achieve remarkable wholeness and self-expression.

2) Forward *thinking* is great! Discussing shifts in consciousness *theoretically* is great. *Learning* innovative theory is great. But I've created tools—new modalities of healing and empowerment—that radically change people's emotions and behaviors, so that they can *live* that theory. Ideas aren't always enough to change us as deeply as we want, let alone in ways that are still in effect years down the line. Some of my methods are here. (They are part of a larger curriculum called *Another Step*. See *Resources for Illuminated Lunatics* at the end of the book.)

   It shows immense progress to approach our challenges and opportunities by addressing the whole self—mind, body, and spirit. Perhaps you use a therapist, exercise regularly, eat well, and meditate. Excellent! But it may not have brought you the last nine yards, whether your goal is serenity, starting a business, finding your soul mate, and/or whatever else you might pursue. As innovative as we have been by coming at life from a variety of angles, there is another step needed. So I developed new methods. This paragraph does *not* mean my material is inappropriate for inner-change newbies. They won't have to waste time on tools that don't take them far enough fast enough.

3) I've numbered the points, for clarity's sake, but within each item are all the others. Within each dot are all the other dots. You know that a main theme of this book is

drawing on *all* your inner resources, *all* your emotions and ideas. This holistic sense of self has often been promised to readers. I try to reveal why we, as a culture and as individuals, haven't yet been able to become holistic *enough*. Healthy madness helps us be *truly* well-rounded, integrated, and able to embrace our own *inner* diversity of thought, emotion, and talent. As such, we learn to recognize and draw on more of our innate powers.

4) People no longer have purely religious, political, sexual, or psychological dialogues. They talk about a million topics simultaneously, while applying a million different disciplines. They don't want pieces, they want an integrated *whole*. I am lucky to follow the tradition of Holy Trickster, whose voice is exempt from censorship on any topic. (People *do* try to silence me. Constantly. Viciously. It is frightening and makes life hard. Nevertheless, my spiritual lineage is a real strength that helps maintain me.) I hope my interdisciplinary approach echoes *your* multifaceted being and affirms that your many assets make you up to the challenge of life's ever-updated chaos.

Drawing on any useful discipline includes using pop culture fun—instead of dry academic lecture—as self-help. I grew up on *I Love Lucy*. TV is relaxing and easy to imbibe. At the end of a hard day, not everyone has it in them to mentally dig their way through obscure boring material. (I don't!) But Lucy, though fun, didn't give me enough meat with my potatoes. I believe that easygoing entertainment can convey substantive material. Think about *Buffy the Vampire Slayer* (yay, Joss)! Consider the long tradition of Chinese opera. It was for the "common folk" and had an incredible degree of artistry. Consider my friend who teaches beading classes; on the surface, they're just for entertainment but, the way she teaches, students learn confidence, serenity, and self-respect. It insults viewers and readers to think that depth can only be conveyed through non-entertaining mediums. The Holy Trickster's antics in sacred circle were often frivolous and slapstick.

5) Directness about life's issues is needed to change our personal lives and society. We can all be mad(wo)men, allowed no-holds-barred talk, saying what we need to. This book fosters and is part of that dialog. "Sanity" is not always the best option.

6) The alternative community just isn't alternative enough. Don't misunderstand—I love this community, and I realize it is simply a matter of us having more work to do. Being human means needing to improve. My community is not unusual in the fact that it has faults. My community is unusual in that it has enormous potential for overcoming its shortcomings. Crazy Sage wisdom can reveal and heal many flaws that suppress this community's potential. Example: We are amazing about honoring diversity, but it is an area that still needs a lot of improvement. For one thing, some people

are left out of dialogs about creativity and innovation if they don't express these things in easily recognized ways, such as artistic hobbies. I hope they have their own styles of originality affirmed in this book.

7) To grow past where old innovations brought us, we must live in a *culture* of the new consciousness,* walking in a new world. The important words here are *world, culture,* and *live.* I tried to write a book that, when you are reading it, you *live* in a new paradigm. That environment will cause an inner shift that an intellectual journey can't. I reside in that cultural matrix daily, as may you—a lot of people do—and when I show you *my* part of the terrain, it helps you know *yours* better.

   Life is not a modern highway speeding directly from here to there, with well-marked signs and a clear map. Life is a twisting road. No, better to say it's a road that *swirls* through plains, valleys, and mountains, then swirls up off the ground and into space, its spinning making you dizzy. A book that lays everything all out in theory, flat on the ground, feels safe: Whew, you know what to do! And no risks! But it is a useless approach in some ways. Learning by being in a cultural matrix is just that: *being,* not theory. You *live* that culture. This bumpy joyous ride—sometimes puzzling and even painful—transforms you deep down. And that

---

* A lot of people talk about "the new consciousness," using the term to mean different things. For our purposes in this paragraph, it refers to cutting edge thoughts and modalities of awareness.

is what I have tried to provide herein, in Toad's Wild Ride.

I did not discuss *all* my goals at the start of the book because, when you begin with theory alone, it is hard to then shift into *being* instead of *thinking*. The means is the end. So I explain a bit here and a bit there. Having integrated more of the book's overview *now* adds facets to the experiential process that this book constitutes.

Two sentence summary: My work is an interfaith, interdisciplinary intertwining of newly-evolving DNA. It is *experiential* mysticism.

By and large I fulfill this overview without pointing it out. Creating a transformative *experience* for you means leaving out things that might distract. Most of my theories that are relevant to this book remain unspoken. Being implicit in everything I *do*, they are conveyed subtly, but far better than if I delivered them overtly. My readers are intelligent. If they *care* to know my theories, they've the smarts to figure them out. But it is not something they need to do to benefit from my work.

Faerie Nation

A few years back, I imagined a global tribe. Of social innovators, spiritual outlaws, poets, clowns, and other originals—the lunatic fringe of the alternative community. Add folks who identify as fairies, dragons, witches—people who happily, fruitfully live *in* myth, *as* myths—sanely insane. (I'm a fairy-dragon-witch-bunny! If you identify as any type of otherworldly being, or as a wolf, eagle, or other animal, this is tribe that you'll fit right into.)

I imagined a spiritual focus that's not religious; it is earthy mysticism. Tribe members might be pagan, Christian, Buddhist, or be happily *without* a tradition.

I imagined people who refuse to be bound by dogma or other limiting restrictions, and who nevertheless realize the power, fun, and necessity of tribe. I imagined our tribe celebrates the lone wolf; and we are a *pack* of wolves. We are paradox, the split second between boredom and fear: ecstasy.

So I founded Faerie Nation, where we each create our unique path, and join together—in a new way that people who never join anything can join—in celebration and cooperation.

Mind you, the above also describes the Another Step community. People who study with me or whom I counsel tend to be like me—the alternative movement just isn't alternative enough for them. The same goes for my close friends. All these folks are the most wonderful folks I could imagine.

However, someone may want to join our lunacy, but not study with me. Many lunatics feel isolated. What's more, I *personally*, deeply need a *global* community of wild mystics; I had that before Faerie Nation, through Another Step and other avenues, but the more the merrier. So, both for myself, and as middle management for chaos gods, I started Faerie Nation (FN).

Don't fit my description of FN members? This Fey-touched tribe is for anyone who wants to join it. The merely curious, wildly confused, thoroughly hostile, perfectly cynical, and "I-won't-join-because-I'll-never-fit-in" folks have a place with us. Even fundies are welcome. (But we might put bells on you so you can't sneak up on children.)

Participate how *you* want. E.g., if you just lurk on our on-line list, awesome! No forced activities in *our* tribe.

What do we *do* in FN? We play together, change the world together, do ritual together, heal our spirits together—or not. It's according to each individual's inclinations. This list of activities is not a comprehensive view of what happens in FN. We're too diverse for that.

This piece about Faerie Nation describes a community, yet it is in a self-help chapter, instead of in another part of *Share My Insanity*. All the dots . . . A gorgeous evolution will allow lone wolves to run in a pack. The same radical shifting of our cells and DNA is necessary to go the last nine yards toward our dearest personal goals, protect human rights, and save Gaia. Without a tribe of folks who don't usually join groups, neither Gaia nor our species will survive.

I don't insist that others agree with all this, but I'm passionate about it. I've prepared for lifetimes to develop and teach innovative material that helps stars drench the atoms of your being, and creates rapid, joyful change at a cellular level. All my classes and books create this evolution, even when they're not specifically described as such. This is past the most authentic ancient shamanic paradigms. And I trust *those* paradigms more than I trust almost any other. I'm breaking new mystical ground.*

---

* Questions to ponder: People acknowledge scientific and psychological discoveries. However, spiritual innovation is thought impossible. The same

Accept no substitutes. My teachings aren't the only way to accomplish what I'm proposing, but stay away from teachers who worry about their "market." I don't want them to hurt anyone. You can spot them: Do they imitate descriptions of innovative curriculums or books, but use the same old approach, so can't achieve new results? In other words, is there new rhetoric without ground-breaking methodologies? Do they walk the new talk, or does their behavior feel off to you somehow? Perhaps "better than thou?" New Age or personal fundamentalism? (Below, "Afterthoughts" defines *personal fundamentalism.*) Trying to create a monopoly by gossiping about teachers unlike themselves? Good grief. (Some leaders tried to blockade my work. I prayed with friends, "May I be able to continue helping people shine in their own truths and authentic paths." Our prayer was answered.)

Nothing in the above paragraph is meant to denigrate old theories and methods that are tried and true; I honor, teach, and personally use them. But they can't do it all. We need both old *and* new ways, to address not only the immense inner change mentioned above, but also many other concerns and challenges that mystics, artists, pagans, social innovators, activists, and other independent thinkers might have.

Stardust is falling on you, every moment. Grab it.

---

goes for mystical and psychic breakthroughs. What does this say about modern society? What does it imply about potential for an evolution of the human spirit? Yes, *anything* discovered has likely always existed, but why do we refuse to credit the person who first notices *spiritual, mystical,* or *psychic* facts? Why are we more likely to say, "There is nothing new under the sun" if we're looking at spiritual, mystical, or psychic work?

The book's resource guide has contact info for Faerie Nation.

Afterthoughts: To create crazy-camaraderie for yourself, make an environment where wild souls can run free. Here are a few ideas.

Wild souls bolt if you're unkind. Don't attack. Being gentle won't squelch your heathen spirit, but instead provides the caring a wolf gives its cubs. Freedom doesn't = meanness. Next tip:

No fundamentalism: Christian, Buddhist, Wiccan, political, academic, or personal. By *personal* I mean beliefs of one's own devising that one holds as the only truth. If you think this is irrelevant to you, consider. If you've had to fight to honor your own ideas in the face of intolerance, it's easy to become intolerant or suspicious of someone who has good *reason* to disagree with you. I mention this elsewhere herein, but it's a major block to independent thinkers supporting each other, so it bears further scrutiny.

Society as a whole doesn't support people thinking for themselves. Free spirits can go from that extreme to the other, by seeing any challenge to their ideas as an invalidation of them. In a roomful of this type of person, each one may think he is right. And he *is*—for *himself*. But what *could* have been a chance for mutual support between diverse thinkers turns into *more* painful squelching of their views.

For example, a person who's fearful of once again being told "Put a lid on it" may try to protect her own opinions by arguing for them in a way that's mindless of others' feelings.

She may not realize she's doing it. In other words, determined to stand up for herself (which is a *good* thing), and caught up in her nervousness, she can't see that her tone and/or choice of words cause her *listener* to feel invalidated! Subtle stuff. The last thing she'd ever want to do is stifle someone!

It can take a lot to change this pattern. Here's part of the solution: Watch for your fear of invalidation, and calm it before you speak. Then, speak not to the beliefs that are on the table but to the heart. Support the heart. And support people's efforts. Maybe even forget the topic of your ideas, the other person's ideas, and the difference between them.

Also, listen with your heart, not your head. Listen to feelings and experiences. Listen for commonalities in them, instead of differences. Share *your* stories, too. Stories create a community where, organically, almost as a by-product, each person's allowed their own thoughts. In some of these conversations, it is most helpful to you and others to forget *ideas*, and share your *journeys*. Star-drenched!

Remaining Crazy—By Choice

I forget easily. I forget that God loves me. I forget She has a plan that includes my happiness. I forget that the insanity I confront daily—heartless insanity of bureaucracy, cruel insanity of social mores, ruthless insanity of enforced mediocrity—need not rule me. I forget I can live in another world, one not defined by these insanities.

Today I choose my *own happily* crazy world, where love is priority, where creativity is honored, where miracles are alive and working effectively, where beauty, helping others, and fun reign. (In some ways, miracles are the equivalent of magic. Oh, Disney, I love you! Despite all I cannot stand about your corporate policies, I'm grateful that, amidst the blandness of our world, you keep pumping out fairy tales about wizards, wonder, and enchantment.)

I can live this choice if I do not live in anger at the insanities of others. Anger keeps me living in their world all day, living according to their rules and defeatist beliefs, living in their confusion, bitterness, and mistakes.

I release the anger now, and so now live where love is priority, creativity is honored, miracles are working festively. Beauty, service, and fun become all. I will remain happily crazy—by choice.

Afterthoughts: Anger is God-given, so I do not suppress it or shame myself for it. I feel it. *Only then* can I let it go.

If you've been invalidated or shamed about your anger or other emotions, you may have buried them deep inside, so you lost awareness of them. We get many negative messages about feelings: "You're bad to be angry." "Why should you be sad at *that*?" "You shouldn't be hurt just because someone was rude." "It's silly to *ever* get upset."

We stifle anger and other feelings not just because they've been *invalidated*, but also by *validating* them to ourselves. Justifying them can smother them just as well as thinking they're *not* justified! In other words, if I start to get angry, then focus on justifying that anger, even silently to myself, I'm too busy to *feel* it. I'm not giving it the chance to just be. And if it's an emotion that will cause trouble should it stick around—like anger—I'm like most folks: I can't release it *until after* I've *felt* it.

Another way to suppress emotions is to invest them with indignation—"How dare they treat me that way? No one should be treated like this!"

Just as effective at interfering with our emotional process is the high moral ground: "What a terrible person she is, how horribly she's behaved to me!" A subtler righteous indignation is, "I may have shortcomings, but at least *I* wouldn't behave that way."

We can also suppress ourselves by trying to find meaning or decision *within the moments of experiencing* a feeling. For example, in the actual moment of your grief, if you try to find philosophical meaning in it, or try to use it as the basis for an important or even minor decision, you're not letting the grief *happen*. Don't get me wrong, feelings are important factors in decision-making. Our emotions inform us in vital ways. We need to listen to our feelings in order to make major life decisions, because otherwise we're only living in our head. But in *the moment of having the feeling*, we need to *just have the feeling*. Then, *afterwards*, try to let it go, analyze it as much as you want in order to use it in decision-making, write a novel about it, or whatever.

So-called negative emotions—anger will be the example—have an important place. But holding onto anger about a particular person or event can hurt you, in the way the above essay describes. And anger can't eventually leave until you feel it fully. How? Experience it as physical and/ or emotional sensations, operative word *sensations*. Just be aware of it, the way you would a breeze against your cheek or a stubbed toe. This is simple but can be difficult if it's a painful emotion, but *afterwards* I can realistically try to release it, truly leave it behind! I can move past it into a beautiful day.

Chapter Four
Cock-eyed, Out of Your Mind,
and Having Taken Leave of Your Senses

Let me reiterate: Cleaving to your dreams affects every part of life; therefore, your fantasies are touched on in all chapters. Now, however, we'll focus *specifically* on creating one's dream life, and the dreams that lead to it.

Believing in the Ridiculous
Written before I moved from San Francisco

There's enormous power and virtue in listening to the absurdities that spring forth from your own mind.

In preparing to move from urban apartment to rural house, I've pictured myself growing vegetables. An economically smart act for a woman without much money, plus I love gardens. Kind of a nice picture in the mind, too.

But yesterday, I remembered: I love gardens, but hate *to* garden. My urban garden is fabulous only because friends do a great deal of the work for me—I'm too disabled but, since I'm basically housebound as a cripple, my garden is my sanity, a sanctuary with bees and roses where I escape my apartment's confines. My friends realize how crucial this patch of vegetation is to my mental health—the greenery barely existed before I got sick—so they generously tend the plants.

And I do what I can.

Even were I healthy, I'd still hate gardening.

So what on Goddess' green earth made me think I would enjoy vegetable gardening?

Realizing I had been delusional, I asked myself what I *really* want in a garden. I let my mind drift through the years of my childhood, teens, and twenties. An absurd mental picture appeared from childhood days. The image ignited me with joy: a witch's garden, like you might imagine in an old country story or fairytale. Weedy and overgrown, filled with nettles, roses that climb all over trellises and old chairs—a chaotic, joyous, and quiet mystery.

"Why not?" I thought. Lately I've allowed the absurd images, desires, and ideas—ones that I left behind as youthful follies—to take root, so that I could see where they might lead. When I can't *literally* fulfill that absurd image, desire, or idea, I know that, deep down, I would not want to. Often, nevertheless, the fruit is a realization that there's not a single darn reason I can't live that absurdity, full-tilt and happy.

In other cases, my openness to the absurdity leads me to a very fulfilling adaptation. Or I at least get the satisfaction of some bit of my dream. (That's so much better than having no part of it!) Other times, validating the ridiculous allows me to find out what it symbolizes to me and, whatever that is, *it* might be attainable.

As to my future garden, with its nettles and weeds: Dandelions and nettles are marvelous food, not to mention strong medicine. So right off the bat, I've got a bit of a vegetable patch growing, and won't have to fuss in the dirt much for it. And I love tea made from roasted dandelion root.

I remember my Italian grandmother out in my childhood backyard, picking dandelions for dinner. I like to think she'd be proud of me.

As to the rest of the garden, forget the doomsday recitals of those who declare, "Roses are *so* hard to grow." That's only the new breeds. I've got three of the old variety that will make the move from city to country easily. These are the type of roses that you could jump up and down on, and they'd still flourish. Or so I'm told. I'm kind of new at gardening.

I called a friend who has a green thumb and told her about my witch-in-a-fairy-tale garden. I asked what should go in it. She said, "Daisies. Cosmos." Perfect! Plus there has to be lots of ivy, climbing all over everything. I love ivy and have four stunning types in my urban garden right now. All of them will move with me. As will my mint—easy care, and I use huge quantities of it, as opposed to carrots, which I *do* eat a lot of but are far cheaper to buy, and much more of a labor to grow.

Of *course*, God's synchronicity being what it is, I already have mint in my garden to transplant. As I do sweet grass, ferns, and spider plants—all equally perfect for my dreamscape.

I have an enormous container garden. My outdoor space is huge, but cement. When I move, I will still container garden. For one thing, when plants are up high I can, disability notwithstanding, do some of my own gardening.

My lovely retreat area is filled with brick-supported

shelves loaded with plants. A cement wall around the area holds yet more plants. A six-foot-long planter stands a good three feet off the ground. And so on.

"How will I adapt my witch-with-a-wondrous-garden-in-the-middle-of-the-woods vision to containers?" I asked myself.

I don't know yet.

But with this new plan, I at least won't find myself covered with dirt, wondering why the hell I'm trying to grow carrots, and what ever made me think I would enjoy it. And if I stay open to absurdities, synchronicity, and all other forms of divine intervention, *some* sort of happiness-inducing witch's garden will grace my new home.

I look out the window at my urban garden. It's not the green fantasy I hope for in my future, but I can see the hints of it. Maybe all I need is more containers. A statue. Hmmm, let me hold a picture of that fairy-tale garden in my mind again and see what I see . . . Ah, that magical cottage doesn't have a million types of plants around it, just a good variety as its staples. And a fair number of variables as the seasons change. I already have a great deal of what I need. The ivy and the likes only have to spread more. And I should acquire more seasonals, and find a few types of wee little flowers that look like fairies hide among them.

Afterthoughts: Eight years later, you should see my yard! It makes me happy. Neither my process creating it nor the end result went as planned. For example, the ivy I wanted is a no-no because it's an invasive plant; and I worked too hard, forgetting that growing an easy weed garden was my goal.

But I've learned to be a lazy gardener! Moving on:

Let me sum up: A "crazy" childhood love of wild, overgrown fairy-tale cottages solved a problem of mine, and became a jumping off point for an easily maintained, environmentally sound garden of edible weeds. I love being crazy! And love you for *your* craziness. Here's an exercise to help you draw on the "ridiculous" wonders left behind in your youth, and use them to solve problems. If you're used to self-help or imaginatively finding your desires or the like, I suggest you try these instructions anyway, exactly as is. Students who come to me, and are old hands in other self-growth systems, or have created their own ways of dealing with such things, will concur that they still needed to do things my way. (I have the oddest history of people who will not do what anyone else tells them to do nevertheless doing what *I* tell them to do. I don't understand it.) For one thing, a lot of my 101 basics are not the same as others' even though they may look similar on the page. You can't tell the difference until you actually use the instructions. For another thing, my material meets you where you live. Example: Let's say I give an exercise to a newbie. As she carries it out, she'll find her concerns experientially addressed. A spiritual journeyer with many miles under her belt will find that the same exercise touches her more informed concerns, current inner blocks, and the likes.

Ah, the Fruitfulness of Wacky Wisdom

Step 1) First choose your question: What do I really want in a

garden (home, job, mate, self, spiritual path, or . . . ?)
Fill in the blank with only one item.

Step 2) Let your mind drift through your childhood and
teen years. Operative word: drift. This exercise does
not work if you do it with laser-like concentration, a
laborious effort, a sharp focus. Rest your attention
gently on your younger years, the way your head rests
gently on a pillow at night.

Step 3) As your mind drifts, let images, desires, and ideas
arise. Don't discount any. Just note them, without
worrying if they're useful or not.

Step 4) If your mind drifts to other things, or starts getting
sharply contracted onto the matter at hand or into
fierce worry, don't think you're doing the exercise
wrong. Just reread and use the instructions in Step 2
again. It's hard to have that gentle focus. One reason
Step 1 says to fill in the blank with only one item is that
more can overwhelm, making you have to think *hard*;
this exercise has to be done with some degree of ease.

Step 5) Brainstorm about the images, desires, or ideas. This
could go several directions. Maybe it is as simple as
just making practical plans to implement what came
up in Step 3. Or, if you can't fulfill what came up,
figure out how to adapt it so that you can have what
is possible. *Then* make your practical plan. Or ask
yourself if the absurdity is a *symbol* of a deep desire;
if so, then make your plan. If nothing that rose from

your mind seems useful, let it go, but stay open to it. Later you might see its worth. And if it has none, a completely new image, desire, or idea may come when you least expect it—a month from now!—and be just what you need.

Step 6) Implement any plan you come up with. Repeat the exercise with the same question when you need more ideas about this plan.

Do not feel discouraged and a failure if you get nothing from this exercise, or cannot do it with a relaxed ease of mind. Simply trying all the steps calls forth the childlike wonder that is in all of us, even if deeply buried. In fact, if you feel nothing when you do the exercise, it has its effect, whether you ever note them as such or not. For example, you may in the future weeks suddenly feel a bit more hopeful, open, or trusting of yourself.

Mirror, Mirror, on the Wall
An Allegory and Exercise

The above piece's discussion about following your dreams leaves the question, "But what if you've lost them?" "Mirror, Mirror, on the Wall" is an allegory about a fairy who creates miracles until she loses her magic. The renewal of her power shows crazy methods—as well as the wholehearted commitment needed—for regaining optimism, bravery, and lost dreams.

Once upon a time, there was a fantastic being—in every sense of the word *fantastic*. She was magical; with a flick of her wand, or even of her wrist, worlds were created. She was brave; the risks necessary to save souls in distress, the risks of following her dreams—she took these on, despite the trembling in her heart and knees. She was optimistic; naysayers and social absurdities did not stop her from her delights, laughter, missions, and love of all beings. She was also a dreamer; living in dreams worked well for her, because she imagined them so wholeheartedly, and lived in them so thoroughly, that they came true. In other words, she came to live in them on the mundane plane, you see?

But she forgot how fantastic she was. A diet of bad food made her feel heavy and grey-minded, which is not a light, magical feeling at all. In addition, some of her risks were exactly what risks can prove to be—acts that result in awful problems. That was, of course, very discouraging for her. Also, she started thinking pessimistically when people she loved, people she'd made sacrifices to help, became afraid to associate with such a dreamer as she. So, yes, she forgot how fantastic she was.

Well, not entirely. She kind of still knew. But rarely. Not enough to construct worlds or make dreams real enough to successfully dwell in.

She tried to become her old self. It was too difficult. Finally, she realized that it would take everything she had, and everything she was, to be the way she had been before: She had to *live* as much of the day as possible in fantasies of her ideal life. She had to *risk* being such a dreamer. She had to *love* as thoroughly, selflessly, bravely, and constantly as she had once. Live, love, risk. Selfless, brave, constant.

And she had to flick that wand—or wrist—all day long. Because *constant* fantastic thoughts and acts are what she had previously done, before her powers had gone missing. She'd lost them through lack of use!

However, this realization wasn't quite enough to get back on track. Then, one day, she was gazing at herself in the mirror. And she didn't like how she looked, thinking she was too tired, ill, discouraged, lonely, and old to be pretty.

That pulled her up by the short hairs. If anyone had offered such an opinion, she'd have been so hurt. And she would have known to say, "Don't you dare talk that way to me!" Yet here she'd been wounding *herself*, with a message that would've been outright cruel coming from someone else.

So she looked and looked and looked at her reflection, trying to find a happy, positive statement about her appearance. And, finally, there it was: She was *fantastic*! A magical, brave, optimistic dreamer! She could *see* that. But she could also recognize that hers was the face of a magical, brave, optimistic dreamer who wasn't being magical, brave, optimistic, or dreamy *enough*. This showed in all her features: They held fatigue, sorrow, resignation, disappointment, and bitterness. And suppressed power, which gave her mouth a frustrated twist. So she appeared a fantastic being who'd been crushed and had lost her powers.

But at least she was on the right track. So she looked into the mirror again. She looked and looked. Every day. Stared and stared. Every night while brushing her teeth before bed. And she found every bit of bravery, magic, optimism, and dreams she could in her face. What she couldn't find, she imagined was there, until, in fact, it was. So, lost dreamer you, you who lost yourself to worry about house payments or health, or to heart-break or other disaster, or to unrealized hopes, or to simple weariness, look in the mirror. The same way she did until she found herself again. Every day. Until you're you, once more. Yes!

A Bug's Life

Many acts or ideas that have saved lives, solved national conflicts, created new art movements, triumphed over the "insurmountable" in someone's personal life, or initiated vital scientific advancements were *initially* called insane.

Even *inner traits* that cause tremendous change—traits like optimism or bravery—are often lauded when discussed theoretically, but are scoffed at and suppressed by being called *nuts* when displayed in real life. When we exhibit bravery, hope, creativity, initiative, confidence, or even *voice* an inclination toward them, *regarding a specific, concrete action we might take in our actual lives,* someone is sure to say, "You're out of touch with reality."

Examples: Say, "I think we should vote, because it makes a difference" (which exhibits hope and optimism), and *someone* will tell you to be sensible instead.

Insist, "We can't just stand here and do nothing" (bravery, optimism, self-confidence), and someone will tell you you're unrealistic.

"I want to be a film director" solicits remarks like, "You're just being starry-eyed," when, in fact, being starry-eyed is exactly how art is created.

Almost every film that exists has a hero in it whom, as a nation, we cheer on, and identify with. Yet, if anyone acts as bravely or daringly, in our own face-to-face lives, we tend to pooh-pooh them (until they've succeeded, that is. More on *that* in a second).

The eccentric outsider portrayed in movies is also adored and, again, identified with. Does this mean we *all* feel like that loner misfit—crazy and marching to our own drummer?

A lot of films reveal the human tendency to ridicule and otherwise try to crush innovators, but to, nevertheless, worship them if they actually reach their "crazy" goals. *A Bug's Life* is a film that stars an animated ant who's an inventor. The rest of the colony pooh-poohs his creations until, of course, one of his innovations saves the day. The movie *Matilda* features a little girl whose family considers her a freak because she, gasp, reads books and is intelligent. The formulaic end of *A Bug's Life* reduces many a moviegoer, myself included, to tears. Our eccentric insect is applauded by his entire colony, everyone clapping and cheering. Does the repetition of this plot in half the films that exist reveal a parallel in our society: Applaud, admire, and honor the outcasts once they triumph, but stomp on and try to crush every last one of them before they possibly *can* achieve something? Thwart success when its first signs appear? That certainly seems the case.

How have we created a society in which so many of its members identify as that crushed bug, that idealistic, odd, and lonely soul? If so many of us feel that way, then who is doing the crushing?

Is it possible that all of us are loners in one way or another, and we are all crushing each other? I crush you, you crush me, oh lonely we shall be. Everyone, join in, sing along . . .

. . . C'mon sing it . . .

. . . because *someone's* crushing all these loners. And if we're *all* the crushed loners, then . . .

. . . Everyone, sing!

Exercise: Support Crazy Bugs

After writing my above thoughts, I realized they reflect something about Cultural Creatives. (Cultural Creatives are people who value independent thinking, challenge their predecessors' beliefs, protect the environment, and emulate "sixties values." They don't focus on acquiring the fanciest house, the most money, or a trophy spouse. They also tend toward volunteer work and meaningful vacation activities.) Research shows that most of them think they're the only one with all the traits that define a Cultural Creative. Despite Cultural Creatives being almost a third of the U.S. population. Food for thought, especially in light of the above ideas.

The traits of Cultural Creatives are not the only ones that people feel isolated about. I get email after email, and hear client after client, saying, "I'm the only one who . . . " and then they finish the sentence in a million different ways. A few examples: They think they're the only one who believes in fairies. Or they feel no one else could possibly have had as traumatic a childhood. Or no one cares as deeply as they do.

Or is as easily hurt. Or has such effective ideas about how to change the world for the better.

Most "I'm the only one . . . " statements represent deep pain. Sometimes that's because the fill-in-the-blank part of the sentence is about something awful that happened. But even if it is not, the person in question suffers a strong sense of isolation. Yet none of the things they fill in the blank with are uncommon.

So here is a suggestion: How do *you* fill in the blank about yourself? Name just one thing. After you've answered that, ask yourself, "How does my thinking this way dehumanize the people I come in contact with?" For example, does it make you feel they are less vulnerable to emotional anguish than you? Or that they don't have your depth of perception? Or that they care less about the well-being of others? Whatever it is, it may dehumanize them in your mind. A painful sense of isolation in oneself can actually dehumanize the people one meets. Which, as I said earlier, leaves you more likely to treat them without all the respect and sensitivity they need; and your acting that way dehumanizes *you* in the process. It also can make you miss opportunities for friendship and support, because you feel no one could possibly be like, or understand, *you*!

This book shows ways we inventive bugs can better spot and support each other. For example, "There Is Always Someone Home" is not specifically about how to treat your fellow innovative thinkers, but its thoughts about being good to *anyone* you meet apply to supporting like-minded loonies.

On another topic, while we're talking about "There Is

Always Someone Home:" It helps one fully embrace diversity among the people one encounters throughout the day, which is part of the *wholly* holistic approach herein.

Many an innovative thinker finds it easier to take the high road about someone whose ideas and lifestyle are miles apart from her own, than it is to accept someone who's quite like herself. The ways that *basically* like-minded person varies from her can provoke every non-acceptance-of-diversity trait *possible* in her, robbing her of friendship (and serenity for days on end). Watching yourself for this sort of bias against those who are "among the ranks" is immensely profitable.

Support crazy bugs!

I'm the Only Genius There Is

I'm the only genius there is. The conclusions I reach come from such a deeply personal place that no one else could *possibly* understand them. Even if someone appreciates my thoughts, or is changed forever by them, said person surely doesn't have my brilliance, or a comparable one of his own.

And that, boys and girls, is a common belief system that keeps otherwise forward-thinking people from working with each other. A person who is committed to living fully has a life so specific in its unique details, so individual in its day-to-day routines or lack thereof, that it's often difficult for that person to recognize that his own inner, immense universe is no greater than that of many *other* people's. It's as if being unique predisposes one to a selective blindness whereby one cannot see someone *else's* unique value.

However, if one, as an act of conscious evolution—yes,

we can evolve through sheer will and thoughtfulness—interacts with others while silently affirming, "The person I'm dealing with has pivotal genius of some kind," then artists, mystics, visionaries, social innovators, etc., can better move from isolation into the power of group action. One's own company has much to offer. Nevertheless, to have the most impact on society or even one's most *personal* situations means claiming every strength possible, including both those of solitude and those of camaraderie. One needn't choose between the two. Today, please try, "The person I'm dealing with has pivotal genius of some kind."

Afterthoughts: Studies—and common sense—reveal that independent spirits have *many* problems supporting (let alone recognizing) each other. *Share My Insanity* addresses a good number of these difficulties. One is mistaking one's own elitism for self-confidence. This can happen not only on a conscious level, but at a gut, hidden level. Don't decide immediately that this isn't true of *you*. It's easy to discount vital input if we're quick to respond. Instead, read the rest of the paragraph. *Then* examine yourself; look deep for the truth. *Do* claim to be God, and amazing, and the be-all-and-end-all; also claim others to be God, amazing, and the end-all. Declaring these things for self and others, and meaning them, constitutes self-worth coupled with valuing others.

Moving on: We've discussed trusting your dreams and having support for them. We'll keep on addressing those topics. But for *now*: What's next is learning how to live your dreams without losing balance. Here's another story about a Fey sprite with something to teach us. Fairies are excellent role models for aspiring Crazy Sages. I mean, could anything be *crazier*?

A Fairy Party
June 18, 2005

Imagine you're walking through the woods. And it becomes stranger and stranger, not in a bad way, though it is definitely so out of the ordinary that it might frighten you. The woods seem . . . well, magical. The color of tree leaves is brighter than you'd ever thought possible. Branches are more sharply defined, as if your eyesight suddenly improved vastly. The air is still, yet somehow also buzzing with a sense of expectancy. Shadows hold secret wonders. And though there is nothing evil about all this, you know in your gut that you should still be careful, in case you inadvertently trespass on a secret meeting of wood gnomes. So you're a bit worried.

Then, as you come to a clearing, your fear vanishes. In the meadow ahead, there is a tiny cottage. It is everything a magical cottage should be. And, deep down, you know that, as tempting and wondrous as this dwelling is, it is absolutely not the work of Hansel and Gretel's evil witch, or of any other malevolent being. You know it is the home of someone very special. Could it be where Glinda the good witch lives? Or where a young loving mother is raising a child in humble circumstances, a child who will grow up to be a great hero in a mythic tale? Who inhabits this hidden place, tucked away in an enchanted forest?

You go up to the door to find out, hoping it will not be an intrusion if you knock. And you see the following sign posted there:

Today's Optional Reading for My Front Door

There once was a fairy who wanted to be like Santa's elves—fairies whose happy work blesses many people. So she started working away, in her *own* way, by creating spells with which people could fulfill their dearest wishes. Though they were grateful to have health and wealth and happiness, the fairy herself became very ill. Too sick to even wash her own dishes.

You see, fairies need a lot of fun to stay healthy. They get unwell when they forget to play. *Our* fairy's dreams about helping humans—the way ol' Saint Nick's elves do—made her work so hard she forgot to have fun.

She had not realized that Santa's elves ignored their tasks a lot. A lot! Not in a mean-spirited way; they were just constantly distracted by the urge to sing, or the opportunity for a teasing jest. Not to mention the scent of hot cocoa that dictated one immediately drop whatever one was doing to consume chocolate. (With marshmallows in it!)

On and on, all day, the North Pole sprites spent more time playing than making toys—which made for better toys than all the hammering, nailing, and painting ever could, because that's the way of elven magic.

This fairy had friends who came and did her dishes and other chores, so that she could rest and get better. But she still worked too hard. Then one day, fairy Timothy visited, then a good Christian minister named George, then a dish-washing bird called Blue. They all asked, unbeknownst to each other, "You don't have any fun, do you?" So she's throwing a party today and, hence, will start getting healthy.

Now that you've read this sign here on my front door: Welcome! You're just in time for the party. C'mon in! I'm throwing a bash to kick off a more balanced life. And maybe the festivities will help you become more self-caring yourself— if you need that. But we'll have lots of fun anyway! And I have chocolate milk! With marshmallows in it. And cinnamon sticks. And games. And prizes. And everyone gets to take a balloon home!

Crazy People Go Nowhere, Part Two:
I've Never Been in Washington Square (That's a Lie)
Written 2004, shortly before the move. I am repeating some thoughts here that I said elsewhere in this book, so that we can explore different aspects of them.

I've never been in Washington Square. That's a lie but, if you say it, many people immediately condescend. Why is it so important to be in New York? Answer: It's not!

I was born and raised in Boston, lived in the Big Apple, and spent a quarter of a century in San Francisco. I've no sour grapes about getting to dwell in a major metropolis. I'm *choosing* to relocate to a town the size of a large sofa, in a part of the U.S. an L.A. friend called "what I fly over to get to N.Y."

My decision to move gave me pause, albeit briefly and illogically. Would I suddenly be considered not in the mix, not up to speed; would people automatically think me unknowledgeable, unsophisticated, or, shudder, unimportant?

As I said, my misgivings were short-lived. The stress of moving had temporarily lulled me into thinking that I actually cared about my "importance." (I'm embarrassed by that slip into an oh-so-superficial consideration. But it was quickly followed by the prayer, "Help, I'm falling, falling," which lifted me out of that shallow but deadly pit. Heh, *shallow*: Get it?) More to the point, the move was motivated by the aforementioned belief that, where the heart leads, the whole world follows. This laid waste to my fears, before they got any real hold on me. However, those worries do serve as the perfect jumping off point for showing that who you are and what you do can transcend anything you might conceive of as limiting, such as your location. Let me explain. (When I focus on the supposed limits of locale, do extrapolate, applying what I say to other restrictions.)

But first, an aside: When I say it is good to ignore limits, someone might perceive me as unaware of the brutal hardships some people endure. I'm not inured to life's injustices. In fact, I've been and continue to be subject to many of them, repeatedly and to such extremes that nothing herein is said glibly. I know about awful severities, how they *can* limit, and how sometimes there *is* no way to overcome them.

Another aside: I could contradict any point I make in this book. It's often a matter of minute distinctions, e.g., the details of a specific context. But if you use your fine mind to dismantle my ideas, you may achieve nothing but a false sense of superiority. If you instead use your intellect to figure out ways to apply my suggestions, you might profit. If not, at least you tried.

Third aside: If I mention a possible foible, your response might be, "That used to be true of me, but not any more." Life is not black and white. You're a gloriously complex person. Perhaps the shortcoming in question is no longer *as* true of you but, if it remains to some degree, it can still impact you. Or if I address an issue—e.g., the need for self-fulfillment—be aware of the automatic response of "I'm *already* self-fulfilled." Again, it can be a matter of degree. Resting on our laurels, no matter how hard we worked to win them, is a dead end. And the internal things that have most plagued us generally need to be worked on at deeper levels as time passes. Okay, back to explaining how who you are and what you do can transcend any limit.

As I write these words, I'm staying at the home of Eleanor and Max. They offered me their place while they're out of town because my apartment is mold-ridden, which hurts my health and is part of why I'm moving. Eleanor and Max live in the quintessentially wonderful urban dwelling. I love it! It's one third of a Victorian on Nob Hill, and has many huge rooms.

Moreover, my friends have created a home that makes me feel like I've discovered a secret garden. Eleanor, like me, loves Victoriana. She writes books on the topic. As literary agents, their home-cum-office is packed with every worthwhile book published. I wander rooms, choosing books on publishing, Victoriana, and anything else I want to know about. Every inch of wall and horizontal surface—floor aside—is crammed, either with books or "stuff."

The "stuff" is in jumbled piles that fancifully tickle the eye. Were you to wander into a second-hand store, and find it to be like they used to be—filled with antique delights, brand new delights, vintage delights, original delights, all of it artfully arranged in exquisite chaos—you can envision this apartment.

Each item unfolds a little story about my friends. Despite their absence, my stay here is in their company, because I'm getting to know them better. This sharp-minded woman who battles publishers for her clients confesses, in a book I'm reading this weekend, that she loves romance novels. Ah, yes, I see Peynet after Peynet here: framed pieces or postcards, ridiculously—yet whimsically and breathtakingly—romantic.

Then I notice a framed wedding invitation, reminding me that Max and Eleanor married *after* being together 25 years. To me, they've always seemed bold risk-takers, with enormous integrity and creativity. The wedding invitation adds to that assessment: Living together, when *they* first did it, was no small thing, in the personal or professional world.

I put a dab of Eleanor's Eau D'Adrien on, thinking—and hoping—she won't mind me trying it out. Voilà, a new favorite perfume.

The apartment is filled with quality. Antique chairs, linens from their constant stays in Nice, leather bound texts. There's also quality from their own craftsmanship. A faux finished fireplace (which it took Max two weeks to notice that Eleanor had repainted with a marble-like pattern). Wastebaskets decoupaged with postage stamps—I leave a note asking Eleanor, "Did you do that? If so, please teach me."

Most important, the quality of the *residents* shines in every chair, bed, print, and plant. These are people who have risked, who have made a difference in the world, who have loved their friends and clients freely and generously, and who have lived full-tilt.

I once complimented Eleanor on the apartment and her aesthetic. She looked a bit puzzled and answered, "It's just a typical New York apartment." (She and Max worked in the publishing business there, before moving to S.F. and starting their agency.)

No it's not typical! And that moves us toward the crux of this essay. Their apartment represents actions that some New Yorkers incorrectly think of as typical New York life. Just like many San Francisco residents automatically— and wrongly—believe themselves to be on the vanguard of grassroots change.

Lew Welch, Beat poet, lived in San Francisco. My friend Kush said that Lew was a rebel and outsider even among the Beats. (No surprise that Lew's one of my favorite poets.) Eleanor and Max have actually *done* what many New Yorkers have only *identified* as doing. Lew did what many Bay Area residents only identify as doing.

In other words, some major metropolitan area dwellers think they're involved in creating new ways of being—social change, art movements, higher spiritual consciousness, and so on—solely because they're at a party standing near someone who *is* making a new world. Or they think they're tuned in because they've fallen for marketing tripe created by mega-corporations who brand their products to make them look oh-so-grassroots: Shucks, it's just us guys making this product in our garages. But it's not what you wear or put in your home, *no matter how "innovative,"* and it's not the events you're seen at, *no matter how "innovative."* It's what you yourself do.

A main thrust of my work is to address the concerns and challenges of many independent thinkers. To do this effectively, I must sometimes honestly discuss their more typical shortcomings. This makes me uncomfortable because I fear that some readers will think I'm attacking them or that I'm insensitive. Know that the shortcomings I cite are often mine. And if we don't face our behavior when it hurts us, we can't live full-tilt.

In that spirit: It's easy to make fun of mainstream types whose self-worth is based on owning a huge house, wearing diamonds, marrying a trophy spouse, attending the exclusive events, and wielding corporate mega-power. But it is no different to find one's value in hipper commodities: *Hip* events, *hip* clothes, *hip* . . . It's the same mindset, with different window dressings.

When someone's healthy ego is not all fluffed up and standing proud, a *false* ego emerges. Let's say one is driven by the fearful—and possibly subconscious—realization that one is not living up to one's treasured standards. One might bolster one's self-image with a false and compensatory self-portrait—the false ego is in the room, gang!—that is perhaps subtle and subliminal. One such picture is that one is "in the mix" by sheer virtue of location, proximity, or clothing. A healthy ego doesn't need that pic. Please please please don't reject this analysis on the grounds that you are greatly developed *already*. Those of us who are self-expressed in major ways can still be partially blocked by false ego. Human beings have contradictory feelings and thoughts. The most accomplished of us aren't *completely* self-realized, so there is always room for growth.

And the false ego forever lurks. It also loves to cite your accomplishments to you as a way to avoid further growth. Otherwise you might oust the false ego for a huge endowment of happy self-esteem. (Read this paragraph again: It's vital to spiritual growth and self-fulfillment in *general*.)

Action Step: If you're not doing something your soul longs for, and this makes you feel guilty, worthless, or otherwise bad about yourself, the solution is not false ego. Nor is it the self-flagellation of *increased* guilt, worthlessness, or other bad feelings about who you are. They will shrink the *healthy* ego more, making you need the *false* ego more.

Instead, start with self awareness. Notice when you aren't doing what you truly want. Notice what you do instead. Perhaps you find yourself falling into purchases that symbolize freedom or other traits you want, instead of making heartfelt acts. Or you're online, "keeping up on vital cultural events," instead of keeping up with your *own* creative projects, whether your creativity is expressed in beading, making a comfy home for your family, marketing your boss's products, or doing anything else that is truly *you*.

Just notice. Don't worry about acting on this new self-knowledge yet. Don't be concerned about changing yourself yet.

After a while, be aware of how decisions based in false ego make you feel. Empty? Frustrated? Impotent? Dishonest? Or? Don't harshly judge yourself for what you find. Harsh doesn't = heal. Also, see if you happen to notice inner road-blocks to self-expression. Again, you may have overcome many already, but if you're not doing every last thing you feel you're put on this earth to do, there are likely more inner barriers. Actually, if you're still *breathing*, there *are* internal blocks.

These blocks might be self-defeating beliefs. You may know better on a conscious level, but your belly might still be full of old nonsense. Or the block might be fear: Again, your mind may tell you one thing, but the fear in your heart may say something else.

Or the block might be that you're unnecessarily accepting limits. There are many versions of this. Here's one: "*She* could overcome her poverty-ridden childhood to become a mover 'n' shaker because she wasn't as sensitive as me. She didn't have to face down the fears that stop me." Another example: "I don't have the money to create art." (I played in top clubs with a cheap guitar that usually would be used by a 12-year-old first learning to play.) Another: "I am not clever enough."

Just note. Do not despair of changing. Part of change is to be stuck where you are, usually far longer than seems appropriate! But you are not stuck.

Be willing to bear the discomfort of new feelings that rise up when one starts to even *notice* the false ego is operating. Rushing to change those feelings can be an avoidance of them. Sure, no one in their right mind wants to *keep* thorny emotions. But sometimes, it's necessary to allow them to just *be* there so they can dwindle away. Pep talks from friends or self are great, but they usually provide temporary relief. They rarely create the gut level change that also changes your actions. Putting up with new not-so-happy feelings—and even really miserable ones—helps get you *un*stuck.

Get the support you need to get through it. Call up a friend; talk to your therapist or minister; look up an old school pal who always "got" you; hug your cat; contact me for phone-counseling. (See back of book for that.)

While going through this period of seeming stasis, be open to the idea that change is possible. By *change*, I don't mean the immediate relief of pain. Heroin relieves anguish, but heroin's not a good idea! Immediate relief isn't always conducive to change. (*Do* look for relief. Just find it in healthy ways if you can. Of course, some of the patterns we've talked about changing *are* unhealthy ways you might *already* get relief. Clearly, from what I've delineated, you may be stuck doing them for a time yet. But look for new ways to do it.)

Be open to change in this sense: When you can't see any possible way things might improve, know that you might see more later. Example: Now you don't know how to make art without money. But if you don't keep insisting to yourself it's impossible, it makes space in the wonderland that is your brain for ideas to eventually emerge. Insisting on "there's no way" keeps the brain too busy and contracted for inspiration to provide a solution. Not knowing something *now*, or not being able to do something *now*, shouldn't be used as an indication of *never*.

Know that, even if something seems impossible—utterly, *completely* impossible—that doesn't mean it is. Be open to change.

Here's how that plays out for me, personally. *Often*, I can think of no resolution for minor and major problems. I've learned that, if I fret and worry about this doom, I'm not only less likely to have the "ah hah" moment of a solution, I'm also miserable. My health can't take that much misery. I mean it! For *moi*, being open to change—being in a *state* of openness to change—means trying to relax. Simply trying to relax instead of worrying or making my head hurt by doggedly trying to figure out solutions. It's an enormously simple spiritual exercise and an enormously effective spiritual practice when it comes to finding ways 'n' means: Relax instead of worrying.

I trust a God that is more powerful than me and *totally* beneficent. If you believe in God, Goddess, Nameless Creator, God Within, Flow of Goodness in the Universe, The Pagan God Fred, or anything else that is hugely powerful and thoroughly enamored with how cute, wonderful, and lovely you are, you're ahead of the game when it comes to relaxation creating a state of openness to change. You can say to Pagan God Fred, "Please show me the solution." Then, if Fred does not give you your answer immediately, your trust of Fred lets you know that instead of worrying and fretting and frantically trying to come up with a solution, or biting your lips about whether you'll even *hear* Fred's response, you can *relax* and go about your business—your mundane day—in the certainty that such a cool deity as Fred will answer you eventually, probably soon.*

After you've done all this for a little while, and even while you're doing it, your cells shift. (Cells are small. That's one reason you don't know you're changing at first—you're undergoing *teeny* changes. But there are innumerable numbers of them: Think of how many cells you have. Cellular shifts happen at the core of your being; they represent deep, long-lasting change. That sort of transformation is worth the patient wait.) This book will help shift your cells further so that you can be *more* you. If you want to then advance *more* with the specific inner growth talked about in this essay, or you lose the headway you make and don't know how to get it back, look me up, for classes or a one-on-one session.

Including this action step in this subchapter was a judgment call. There is *much* more to add to it but, long story short, no way to include it. I feel the oversimplification is okay because its suggestions are so useful. Also, you are a grown up: You can flesh out what I've given with additional steps. That might mean getting input from someone with a relevant background, training, or mindset. (Again, contact me for phone-counseling or classes, many of which would be relevant.)

Grown ups know when to ask for help. (False ego tells us we don't need help or that help is too humiliating to ask for.)

Okay, back to where we left off.

Eleanor worried about my not being in a city with access to

---

* Sometimes, I do have to keep praying for insight about a particular problem. But I can still pray, trust, move on with my day, instead of being all wound up.

its culture. She said that, when she's in the country, she can't wait to return from it. I explained that, when I'm in a rural area, I hate the idea of going back to my urban dwelling. She stopped worrying.

I'll miss museums. I've attended them constantly here. But now I'm too sick to go to them anyway. If I get better, I can go to New York or Boston to wander the galleries. So no big problem, though I'll not get to attend constantly. As to great minds and trends, trends are distractions from fertile silences. And great minds are everywhere. In my urban life, my major dialogues aren't exclusively with California residents.

If you really want to tap into great minds, as well as like-minded friends, you think globally. What's hip and on-fire in your vicinity is not necessarily truly "in." Globally, I have an amazing network that will still exist when I move. Through phone, letters, occasional visits, I'll know what's *really* what. Books written by the greats also keep me alive to my true self. But most of all I, myself, will be in Pennsylvania, keeping myself company there. And I'm where it's really at. So are you.

So are you, if you don't care about looking like you're in the mix, don't spend time keeping abreast of trends and showing up at "important scenes," but instead spend your time doing what the *heart of your being* calls out for. This applies to limits other than location. Instead of buying into *any* limit, no matter how believable, focus on *you*—what *you* think, the actions *you* can manage today, the dreams *you* have. Be crazy! It improves everything.

Okay, there are some limits to honor. If you jump off a cliff because you want to get down from it, you're in trouble.

But often, we see only the cliff, and not the path leading from it to the valley. There are often ways to go where we want that only occur to us if we first reject the apparent restriction.

If you need proof: This refusal of limitations has landed me in—to name a few places—*The New York Times* more than once, and *Cosmopolitan Magazine*. And the spiritual curriculum I developed is used by thousands. So trust me, *please*, when I say that you—you, yourself, right now, in *your* living room, are where it's *really* at. Claim yourself. The fire that Prometheus stole from the gods burns in *you*!

When someone is trying to make a point, their adding an example of it can be the difference between their reader understanding that point or not. Also, Crazy Sages teach through their own stories. Sharing about my move from San Francisco to the country, and about my settling into a new life, shows how well healthy madness works when it *plays out over time*. But I'd like to tell the *specific* parts of *the move* and *the creation of my new life in Pennsylvania* when they're most relevant. That means skipping about chronologically. The following story was written my second winter in my new home.

Chaos Revealed My Hyacinth Bulbs

My new home has a plant room. It's a darling li'l thing tacked onto the cellar, and was built by the property's former owner who used it as a woodshop. The addition is not posh, but I adore it. It receives enough light to keep potted plants alive during the winter. Friends wax enthusiastic about it, commenting that it's ideal for gardening, canning, soapmaking, the works. One of the perks of my move to the country.

Anyway, I just went into said plant room and saw a disheveled heap of pots that had fallen to the floor. Well, fallen isn't quite the right word. There's no doubt in my mind that Ganesh, my new cat, had *knocked* stuff off the shelf. He's been exploring those shelves lately—mostly when to do so interferes with me *using* them. As soon as I start to, let's say, make a dried flower wreath and place a bunch of dried roses on a shelf to work with, he leaps onto them. Smash. Crumble. Flowers not so pretty any more. Sigh.

However, I won't be deterred—I'm trying to live my dream life, remember, off in my little gardening room doing rural things that I never did in the city. I mean, these were dried flowers from my own garden—how country is *that*? I was very firm with Ganesh; soon he was not interfering with my wreath-making.

So, of course, when my back was turned—or, more precisely, when my body was upstairs—he *would* get even. "I'll get on that shelf, and make a mess to boot. I'll show her." I *know* he said that and then went and, as I said, pushed my pots onto the floor—he's just that sort of feline.

However, I also believe Ganesh had mixed motives: Cats have their wisdom and their own, sometimes annoying, way of helping, as pointed out some pages back. While collecting the displaced pots, I discovered two hyacinth bulbs, both sprouting. Treasure!

You see, this is the third year I've forced hyacinths to bloom midwinter but, though it's now snowing, only a few bulbs sit on my sills. The rest didn't survive. Or so I thought. But here they were all along, buried amidst a neat stack of pots—a volunteer had organized my plant room beautifully. Everything's just about *filed* in alphabetical order! I love it. It's part of creating my new dream life here.

And, like all good things, organization has its limits. It takes a bit—or a lot—of chaos to balance one's life. *And to bring it vitality*, a liveliness often squeezed out by our well-intended but over-zealous organization. For example, winters here are long, harsh, and *indoors*; now, because of Ganesh's mischief, there will be more green, growing, lively plants displayed to chase away the winter blahs. There'll also be more oxygen, pouring bountifully into my shut-up winterized dwelling—hyacinths *exude* massive amounts of oxygen—as well as a heady floral scent. In other words, there'll be more *life*. All because chaos intervened when organization had hidden life's bounty.

I've been told that there's a God of Chaos to whom Brazilians build altars, supposed to be kept outside the house so that things don't get too crazy *inside*. I didn't know that Ganesh, the Indian deity whose name my cat bears, is a God of Chaos. A friend suggested the name, and I just went along with it. I thought Ganesh was a *prosperity* God. I wasn't wrong. But it seems that abundance and chaos go hand in hand. Chaos can *reveal* the abundance that's available right there under our noses but that we don't see.

Maybe Brazilians are wrong: You can't keep chaos outside the door. But you can welcome it, benefit from it, and thank God for its gifts.

Afterthoughts: Please bear with a recap of the above piece. Its theme is balance, oddly carried out by showing how chaos helps create it, as follows. (Living in paradox is a privilege—and power—of insanity. Unusual, yet healthily paradoxical, balances are part of Crazy Sage wisdom.) Being a gardener is an important part of my country dream-life. A well-organized plant room helps implement that dream, but my cat tears *apart* my shed. The destruction left in his wake reveals lost hyacinth bulbs, reinforcing a message that I keep trying to teach myself (and others): Chaos *balances* one's life and adds more vitality to it. My cat's skullduggery also affirmed another of my beliefs: Planning too much about how to follow through on our dreams, or rigidly sticking to those plans, can block *fruition* of those dreams. When trying to create happiness, we must plan, of course. We must also go with the flow.

Let's build on all that: Surrender to—and reliance on—God is the ultimate trick of the trickster. Sacred fool, dancing fool! Do you know why a fool so happily dances? She has found freedom.

Freedom gained through the act of surrender may seem a contradiction. But surrender is not: Being a doormat; suppressing your vitality; giving up your unique outlook; forsaking your god-given gifts; being barred from fighting the good fight; or *any* other nana that organized religion has abusively misrepresented as acceptance. In fact, acceptance and reliance on the Divine can help you *fight* for your rights, express your vitality, and otherwise celebrate yourself and life.

Surrender and reliance are an enormous topic. We're

not gonna cover them in one book. They're a lifelong study.

This study cannot be successful if comprised solely of oh-so-brilliant insights. I have *them* all the time—the most beautiful, deep, spiritual realizations, O, I am so profound that it brings tears to my own eyes to hear myself speak such divinely-inspired poesy. Shortly after, I often act like a boob, in exact opposition to everything I've said!

It's not that I'm a hypocrite. I try hard to walk my talk. It's that comprehension is a small part of the larger effort: Surrender and reliance are a *successful* lifelong study only if consisting mostly of the *practice* of surrender and reliance, endless practice. We have to try it over and over and . . . sigh, over. In context after context. And have to find ourselves unable to do it, again and again. And find ourselves *thinking* we've done it, when in fact we've done something else. But we discover how to do it right by doing it wrong first. We learn from our mistakes and persistence.

I hope this book can help you be the dancing fool who's found spiritual surrender and reliance. Let's get more done about it right now. So: the Crazy Sage goes with the flow. That's an oversimplified but very useful way of looking at surrender and reliance.

Here's another. There's a well-known image called *The Fool*: A figure happily stands on cliff's edge, one foot raised as if this person was about to obliviously walk *off* cliff's edge. I heard a tale (I don't know where) that if the fool falls off the cliff, angels will catch him. I use this example to show that surrender and reliance needn't be about puritanical uptightness and oppression of self, but can instead represent taking healthily insane risks because you understand that you're taken care of by something Divine.

Here's another aspect of surrender and reliance: Remind yourself that we can surrender with humor and serenity to the chaos that is life, because we know that unruliness to be God. The Holy Clown's celebration of disruption has deep meaning, yup (or saying so is just my way of justifying my wandering mind and constant stupid jokes).

Back to the cliff and fool (and onto another topic): Elsewhere, this book says it's stupid to jump off cliffs. Contradictions are not always contradictions: Context is king.

Please don't invalidate any idea of mine on the grounds that its opposite is true. Of *course* it is! I don't live in a world where only one thing or the other can happen, or where only one *same* thing ever happens, over and over.

It's *easy* to invalidate *anyone*'s ideas. On occasion, doing so constitutes using one's brain to stay trapped alone inside it. Or amounts to using analytical powers to feel smugly superior. A *real* proof of a fine mind is using it to find *truth* in what you hear!

Don't get me wrong, I love my brain my brain my brain my brain, it's my favorite place, it endlessly entertains me for hours, I enjoy my ideas better than anyone's, and I find my mind to hold the entire cosmos. My brain's as big as the universe. Really, it's *that* big in here, I actually *experience* that hugeness, and wander the stars between my ears! I like living alone because I can explore my mind all day long. But even if all this is going on in you too, you must open to others' ideas, or your brain becomes a small, narrow, and painful trap—

at least for significant lengths of time. Cramped space, ick! Periods during which you don't get to expand out, grow, be free, go where you will.

We become trapped if we do not use our powers of analysis to find truths in others' speech. Even if we glean *one* helpful hint, that wee bit might change our lives!

Afterthoughts: If you feel you don't understand spiritual surrender and reliance enough to try them, try them anyway. You understand them only if you apply them best you *can* figure out. Comprehension of *this* matter happens bit by bit. Be patient with yourself. Also, ask fellow seekers what they think these practices consist of. Dialog is an important part of gaining insight into spiritual principles. If no one nearby is right, read the section about Faerie Nation.

Listen to the Waves

When you spend the day at the beach, you simply enjoy the beach—feeling the warmth of the sun on your skin, letting the rhythm of the waves calm you, and drinking in the peace that comes when city noise is gone. You just be there.

Think of this book as the beach. Don't try to puzzle out the surf, the seagull's cry, the honey-warmth of sun. Just be here. This book is a place. Feel that last sentence with your heart, instead of your head. This book is a place. Just be here with me.

This is a place of healthy madness. That's one of its many layers. This is also a place of wholeness, peace, and multi-faceted being. It's also a dream world. This chapter focuses on creating one's dream life. The whole book is a dream. Yes, it has stories of my everyday goings-on. But a privilege of madness is living in your dreams so thoroughly in your ongoing moment-to-moment existence that the dreams are manifest realities. Mad me sharing my mad life can often = my time in my dreams, a world you and I walk in together as you read.

This is also a place of chaos. As such, it's not a *discourse* on chaos, but it *is* a tiny bit of an embodiment.

My theories are implicit, though my casual tone may make it seem otherwise. At the shore, trying to mentally puzzle out the sum-total of the sun's warmth, the surf's sound, and the bird's cry is fruitless. Experience each, and somehow the whole emerges, experientially.

Sometimes, giving an advanced lesson on utter integration, I'd take a student along with me while I shopped for groceries. I wouldn't say it was a lesson. I'd talk about a new dress I might buy. Or about an annoying neighbor. I might pick the student's brain for their favorite recipes. What we said did not matter. Our presence—that was the thing.

One student was insulted, thinking I demeaned her, wasting her time.* Others thought I was offering friendship—which I was—but missed the rest of the offering. And some saw—and hence received—it all: A mystic gives lessons that are sometimes lectures, sometimes shared meditations or other spiritual exercises, and sometimes, ostensibly, only visits.

---

* She didn't realize the shopping trip indicated that I thought her possibly exceptional. I only did this experiment with students I thought might connect to the heart of the exercise.

I carefully chose what to write about in this book, and I rewrote endlessly. However, in a way—in a *way* only—I could've written about anything. Listen to the waves.

Share my insanity through living it, instead of through a deliberate cerebral dissection. Share my insanity through living a certain way in this book.

I often teach by inference, letting you arrive at the lesson somewhat on your own. Because I'm living it, it's not always sequential. Reality doesn't proceed in a man-made "order." Wacky Wisdom helps us draw on the natural unfolding of events and allow the natural unfolding of inner strength.*

I want to help you be *you* instead of talking about being you. So I must do the same herein. I don't share my stories because I think I'm a high 'n' mighty perfect being. (Egad, it's *obvious* I'm *not*.) I share them because that's all I have to share: me. Good, bad, or indifferent, all I can share is me. (I also share my life because my insanity has improved so many things for me—including overcoming dreadful challenges that other approaches couldn't conquer, at least not all by themselves—that I want to say what worked for me, in case it helps you too.)

Be *you*, instead of talking about being you. Be kind, instead of talking about kindness. Demonstrate your spirituality instead of explaining it. There are acts for which no words

---

* In oral tradition, when my students arrive at the conclusions I've been implying, some think they're the only one who's figured out the lesson. They think even I didn't get it! We thinkers can be *such* snobs! Myself, I'm always the only truly deep person in the room.

can substitute. It's about action and being, not talking and identification.

It is about hidden power. It is about simplicity.

There is only now. And now is God. And He will always take care of you—every minute. This *very* minute. Then next minute. Then next minute—you're always safe if you fold yourself into God's care. Listen to the waves.

Whether we want to or not, whether we notice it or not, we live in dreams. Many philosophers say the world is a dream. So does that campfire song, in its line "merrily, life is but a dream." Not that I trust Girl Scout ditties—no offense to you who collected badges. I have a few myself—but my mind does wander. (I will resist the temptation to create a "Row row row your boat" metaphor built on my "Listen to the waves" remark.)

There are more kinds of dreams than would fit here. There is the bland grey expanse, where we exist like specters, having the same anxieties repeatedly. There is the dreamscape of nightmares. There is the futile dream of never being fulfilled. And there is the dream realm of one's own happy imaginings. I choose happy. I strive to live in daylight dreams of my own choosing.

Simple Exercise

Ask yourself, "Francesca said she'd remind me to go along with the book's flow. But why wasn't the *above* reminder sooner?" You only need to find one answer, even if you think it's a bad one.

Chapter Five
Lovers Like the Full Moon,
It Turns Them into Werewolves

Let's deal with romance, a part of life too loony to deal with rationally. In that spirit, first comes a recipe for Vanilla-Creme and Peach Punch—a sensory delight that inspires me to believe in love and continue to indulge in its madness, without which love isn't love.

Vanilla-Creme and Peach Punch
A dessert beverage for after the meal

This recipe for a smooth, elegant drink is accompanied by a recipe for a smooth, elegant, and confident *attitude* about life—whether or not it includes a partner. Food and l'amour are a good combo.

Ingredients

◊ one 11.5 oz can of Welch's White-Grape-and-Peach frozen concentrate. Look at the label carefully. Welch's various juice *drink* labels look so much like their *juice* labels that my perfectly intelligent friends always mistakenly buy one instead of the other. The concentrate for this recipe is basically all juice; it's sold to make *juice*, not a juice "*drink*."

◊   water

◊   one whole Tahitian vanilla bean

◊   a tiny bit of rosehips. To be more precise: Use lots more
    than a pinch, but *really* just a little.

1) Pour the juice concentrate into a big pot.

2) Fill the pot almost to the top with water. Do not worry
   about fully diluting the concentrate. In fact, if there's
   any issue about it, *under*-dilute til you're at the step that
   asks you to dilute to taste.

3) Snip the vanilla bean into teeny pieces. Kitchen scissors
   do a better job than a knife. I like to cut the bean
   directly over the pot. If you prefer, put the vanilla bits
   into a tea ball.

4) Add the rosehips to the tea ball or straight into the pot.

5) Bring to a boil, covered. Then turn the heat off.

6) Steep covered, overnight at room temperature.

7) Taste to see if further dilution is needed.

8) Reheat to serve. Don't let it boil.

Serve after the meal—or any time as a treat. It makes a nice
change for a holiday gathering.

Afterthoughts: Serve with pride. As I said, this beverage is
elegant.

   Using fine linen and crystal is great, but they're not
the essence of elegance. It's not about being fancy-shmancy,
pretentious, or making guests feel dumb because they don't
know which fork to use. Quite the opposite!

Elegance is a simple, honest focus on your guests' well-being. It is thinking about their needs and fun so fully that there's no space in your brain for a hostess's self-obsessed, "Am I failing as a hostess? Will people hate me tomorrow if my party flops? Does my house look stupid? Is my dress on backwards?"

Do not apply my above idea by constantly asking yourself, "Am I failing at making my guests feel great?" That's still hostess self-obsession. Instead, the only thing you keep asking is, "What can I do to make my guests feel great?" Vary it as needed: "What can I do to make this shy person feel welcome? . . . What can I do to make my guests feel great even though the roof just caved in?"

Try it, because it may not seem worthwhile until you use it. When you do, the result is amazing: You become calm, unworried, elegant.

This ties into romance. The serene, caring hostess automatically displays a grace that draws suitors like soldiers to a virgin in a Victorian novel. (If you're a *host*, the same idea applies.)

My hostess idea applies to any social gathering you attend. All through it, keep asking yourself, "What can I bring to this event?" If that doesn't draw a prospective mate, you'll at least not be miserable the whole event. You might even have a great time sans a love of your life—*imagine that!*

Elegance is also self-respect. Increase yours simply by slowing down. A frantic pace, though perhaps started by self-doubt, can *increase* a lack of confidence. Instead, take a deep breath, assuring yourself that you're fabulous just the way you are. Then talk slowly, act slowly, breathe slowly. Belief in what you're doing—and just slowing down *period*—creates internal elegance and self-possession, which show in every move and breath. It draws the soldiers too! And helps an enjoyment of life whether mated or not.

Also, if you trust that the Divine takes care of you, it can strip you of the terror that life instills. This may not be relevant to *you*, but it helps *many* people. When they trust Divine caretaking, they can breathe deeply, breathe regularly. This slows their pace, and their senses start drinking in. So they enjoy their work, their chores, and their adventures. That is elegance. That is wealth. And it's important in the area of romance: Humans easily forget their spirituality, becoming completely unhinged, the moment they spot a possible significant other, or deal with a grumpy, *current* mate, or start to think they may always be single.

If using my above suggestions or any ideas in this book, don't expect to change all at once. Note any oh-so-tiny shift, the wee improvements, because inner transformation often happens so subtly that we cannot see it at first, and might think we are just too "messed up" to ever change enough. In the case of my above suggestions, you *can* bit by bit be carefree and confident.

The next essay offers more Wacky Wisdom Ways to develop confidence.

The Modern Goddess' Guide to Flirting

In the middle of a deep meditation on the nature of romantic love, I received a vital message. Here it is—the modern

Goddess' take on flirting. The heavenly directions consist of whimsical—but useful—instructions in the art of flirting. It's the way to garner worship. For the Goddess—or God*—in you! The modern Goddess doesn't leave anyone out—flirting tips for guys are included.

Being a Goddess or God means that, though others may adore you, you are under no obligation to adore them back—let alone date them, marry them, or even listen to their insufferably boring poems about you. Therefore, flirt all you want.

Flirting is done for its own sake anyway. We do it because it's fun, both for the flirter and flirtee. It also bolsters everyone's ego, and is a harmless, no-obligation way to vent one's propensity for romance and sexiness.

Of course, it's only harmless if both parties understand all that. If the other person might misconstrue, a Deity's obligation is to refrain. It is *not* divine to hurt someone's feelings, by flirting with a person who thinks it might go somewhere. And if you have your own hidden agenda that romance might follow the flirtation, it will show no matter how well you think you are hiding it. A heart—or hearts—*will* be bruised.

With that, how does one go about flirting? Most modern Goddesses, perhaps yourself included, might think dropping a lace handkerchief too old-fashioned. Not me. It's too funny a practice to forgo. Whenever I picture myself letting

---

* If you're like me, with both God and Goddess within—heh, spiritual genderbending!—adapt the flirting ideas accordingly.

a little piece of cloth slip from my grip, I just about have to hold my sides because I'm laughing so hard. It's an absurd act! And flirting, if nothing else, is about humor.

Therefore, smile as if you're involved in a bit of sportive mirth—remember, flirting is not about getting a date but about having fun—and drop the hankie, after which you should pause with a secret smile and expectant look on your face. You're not risking anything—the whole thing's so silly that if your targeted hanky-picker-upper does not respond the way you had hoped, you can just laugh it off as the joke it is.

Most folks neither own nor regularly carry a cloth handkerchief, let alone a laced bit of nothing. But dropping a Kleenex tissue just isn't the same! Buy a feminine hanky for special occasions.

A handkerchief is not the only good prop. It *may* not be your prop at all, if you're a straight guy, butch gal, or <u>if needed, fill in the blank in a way relevant to you</u>.* A fellow's best prop might be a toolbox. Mind you, its use goes past flirting; it may inspire actual romance. Beholding someone's capability with tools kindles an instinctive response of, "I'll be taken care of. Sigh," followed by heart flutters. Gay gals and anyone else who might be looking to ignite romance with someone who'd be touched by displays of tool-belt-ishness,

---

* Note I said "*may* not be." As to filling in the blank: There are so *many* ways people might fully be themselves that I couldn't cover all the subtle gender variations, partnership possibilities, and the likes! The alternative community's use of "GLBTQI" has been an important attempt. But using the whole *alphabet* as abbreviations wouldn't cover all styles of romance, gender, et al, because each person is unique. The term *GLBTQI* helps a lot of folks, but *many* still feel left out. Trust *your* "crazy" gender permutation, types of romantic pairing, etc.

note that possibility! Primate courting rites haven't been replaced by centuries of civilization. Showing an ability to fend for someone still wins a lover. But we've wandered from the topic of flirting to that of procuring a mate. Back to the topic:

You *can* use hammer, nail, and their pals to flirt if you approach it correctly: They give you the chance to make self-mocking jokes about your abilities. And that is charming, as long as the jests don't reflect any real lack of self-worth. The point is: The tools give you a chance to display charm and wit, which are the heart of flirtation. Just be careful to not *at all* seem as if you want an actual relationship; the power of the tool belt is mighty, and you don't want to accidentally use it uncaringly!

Onto another prop: the fan! If you do not own a fan to peek over coyly, a magazine, dinner plate, or other flat, similarly sized object will do. However, watch out for printed material: Peeking out from behind a magazine with a cover that shouts, "Meat prices soar!" just doesn't come across as cute.

If you lack coyness, don't despair. Try a self-mocking look that implies, "I look absurd peeking over a fan, but see how charming and roguish I am nonetheless?"

Other props and their uses: Cup a coffee mug in both hands and, having brought it to your lips, gaze languidly at your flirtee. Lean dramatically against a fireplace mantel and fuss with a scarf that's around your neck or with a brooch on your lapel. Don't forget your hair as the best prop of all. Playing with it or tossing your head around to supposedly get hair out of your face are both dynamite.

Prop-free flirting often entails words. "Oh, look how *strong* you are!" can be announced playfully enough that your flirtee will enjoy it but not take you seriously. Watch corny, old, romantic movies. You'll find all sorts of perfect phrases. Whether they're used seriously or not in the films, be sure *you* deliver them with a tongue-in-cheek style so that they work yet, again, no one gets the wrong idea.

Next, let's discuss how a Deity responds to flirtation from others. If you're startled when someone initiates it, let your shock show—part of the game. Say, "I am abashed!" in a tone of good-humored, mock outrage, or try "My *dear*, I hardly know what to *say*." Or, "Ahem, my dear, I fear I'm not equipped to handle someone as charming as your*self*."

Flirting is somewhat a matter of matching wits. One can become stumped easily. If that happens to you, fall back on the sort of lines that are in the previous paragraph: "Goodness gracious, how you disarm me!" Luckily, matching wits in this context is not a matter of outdoing the other participant. It's about staying cool, keeping it light, and having a grin. Think of it more as wits meeting than as wits matching.

Note that the phrases I've suggested have a Victorian flavor to them. In the Victorian era, all that repression and prudery demanded folks have an outlet, which demonstrates to us that flirting and follow-through need not go hand in hand. When making up your own phrases, you might think Victorian. You needn't use the period's language correctly. This is not about linguistic accuracy but about getting the flavor across.

Should someone start to flirt and you do not want to play, stop it dead in its tracks. If you try to do so with a joke, the other person may think that's simply part of the game. So, pretend the offered flirtatiousness swept past your radar, and don't even ask what was meant. You don't want your question taken as an invitation. Act as if you didn't hear, perhaps immediately introducing a new topic.

A last word: Flirting *can* of course occur between two parties who both want romance. But, even then, the point is fun. And be assured: No matter how rampantly involved, completely flattering, and totally adorable the other party might be in the game of flirtation, it *is* just a game and it *means* nothing. Don't fool yourself.

Instead, enjoy the thrill. Flirting gives us a certain amount of celestial confidence—something every modern Goddess and God should have!

For more guidance from the modern Goddess about other parts of life, see info about *The Modern Goddess' Guide to Life* in the resource section.

Romance in Grubby Garments

Let's continue the theme of confidence *by* pondering the question, "Why do men tend to find me more attractive when my fashion statement consists of dirty sweats and unruly hair?" This query implies a modality of becoming attractive that is so tangential to the suggestions in my article on flirting that the two approaches *seem* opposed. That does not mean they don't both work. Consistency is not always ideal.

Elsewhere herein, I mention that my makeup tends to be opulently eccentric, including lots of glitter on my face. My day-to-day drag often matches, with an approach to clothing like that of an eight-year-old playing dress-up.

However, I have another, totally different way of garbing myself, one that I *also* tend to wear constantly; most artists, mystics, stay-at-home mothers, shamans, and professional writers know it: grungy pjs or sweats—that have been worn for three days and nights straight—plus unruly hair, and an expression of either manic concentration or addled exhaustion.

What's odd about this get-up is that men seem to find it attractive. At least, that's been my experience. Someone please explain this to me. I mean it! Someone explain!

For example, years ago, dining out with my boyfriend-of-the-moment, I was distressed about my appearance. I'd had no time to brush my hair and change into reasonably attractive clothing, let alone slap on some make-up. Okay, I'll be honest: I was wearing clothes I had slept in.

I didn't mention my worry, but the committee of sneaky gods that runs my life was listening to my thoughts. Boyfriend and I ran into friends. And he announced, "Doesn't Francesca look beautiful today?" Huh?

Is it the tousled hair? Because it just looks like a ratty mess to *me*.

Or is there truth to the cliché about guys liking brainless women? I mean, if I'm not grooming, it's because work took all my time; and that degree of busyness leaves me so tired that I'm *stupid*.

I'm telling you, I don't understand it. I doll up, I might get attention. But when I used to run to the store in true grubbiness, men went into their pick-up routines with me big-time.

Or did I just, in my careless haste, repeatedly leave blouse buttons open? Or what? Someone explain to me the romance and appeal of grubby garments.

Afterthoughts: We can at least extrapolate a lesson from the above: Women and men should be themselves, be comfortable, be busy with their own lives, and, *thus*, be desirable. *That* is confidence.

My Funny Valentine

February 18, 2006: four days after America's second-largest greeting card festival

It started with the sort of sniff that someone makes when they have a cold: "<Sniff> Well, this is, uh, the Kush, and I'm, uh, sending you, uh, <sniff> Valentine greetings. Of course, there's a wide margin, hopefully, to Valentine's Day, that can be celebrated 365 days a year. I hope you're okay. Um. Just have had a lot of colds and just getting through everything, uh, and I still have to rush out tonight and do yet another shoot. But you take care of yourself <sniff>, Valentine, take care. This is the Kush. Take care of oneself. I love you."

That was the message on my machine today. The "I hope you're okay" was because I'm so ill all the time, and none of us know if I'll keel over *tomorrow* from it.* However,

---

* At the time of writing (some of) this piece, that was true. It's 2011 now; things have changed. We can reasonably assume I've another ten to thirty years in me.

the possibility of my imminent demise is not the matter at hand. It's that the rest of the message is fairly strange, given that I've not seen Kush for ballpark five years! But remember this book's title. I *like* strange.

Kush is my soul mate. Not the love of my life—*that* was a man I knew briefly, a guy too crazy to stay with (yes, even for me). But, *with* him, I had the joy of giving to a significant other as selflessly as does a mother or a saint. Kush is another matter; if we were two heterosexual men, folks would probably easily understand our relationship. I probably would as well.

We *were* lovers, about twenty years ago. Since then, we're a friendship, one that I'm not sure I could do without, though it consists entirely of phone calls and letters nowadays. The boyfriend-girlfriend thing was just a moment in time, because the core of our connection has always been the friendship.

Before my illness had me housebound, we did see each other, but only rarely. *Rarely.* Now that I've moved here, I don't know if we'll ever be eyeball to eyeball again. And we did have sex again, about nine years back, a one-nighter because I desperately needed someone to cling to that evening.

Kush and I have navigated a 20+-year friendship, long after our brief romance ended. I attempt to understand this situation, in which we provide crucial support for each other regarding our respective community work. And I feel I finally *do* understand it. The attempt at comprehension illuminated the importance of transcending *accepted* definitions of emotionally healthy love and, instead, listening to my heart, head, and gut.

We who are "odd" may make odd relationships. Others naysay them, declaring our style of companionship chosen out of contrariness, stupidity, naïveté, or insanity.

The norm of what is "right and reasonable" is so prevalent and deeply ingrained that it can make us doubt that we made these choices out of legitimate ways of seeing and being. We might feel we should hightail it out of the reach of much-needed companions. And even if one trusts oneself in this area by and large, one might have parts of oneself still in doubt. Those parts can keep one from trying for *maximum* joy and support in a friendship.

Instead, share my insanity. Know the beauty of your mind, be free to follow its brilliance. Listen to your wild heart. Love who you will, how you will. Love *fully*, be *loved* fully.

Let me talk about my experience with my beloved Kush, because it has provided crucial love, support, and companionship, all possible because I ignored what love is "supposed to be." Maybe my tale will help you do the same, or do it more deeply than you previously have.

He won't take the romance out of our friendship. I could say, "Men! They always do that with a woman!" However, I, in return, am still in love with him in some way.

Of course, Kush is lusciously safe to love, since he is distant from me physically. I could focus on that, seeing our relationship solely as a dysfunction. Surely, that is the case with some long-distance relationships. Think of what happens on the web: Some (not all) people create an on-line, false sense of connection, because they lack the social skills for something real. Or, traumatized by awful childhoods or other disasters, they lack the emotional strength for face-to-face interactions, risks, and intimacy.

But applying that measure to myself, I realize that you know something by its fruit. The fruit here is good. This has been proven over time. An additional example: Juliette stepped out on her spouse, occasionally visiting a long-distance lover. She felt she was doing everything I've described thus far. But the fruit of it was so much hidden stress that her children had nightmares. She went through a series of emotional highs followed by feelings of dark emptiness— drug-like stupors that wiped out all joy. Perhaps someone else would be following their heart by doing what she did. You know by the fruit.

The fruit is not the immediate thrill, the pressing longing of heart and loin, or the sense of freedom when one has run from one's responsibilities or accountability. (And loving *fully* can mean never seeing someone ever, instead of meaning a rush into someone's unsuitable arms and unsuited life.)

There *is* probably some truth to the dysfunction idea when it comes to Kush and moi, but *all* relationships have their weaknesses; and it would be insane (in a bad way) to use its weak points to invalidate our pivotally nurturing alliance. (Ditto, beneficial on-line companions.) I won't let someone invalidate us on poorly-applied psychological grounds.

In the same vein, Kush tends to be the archetypal male, bending and bobbing, like a fighter avoiding punches in the ring, saying almost every time we speak that he is extraordinarily busy, oh so busy, (hidden message: So if you don't hear from me for a while . . . otherwise known as the masculine cry of "Don't tie me down, don't fence me in!"). However, it seems almost an unconscious reflex on his part. I'm not trying to build a cottage for two with picket fence, or even some hip variation thereof. More important, *he is constantly there when I need him, and is otherwise all around available when I call him.* Again, I know the fruit, so can ignore the messages from small minds (there is no *room* in those minds to hold a lot of thoughts).

As I said, if we were two heterosexual men, the relationship would be apparent. We are both poets and mystics. Books portray friendships between historical literary figures and innovative thinkers. Whether Kush or I are worthy of history is not the point. The point is that we are enormously powerful as to what we each accomplish for our communities, and part of how I do it is by creating paradigms used globally. And *that* is what we discuss: our work! It makes for *big* ideas flying back and forth furiously. I need him shoulder to shoulder with me, because he is someone whose big ideas are backed by big action.

I don't crave big ideas per se. But I need the very specific bigness of the ideas we share, bigness defined by the following aspects. First: Many people talk big, but do not act on it. Big ideas from the mind of a person with follow-through may be shaped differently than pure theory or ego-driven dialog or good intended plans made by someone too fearful to execute them yet. (But that fear can be overcome, ya, ya!) His work is different from mine but we share the same type of mind. Second: We're both extremely ambitious, but not for our own gain. We are *obsessed* with changing the world. We are ambitious about it, coming up with goals that would constitute megalomania if time had not proven us capable of achieving them. Our urges to improve the lives of our entire human species *and* the other residents of Gaia cannot be ignored; they consume our respective days, our hearts, our souls—often joyously, and often painfully. Again, this makes for specific types of exchange between us. Third: Another commonality is that we both approach this daily occupation from a mystic's viewpoint.

I am blessed to have found someone with whom I have all these things in common. I don't know what I would do without this common bond. Nor should I invalidate *any* enormous blessing God has given me.

Historically, movers and shakers have associated with peers long-distance, by which means they derived support and camaraderie. These affiliations have been portrayed in book and film as mythic, the epitome of human companionship. But if it happens between man and woman, long-distance or in person, they create a portrait demeaning to her. Gender bias generally rules out *this* sort of camaraderie happening between the sexes. Suddenly, the man is the mentor, and *her* great achievements do not represent her genius and hard work, but are seen as derived from *his*. Blech! That's dumb!*

Or their dialogs in film are portrayed as her beauty,

---

* If we were two straight *women*, most people would not imagine us discussing big mover 'n' shaker ideas. They'd assume we were talking about *men*. We'd support each other through the heartbreak caused by our *men*, one of us holding the other who wept because of *men*. Or one of us advising the other about the best way to *attract* men. Once more, *blech!*

wild grace, and selflessness inspiring him to great creative height. Again, *blech!* Oh, and she patiently suffers his long absences, as he runs around the world saving babies from plagues with the serum he's invented. When he arrives home, she waits on him, hand and foot, quiet as a mouse, lest he be distracted from his brilliant musings. She *believes* in him, even though she cannot fathom the depths of his intellect and creative discoveries. The movie ends, "Martha, I could never have accomplished all that I have without your endless and tireless sacrifices. You never stopped *believing* in me."

"Oh, John, I have always loved you," she answers, a single tear falling down her now weathered and aged cheek. *Blech, blech, blech!*

Instead here is an example of our chats: One of us starts talking about an idea, and the other excitedly interrupts, "Oh, yes, I have been thinking those exact same things." Then we each give our piece of the puzzle to each other.

Or one of us will bitch about current struggles we have in trying to "change the world," then the other of us makes consoling noises. Kush often says to me after one of my many complaint binges, "Just keep on doing what you are doing. It is important." It's the exact same words, again and again. Which is the right thing for him to do! Without that exact remark, I might be screwed. It keeps me going, keeps me fighting the good fight! When illness, naysayers, corporations, and pirates waylay me, I must hear his "Keep on . . . It is important." And I must hear it from *him*, because I trust it from him, since he's facing down the same sort of interference from naysayers, corporations, personal challenges, and . . . okay, there are no pirates, but I love the image of fending them off. It makes us sound so noble, so Errol Flynn.

One point of my last few paragraphs: Be insane; embrace the people who actually support you. Okay, I cannot have just one or two themes in an essay or even in a paragraph sometimes. All dots connect. Theme: Foster your inner crazy sage by hanging out with folks who *like* crazy!

Theme: The above discussion about my doing "big" things touches on this book's focus on living fully, drawing on all your inner and outer resources, expressing all your aspects. Without Kush's pep talks, without knowing that he and other of my friends are side by side with me as we put our butts on the line in our community work, without someone to tell my big ideas, I do not know if I could keep on with this bizarre career I have, a profession of community service that expresses so much of me. Ignore the small minds who try to keep you away from *your* "Kush" by ridicule or any other means. Ridicule bad, crazy good. Be *fully* you. Not that doing so necessarily means professional community work. Have your own definition of *big*: Perhaps it's the way you parent, or how you manage the people under you at work, or *whatever* you define as big.

Moving on: Perhaps one reason that our long years together have been hard for me to figure out, let alone portray, is that they have been multifaceted. (We're now on to *another* theme of this book, boys and girls—the many facets of the gem that each experience constitutes.) This makes it confusing for me sometimes, and surely confusing to anyone looking at it from the outside. Especially anyone who wants everything tied up in a simple package, with the label "I feel in control if nothing gets complex!" For example, Kush was briefly a mentor to me when we first met. Even with that, the friendship was what we were really about. But some folks don't realize that peers can mentor each other. Sometimes, mentoring is more a *function* that either person involved could take on, rather than a lack of equal knowledge. So, when I briefly studied the anthropology of shamanism with him, we agreed I could have taught his classes myself. But I loved his mind! And—more complexity—the writing lessons he gave me for a bit consisted immediately—and mostly—of throwing me head first into the professional writing community, with the insistence that I was an accomplished writer, and "You don't need to *learn* how to write!"

Mind you, I am not belittling his mentorship! Up until him, the few writing teachers I'd had did everything they could to convince me I could not write! So I went to Kush, nervously saying, "I am a novice writer." I will always be indebted to this professor who simply answered, "You are not a novice. You can *already* write." It was no small thing to me. Let alone that his words were not empty: He backed them up with action, almost dragging me into the writers' community, once introducing me with the line, "You two should meet, you will both be famous someday." Lawd! And his anthropology lessons were a saving grace, because they showed me I was not alone in the cosmos with my odd viewpoints and fervor to "save the world."

Trust multifaceted complexity. It thwarts naysayers who insist on simple explanations for *everything*. Often, simple = good. Other times, it is a crying shame, a bad bad thing that hurts many people! (Bad kitty, bad bad kitty! Um, sorry. My cat just knocked over a vase.) Glib analysis is an effective way to deny the facts of a situation. Even someone in touch with his own intricate internal landscape can be guilty of this, sometimes thinking himself more complex than those around him. (I do it myself; sometimes I find myself thinking that I am so deep, much deeper than anyone I know. Eek. I am embarrassed to admit it, but there it is. Bad bad kitty. Usually, this is a subliminal message, because on a conscious level I know better. Important interruption: Look for your own subliminal messages, in this and other areas of your life. They are one of the major challenges of someone who has done a lot of work to create inner change. Despite all your headway, there can be bits of yourself telling you the exact opposite of your new beliefs, subtly sabotaging you. It does not mean your hard work was a waste. You may be *living* your beliefs quite well, by and large. But there can be a bit of touch-up work left, which will help you progress even further, going the last nine yards toward your goal of finding a wonderful mate, writing the great American novel, having serenity, or whatever. The subliminal message may not be words. A negative idea can reside in you as a subtle and vague sensibility. In the same vein, instead of a message, you might want to look for a self-defeating feeling that you almost do not sense, but that needs to be addressed as part of the touch-up work. Read this interruption again. It is an important tool for a committed spiritual seeker to apply to any part of life where he feels he needs more work in order to live as fully as possible.)

Back to our guy who is so much more complex than those around him: When he falls into this trap, he is blind to the facts of others' lives and, hence, their needs. Applying what I'm saying about oversimplification to those who try to stop your health is important. Equally important is looking into yourself to see how you might be doing the same. In fact, look at the whole essay to examine yourself about thwarting others' healthy bonds. You might perceive ways you can better nurture the wild souls you know. Doing so will enlarge your community of wild souls, or at least strengthen your bonds with a wonderfully mad someone, giving you more of the camaraderie *you* need.

Moving on again: I once said to Kush, "You are still my soul mate." I was referring to the fact that we "share a brain," coming up with many similar concepts—repeatedly ideas I've never read, even in the supposedly most forward-thinking writers. I need someone who thinks like me, not only so I can hear him add his ten cents, but also because I cannot bear the thought that no one is in this journey with me. By "this journey," I mean the following:

A colleague of mine once told me, "People love what I write, but would never travel the journey with me that I have to go through to *arrive* at what I write." I understand. It is similar to what a minister said once: "Talking with God makes you crazy." He meant something very specific by that; his context was that his parishioners get to just sit in church and hear his sermon, but they do not know what that sermon costs their minister. The writer friend, the minister, and I (all walked into a bar?) are all walking a solitary path; it is the pursuit of the heart of the matter, of the plugged-in moment, and of the expression thereof.

But Kush *will* walk that journey with me. Yes, we are each alone on it, ultimately and daily, but phone calls are shared moments on the path, a time of "Ah, yes, someone *is* like me. We may each be walking alone, but we are both fighting the good fight. I had forgotten that I am not the only one in this battle." And, as mystics, we are solitary explorers in an additional way, each alone walking the lonely distances between stars. But sometimes we pass each other, waving hello via Alexander Bell's invention, affirming that we are not alone in that vast empty darkness of space.

No, I will not let any so-called norm convince me I'd be better off without Kush.

My soul mate remark was also in reference to our shared mystical viewpoint, which is so similar as to be freaky. As a spiritual teacher, I talk to mystically-inclined folks all day, every day. So I *know* that Kush and I sharing our viewpoint to such a degree is rare. No, I will not forsake this life's blood (hm . . . um, "life's blood" seems kinda creepy right now, because I was reading a vampire novel last night).

Of course, after I proclaimed him "still soul mate," I was concerned he would take this as a romantic impingement on him. So I hastily exclaimed, "Um, I don't mean that in a *romantic* way."

He responded," Oh, let's not take the romance out!" After not seeing me for *years*. He is my funny valentine, who left that wonderful, odd phone message.

Ah, yes, its multifacetedness has made our bond a

puzzle. It has also made it precious.

The human animal longs for connection. It is a basic necessity, an irrepressible longing instilled deep in our cells. People suffer immensely when they lack connectivity with others, with the Divine, with Mother Earth, with community. (This book tries to help all those happen.) Our *type* of connection with each other helps Kush and me have all the aforementioned ones. You, as a unique person, possibly need unique friendships. Instead of letting them be pathologized or otherwise invalidated, embrace the various sorts of camaraderie that are right for *you*.

If you can't find folks like yourself, check out the subchapter, "Faerie Nation." Also, use thoughts on global community in this book as reminders to find ways to make beneficial long distance companions.

Okay, the above essay was as much about community as a whole as it was about romance. And this is supposed to be a chapter on romance. I am constitutionally incapable of having one theme at a time. And I like that about myself. But let's get back to romance per *se*: courtship, marriage, and everything in between—all of which are crazy—as well as some of the options tangential to that spectrum.

Self-assurance when it comes to love is important, so I give ideas about how to bolster self-confidence. If things go wrong *despite* all your confidence, the next subchapter can help. It's a remedy for lovesickness and other ailments of the heart.

Cosmic Soup: First Add One Chicken

Need something to get you through the interminable wait for him to call? Or soul-healing after a break-up? Eat chicken soup. Here's my reasoning: I started to write down my mother's chicken soup recipe for a friend, when it occurred to me: Chicken soup is cosmic.

I mean, Jews, Chinese, and hippies believe it's healing. People of various faiths enjoy it. And Maurice Sendak waxed so eloquently about it in his classic for children, *Chicken Soup with Rice*, that years after my daughter's grown, I still recite the book, insisting my friends listen to this sing-song praise of poultry and grain!

What is it about the soup?

Well, here's the recipe for Italian chicken soup, then we'll take it from there.

Dump one chicken in a pot. If you prefer, gently and lovingly place the fowl into the pot and fib to it, explaining you're only tucking it in for a nap.

Cover it two thirds of the way up with water.

Add three carrots, three celery stalks, and one whole onion. Chop them up first, unless you're willing to eat them whole. The onion'll fall apart anyway.

Then add the amount of parsley, sage, rosemary, thyme, basil, and oregano that you would use for this much spaghetti sauce. Also add a bay leaf, two thirds of a small can of tomato paste, and a half cup of uncooked brown rice.

Cook til the chick falls off the bone. You may have to turn the chicken over a few times, using a huge fork.

Add salt and pepper, and serve with grated parmesan cheese. Insist everyone grate lots of cheese in their soup bowls.

Don't choke on the bones. (You can let the soup cool and take all bones out before serving, if you prefer, then reheat. I'm not sure you'll be able to find them all though, amidst the rice. So be careful to not choke on them, anyway.)

This is a bastardized version of my mother's soup. It is cosmic. And guaranteed to be loved by all who enter your home, when they come to comfort you in your heartbreak. Except for vegans—have soy ice cream on hand for them.

And why, to repeat my earlier question, is chicken soup so universal, so capable of crossing innumerable borders of humankind?

Maybe it's because poultry is relatively cheap.

But maybe it's because so many of our moms made it for us when we were sick as children, and our adult selves don't completely forget the comfort of that.

And maybe there are scientific explanations delineating a chemical health-giving property that is alchemically created from stewing fowl together with other standard soup ingredients.

Or maybe it's because—and this is my favorite theory about the matter—each chicken is a manifestation of the His Most Holy, Great, and High Muckety-Muck Cluckety-Cluck Chicken God. Yes, each chicken is sent here as this mighty deity's presence on earth, to nourish, heal, and calm us in our times of need. Sent to help us celebrate in our times of joy.

Chicken soup—cosmic!

If you're single, the next piece proves that having a partner isn't always as necessary as you might think.

Romantic Weekend, Straight Up

I fondly reminisce about the perfect weekend. In an ocean-side tourist town, I lazily passed the time, stayed abed late, walked along the beach, and ate by candlelight. And felt, by Sunday night, the lovely warm glow of a romantic weekend tryst. However, I was alone the whole time, having gone off to get some peace and quiet by *myself*. I was shocked by the result!

My surprise was a happy one, though. I was delighted that many of the marvelous feelings experienced during a romantic getaway don't necessitate a partner—they come from the getaway itself. (Publishing this info is going to thwart a lot of seducers.)

You may want to try it. But I'll warn you, people kept asking where I lived. (It's just something one asks in a tourist town.) When I'd respond, "San Francisco," they were shocked, because S.F. was just over the bridge. I was only a half hour from my apartment! No one could fathom my spending a holiday weekend so close to home, let alone by myself. I didn't care. Besides, they kept saying, "I'm jealous" with immense longing in their voices. They so wanted what I was having.

Don't wait for love if you have no mate. Love *yourself* and do it *now*. Make memories of fabulous holiday weekends with or without a significant other *now*. You might even meet your soul mate while you're gallivanting about. (And I got to make lots of folks jealous, instead of just one significant other.)

Afterthoughts: Okay, so enjoying life with or without a mate is relevant to everyone. Even if we have a significant other, we need to be happy in ourselves, or we can't be *fully* happy with our beloved. But the way I *personally* go about it, well, it gives me pause—see below.

When it Comes to Romance, I'm Not a Normal Woman
Dec 2010

Years ago, I attended a luthiers' convention (luthiers build stringed instruments). I walked into the main exhibition hall, and went into a dead heat. Not because of all the fine dudes there. It was because of the *guitars*! I was *stunned*—completely shocked—to find out I could feel that way about them. But it was then I realized, I am not like other women!

My relationships with my guitars and my mandolin just ain't right.

Multiple Sclerosis (that's as close as we've gotten to a diagnosis) has made holding a guitar too difficult. I really missed it. (I name my guitars. My vintage Gibson semi-hollow-body electric was called *Blondie*. She's living in Arizona now with a drummer.) One day, a friend dropped by after his gig, toting a mando. I asked, "Put that in my lap, will you?" (It can be too hard for me to reach for things.) Lo, its weight was not too much on my thighs, and it was not too big for me to bend my torso around.

An aside: I found out later it's a really small, lightweight mando; if any other had arrived that day, I would not be playing mandolin now, because it would have been like guitars—too heavy, and too large to wrap myself around. I guess God AKA randomness was looking out for me. Trust the flow, Luke. The flow of events in your day, that is. There are gifts all around, if you watch the moment by moment with the understanding that it is God. There is only God, and God is now.

There is only now, and now is God. And She will always take care of you. Every moment.

I usually wouldn't have asked to be passed a mando. I assumed I couldn't manage it physically. But just couldn't stop myself! Again, lo, it turned out way great—unlike some guys I dated whom I thought I *could* manage! Maybe my impulsively saying, "Put that on my lap, will you?" was a bit of the Divine too. The Gods of Chaos do use every part of a person toward Their agenda of us having immense joy.

Back to the story: My friend offered to lend the mandolin to me. However, it was his dad's. I insisted I could not accept it. But deep down, I'd fallen in love. I was lusting after *another man's mando*! I mean, that's actually how it felt to me, like I was breaking the tenth commandment, "Thou shalt not covet thy neighbor's wife" (or his musical instruments either, in my case. Wait, now that I think about it: The full version of that commandment isn't solely about wives. It's also about coveting property. If craving someone else's belongings is so rampant that Jehovah had to make a commandment against it, maybe I'm a *little* normal.).

My friend would not take no for an answer. I finally accepted his kind offer. But honest-to-goddess, I felt I was cheating with his wife.

Since then, he's generously given me the mandolin. The mando and I have a legitimate relationship now. I am *not* normal.

And recently, there is my crush on Jacquard products. I won some of them in the TeeJuice contest (www.teejuice. com). I called Jacquard a few times to ask something about their merchandise. In maybe my *second* phone call, I suddenly found myself asking if they had a job opening.

They had no position available, and it was a crazy request. I *have* a job. And am not suited temperamentally to hold any position there. Besides, they're in California, I'm in Pennsylvania. *Plus* I'm too disabled to go to an office. (I break easily. Seventy percent of the time I'd leave the house, I'd end up injured. So I happily live, love, and work, all at home.)

But I was acting impulsively because I'd fallen in love— with *product*. And with a company of really cool people. I wanted to be part of that family.

I still do, and am trying to make it happen. (Is this a courtship?) I figured one way I could contribute to their work would be as a writer. I submitted three articles to them (they accepted the third! Yaya!). I mention Jacquard products on one of my sites for free. I will keep offering articles.

Another reason I adore this business is that I owe them big-time! In summer, 2010, their products taught me that I can draw 'n' paint. Doing so has been a huge blessing to me. And a huge deal. And (delighted) shock! It was so unsuspected previously, that it was a matter of "I can draw? Huh?" *Suddenly* I was able to paint things like a face—huh?—and these pieces of art immediately started to sell. Again, huh?

This was freaky to me.

But it's making me happy. As a child, I didn't have good art supplies. Not my folks' fault: No kids in my neighborhood had them. Well, I *won* a Jacquard high quality silk painting kit that made me see what I can do. I also found out that I can manage silk painting and some other dye-arts despite my disabilities. This means I have an additional way to put my energy out into the world—via this art—even though illness keeps me homebound.

Again, I can't believe it, my paintings immediately started selling. This was weird: Expressing, and getting to share, a part of me that I did not even know was neglected! I can't wait to see where this will go! I am always looking to express more of myself, not only for my own sake, but also for my students and clients: The more of me I know, the more inner resources I can draw on to help you express more of *you*, whether it is your artistic talents, your inner voice, your full range of ideas and emotions, or anything else. I also hope you'll let me share my drawing adventure with you. If you're interested, look at the book's resource guide.

So Jacquard started an adventure for me. They're a bunch of people whom I perceive as doing something remarkable: the highest quality product, highest quality service, and genuine caring. Their TeeJuice contest is generous with prizes. I rely on it for some of my art supplies. I get to have the best possible stuff, which I could not otherwise afford. I want to be part of all this, support it any way I can. When someone has a project I think highly of, I tend to get involved, do my bit to support it. I also want to give back to them for all they've given me.

Still, a love affair with an inventory and a group of people is odd, no matter how amazing the merchandise or how awesome the people. It's ridiculous. Aren't I supposed to feel this way about a *man*? Or woman? Or polyamorous group? Is something wrong with me? Or am I instead passionate, focused, and capable of being in love with *all* of life? Yes, I like that explanation better.

Afterthoughts

1) As a mystic on an ecstatic path, I really do find myself in love with all of life. There are moments of stunningly beautiful connectivity to individuals, or to a group I'm teaching (in the latter instance, I'm also feeling connection with each person). Or, during an Another Step exercise, I bond with all the dots in the connect-the-dots painting that is the cosmos. During all these unions, I'm in love.

   It's part and parcel of what I realized long ago: I'm in love with my closest friends. But it isn't a bad thing. I adore them, worship them, try to treat them as a beloved. It's wonderful for them. And for me.

   This style of friendship is not something I chose; it's just how I innately do things, before I even recognized what I was doing. In case you misunderstand, I'm not talking about wanting to make love with them, nor do I put someone on a pedestal or otherwise set myself up for short, disappointing alliances. I am a loyal friend, with lifelong friendships.

But they have a strong element of romance.

The world is my divine beloved.

2) Some people live happiest single, some married, and some do well with altogether different options.

One of my particular gifts as a spiritual teacher and counselor is to help people live *their* authentic self. So I'm able to guide them to choices other than my own. When I couple counsel, I rock! Yet I am single. Repeatedly, people who come to me looking for help finding the dream mate end up happily and long-term married.

We all have our own path; supporting each other along it is not about being identical. It's about honoring the Divine Spark shining in each of us, by respecting whatever supposedly *bizarre crazy* way it manifests.

When it comes to romance, that might mean helping each other create new ways of being married, single, and everything in between. And new ways of the options tangential to that spectrum.

After all, love affairs with guitars, cheating with another man's mandolin, and a crush on Jacquard products and staff? If that makes me happy, who knows what might fulfill you or a friend of yours!

Chapter Six
Parenting, Potato Chips, and Postal Carriers

This chapter scrutinizes my relationships with family, friends, and colleagues, hopefully illustrating mad methods you can use to come out on top in your *own* circle of loved—and not so beloved—ones. We'll also look more at ways to create, strengthen, and/or better draw on friendships with fellow dreamers, innovators, and other mad folk. And how to support those folks in turn. When you need info on any of these topics, remember to look in other chapters as well. All dots . . .

Potato Chips

I adore potato chips. Because of my food allergies, there is only one type of potato chip I can eat. Luckily, it's exceptionally tasty—none better—but it's sold in a national chain that has no stores nearby. Friends all over the country send me bags of this crunchy bliss. A bag or two arrives once or twice a year. People show their love in many ways. I'm sent yummy greasy containers of it.

This may end up being a short essay. I have to go eat my chips. I am eating their love. I can really get into the "No one loves me, I'm gonna eat some worms" blues. So it's important I recognize the love I'm given. When someone loves me, even if it is not the *way* I most want to be loved, or the way I *think* they *should* express their love, I try to remember to eat it up. Take a moment to dwell on their love, drink it in. And say a prayer of gratitude. It can be as simple as, "Thank you for this love."

If you feel disconnected from people and underappreciated, please try out these practices, because their results are awesome, and are better than they may seem on the page. Doing them is likely the only way you can see their benefits. It only takes one to three minutes: Dwell on their love; then drink it in; then say the prayer. (Don't try to do all three at once. Do each step separately.) Doing this practice over and over—e.g., when someone gives you the wrong gift, or does you a favor you don't really want, or messes up a chore you asked them to do—might make you feel loved more and more and more, by your family, friends, and larger community.

I am a woman who doesn't lie down and die because of a disability. The pain was terrible when I was first crippled. Sitting felt so awful for the first year and a half that I basically could not do it. It took a year and a half to be able to sit, and then it was only for minutes.

That year and a half was not spent passively waiting, I worked hard to strengthen my muscles, change my diet, etc. Now I sit all day, and am higher functioning than when first crippled.

My physical therapist said that 70% of people who went through what I did never got back out of bed. But I am aggressive about improving. E.g., exercise had to start ridiculously small. My walks began with inching my way along, until I was 30 seconds away from my house, then I would carefully turn around and shuffle the 30 seconds back home. That was a marathon. But I don't cave in easily. For example, when initially "put out of action," I wrote and sold two books, dictating their contents from bed.

My point is not to praise myself. It would be absurd, given my suspicion that some people simply are driven and otherwise innately able to do what I did. It's just who God made me, through no virtue of my own. I sometimes wonder if anyone who can't pull off what I've accomplished regarding my disabilities simply doesn't have it in them, by their very nature. Maybe they weren't built like me. I don't know. Or maybe they haven't gotten the support they need.

What I *am* getting at, though, is: It hasn't been easy. *And* I am blessed: I get support. Including potato chips. I dwell on the love in them, drink it in, and say a prayer of gratitude. Without this support—the crunchy kind and all the other wee and large ways humans love one another—I wouldn't have been able to keep going. The obstacles were so many and so large. Get the support you need. Recognize the support you get. We need every last bit we can garner if we're to survive this mad world.

Afterthoughts: I lack support in ways that are horrendous. I'll spare you the details except to say that people have cried when they've heard them. But I want you to know my suggestion that you recognize any help you *do* get is not empty words.

My work draws a lot of attack. I always say that "they" ain't stopping me unless they kill me. I was born incredibly stubborn; I will crawl if I cannot walk, to keep on working, keep on giving, keep on living. Gifts of potato chips feed my healthy obstinacy. Goddess, may I always watch for moments of love—however subtle—that renew hope, vigor, and spiritual health.

My Family Still Thinks I'm Eight Years Old

Food and its preparation have always been important in my family, making culinary matters an integral part of our family tales. Cuisine figures in half our stories, one way or the other. That's just part of family history. In the sort of house where I grew up, pizza dough flies through the air. *Literally.*

My brothers asked our mom to teach them to make pizza. I wasn't there to see it, but I heard about it. As she coached them on spinning a flattened wheel of dough up into the air, things took a typical masculine bent. Pretty soon, gobs of sticky dough were flung through the air, not in an attempt to spin the pizza wheels, but in an all-out food fight. They must have ended up covered with sticky wheat. Apparently, though, they left Mom out of the battle. Hey, I just realized: *That's* a family food story.

Women and men are so different from each other in the kitchen. Okay, I'm about to get into gender clichés but, still, there is *some* truth to the following. Really young guys learning to make pizza = huge chance of dough made into attack missiles. Really young women learning to make pizza = better chance of "No, no, I'm afraid to throw it high. If I throw it *too* high I might not be able to catch it. It'll land on, gasp, the *floor!*" Guy = "How high can I throw?" or "Can I throw it high 'nuf to have time to clap my hands before I catch it?" Gal

= "Okay, maybe I'll try a *tiny* bit higher this time, because my last attempt had so little momentum it just plopped right back into my hands before it had a chance to spin."

Also, have you noticed how much more "important" it is when a man cooks? With a woman, food preparation in the home is a given. With my brothers, professional cooks all, a rhapsodized account always unfolds when they make a meal at home. "I'm getting Christmas ready. I cooked three turkeys—you know, what with all the guests we're having—an apple pie, a cranberry tart, two mincemeat pies, a lemon meringue pie, potatoes, antipasto, spaghetti with meatballs, and green beans with almonds."

And a partridge in a pear tree.

Then he continues, "I've been cooking since last night." Really? Oh my! I never heard of a *housewife* doing that, *honest*, not ever. Jeez! If he'd been a woman, he'd have been doing all this with a kid on his hip—easy peasy—and, as I said, it would be a given.

You can bet that, at the exact moment my brother Bill plunges his arm into a turkey's body, and he's elbow deep in it, no one asks him to fetch a beer. "Hon'! The game's on. I don't want to miss anything. Could you grab me a cold one?" (I *did* tell you this book would have rants in it.)

The only time I ever asked Mom to teach me how to cook, I was a child. (The pizza escapade happened when my brothers had grown into men, or maybe teens.) She responded, "Watch." In one word, she snuffed the flame of gastronomical education. That was that. I'm a person who can only learn by *doing*. So I walked out of the kitchen.

I have no idea how it is that, by the time I was in fourth grade, this latch-key kid was making meringues when she came home after school. I didn't even realize, until I was an adult, how unusual it was. I just thought cooking was what one *does*.

Therefore, it's almost automatic to include recipes when sharing ideas and conveying power in *Share My Insanity*. And when discussing family foibles, I automatically tend to tell kitchen and restaurant anecdotes. Hey, I was raised in an *Italian* family. Plus it has a lot of professional cooks, including my brother, Bill.

He was puzzled by the prospect of my writing recipes for this book. "How can *you* do that?" he asked.

Of course, there's not a member of the family who couldn't—everyone is a marvelous cook—but Bill's a typical big brother who, despite all my publishing credentials, is puzzled by my being able to write about *anything*—you see, he still thinks I'm eight years old.

It extends to more than cooking. Right after I received the contract for my first humor book, Bill asked, "How are *you* gonna write that? Will you just fill the book with other people's jokes?"

Ah, the supportive family and their belief in you. It really spurs you on to great things.

Is it that older siblings always think you're still a child, or is it gender bias? Or is it simply that my family is a bunch of wackos?

When Bill challenged my ability as a humorist, he'd no idea his attitude was in any way wrong. He'd spoken in an affable tone. I tried for the same friendly manner when I countered, "Billy, when we're sitting around the Thanksgiving table, eating, and all of us are making wisecracks, and they're flying fast and furious, are the jokes you're making your own, or are they someone else's?"

He indignantly replied, "Mine, of *course*."

"Well, Bill, it's the same with me."

I spoke in an agreeable, soft way, but thought I'd better tone down the next part of my statement a bit anyway—gentle it into feather-like softness. End my remarks with something he could feel reflected well on *him*. So I added cheerfully, "We're a very funny family."

But as any child with older brothers and sisters knows, your logical, calm persuasions don't seem to make a difference. Whether it's because of gender bias, or that I'm the baby of the family, or that they are all crazy as bed bugs, my family still thinks I'm eight years old.

Afterthoughts: I hope the above cooking tales from my childhood illuminated some family foibles familiar to *you*.

Maybe I can also share a few ways I stay one step ahead of them. (In my family, it's like the Mad Hatter managing to always stay one seat ahead of Alice at the tea party. Or, just as much, it's like Alice trying to deal with *him*. I never know what someone might do to grab the seat out from under me. Or grab the tea cup I'm about to drink from. Maybe that's why I learned to enjoy cooking a meal for one, then sit down to eat it, peacefully, all on my own.)

Maybe part of how I cope is to write about culinary matters in the context of supporting the black sheep in families, for whom dinner was often a time of rebuke.

Maybe teaching classes on cooking as a spiritual, transformative art is another way I cope.

Meals were hard for me as a kid. It really was a crazy family, and generally not in a good way. I don't need to make you read a catalog of their wrongs to me. Or a litany of how much this hurt me. The main thrust is: Despite all my jokes, I have a lot of awful mealtime memories; many holiday dinners broke out in verbal and physical violence. Wow, I did not expect to be typing this. The above is a light humor piece. But the Muse will have Her way: I seem *impelled* to tack on a more serious afterthought.

So to continue: Cooking can heal the spirit. It took many years for me to find that out. Not only because my crazy-in-a-bad-way youth left me full of nasty dining-room memories, but also because women raised in the fifties and sixties—I was born in 1949—were drilled into submission, so that they would accept being eternally tied to domestic chores, bearing the yoke of making three boring meals a day, one after another, *every* meal, whether they felt like it or not, every every *every* day. Talk about taking the joy out of the kitchen!

Now I cook for fun. I cook because God's in every morsel, filling me with His love and power. I cook because healthy food imparts its health, filling me with sparkly feelings. I cook because preparing whole organic food is a way to take responsibility for my well-being; a large portion of America's health crisis could be averted by good nutrition. All these things heal my past. While cooking, I'm one step ahead of the Mad Hatter at Alice's tea party. (Or I'm the Mad Hatter one step ahead of *everyone*.)

The calm I gain while chopping, stirring, and inventing makes me more able to deal with everyone at the tea party. The pride I take in my recipes and in taking care of my health empowers me to not let old unhappy cooking stories take over my kitchen. I make marvelous new ones.

For example, I take joy in a story one person *told* me about myself. I had a party, and greeted each guest by popping a homemade truffle into their mouth. (I make great truffles!) After this greeting, he said, "I finally *get* it: You're into decadent foods."

I was puzzled by this story about me, until I reviewed dishes he'd had at my home. Homemade truffles. Chilled blueberry soup. Salmon stuffed with hazelnuts. Almond torte frosted with chocolate truffle paste. Yeah, I can see the source of his story. To me, it's not decadence; it's just yummy menus. But I like his tale anyway—it's fun.

Another narrative to replace old sad ones: I had a formal black-tie eight-course dinner for seven of my friends, to celebrate turning 50. Bill said, "You're going to cook your birthday dinner *yourself*?" As if that was a *bad* thing, a bad story. I answered, "Heck, yeah. That will be half the fun." (*Good* story.)

As it turned out, my co-host, also my prep chef, cancelled on the day of the event. Eek! Somehow, I was able to choose to stay calm. All day, I stirred and chopped, stirred and chopped, slowly, slowly, step by easy step, making my way through the feast's lengthy preparation. Serenely, happily, leisurely. It's a spectacularly lovely kitchen memory to replace old miserable tales.

Before starting to chop, I ran to the apartment upstairs. "Jillian, help! My co-host canceled! Can you take his place?"

Jillian kindly and enthusiastically offered, "Oh, sure. I'll get a maid's uniform to serve."

"No, don't be silly. Please, I need you to sit with us: Be a charming co-host."

She did exactly that. A divorcée of a millionaire, she was now down on her luck. But she regaled my guests and me with yarns about rich cowboys, their luxury cars, and their herds of cattle. Hers are more stories that finally replaced long-standing cheerless ones.

As is the fact that my guests knew how much trouble I had gone through: Every one of them arrived in best form, contributing their absolute utmost charm and wit to the celebration. I basked in this act of love on all their parts. And still do.

Another way I stay ahead of the game, when at the dinner party of life and familial dysfunction, is the healing of humor. Joking about my childhood takes the sting out, and makes something good out of past sorrows. Please, oh please, make fun of the things that have caused your deepest pains. Don't do it in a way that makes light of your suffering. But if you can find a *real* belly laugh in past traumas—or even a shy, tentative, oh-so-tiny, but *authentic* lift to one side of your mouth—you also find incredible release and freedom.

Sometimes all we can do is stay one step ahead but, hey, as long as you're ahead, what does it matter? Worrying about tomorrow's cup of tea or seating arrangement never helped anyone.

Whether it's by making your spirit and body strong with yummy repasts, or finding the Divine in your grocery bag, or experiencing the calm that cooking can fill you with, or realizing you deserve to cook fabulous meals just for yourself, the kitchen is a place to make new stories that replace old *heart*breaking ones, and thereby heal your *heart* from the past.

Encourage Everyone's Effervescent Egos

I'm definitely a product of the sixties. We're the ones who believe that our massive accumulation of goods isn't materialistic if it's comprised of beautiful hand-crafted objects and/or of possessions that have deep spiritual meaning. I'll never forget a date I had, during which the fellow in question showed me his meditation room. In it was a pile of sacred objects—crystals, Aboriginal carvings, native weavings, bones, and so forth—creating a mound about four feet high, and covering maybe five square feet of the floor. A huge disheveled heap, like a plunderer's booty. I was horrified, stunned—and judged my companion to be a moneyed Marin fool. (Yes, we were in Marin, where wealth and New Age sensibilities meet, to sometimes embody the worst of both, so that it seems a parody.)

That's another thing we leftovers from the sixties do—feel morally superior. Truth is, after years of alternating between disdain for—and jealousy of—people with gorgeous possessions, I have a home full of them myself.

Many, I made or salvaged myself. For example, I

refinished furniture procured in a dumpster dive, hung my original art, fabricated wreaths, made tiny flowers out of beads then created wee bouquets of them—on and on.

I've really been enjoying the beautiful home I've created for myself. This is a good thing. However, it did recently occur to me that my snootiness about people working endless hours in order to purchase fab merchandise is ridiculous in light of my own endless hours crafting objects for my personal environment.

I'm frightened by any tendencies I display to feel superior, because I've seen the divisiveness and pain caused when a person is like that. Of course, if I'm better than you, if I'm deeper, more sensitive, then my snobbery won't impact your *less* deep, less sensitive being. Right?

Argh!

Superiority also keeps the alternative community impotent. "How could I *possibly* ever work with *you*?" seems to be the battle cry of the immobilized, rhetoric-drenched rebel. (I'm referring just as much to myself as to anyone else, so don't think my remark is a sign of, well, *superiority*, speaking of the topic at hand.)

I've created a new motto for myself: Encourage everyone's effervescent ego.

A *false* ego is sometimes recognizable because it can be contracted, pulled inward til you're like a hard, rigid ball, which occasionally explodes violently and hurtfully outward. A healthy ego is relaxed and expansive—effervescent, moving *outward* from its center in an ebullient, Alka-Selzter-like fizz. A smiley fizz, ever-spreading.

The false ego makes you stand alone, proudly declaring, "I'm so great." The bubbly ego runs around hugging everyone. (It's a healthy ego when you say "I'm great" if you're also encouraging *other* people's healthy egos.)

If you watch for pulled-in, clenched moments, you can better spot dangerous superiority. For example, did you read this piece naming certain people you know as guilty of the traits I criticize, instead of recognizing your own errors? If so, did that make you feel pulled in, tight, discontent? Then stop it! Take a deep breath. Take several. Grin, love yourself—warts and all, because we're all fabulous goofball mistake-makers—and then do the following:

Bubble. Bubble!

Encourage Everyone's Effervescent Egos, Part Two

I wrote the previous piece last night. Felt very good about it: "Look, I can admit my faults and help others at the same time. I'm hot stuff!" There's nothing wrong with self-appreciation. *And* this morning, my basement flooded. As is so often the case, when a human being eloquently expresses their depths of spiritual insight, she very soon has to eat her own words.

So, there I was, in rubber boots, me who needs a wheelchair,* hobbling around with a portable pump before

---

* The wheelchair use is only when I leave the house for anything but sitting in my yard, retrieving my mail, and going on physical therapy walks by my house. But don't think I'm any less disabled for that. In the name of wheelchair users who are misunderstood because we have limited walking abilities: We can be just as ill as, if not more than, someone who's always in a chair. Physical disabilities are often grossly simplified and misunderstood by those without them. Listen to your injured friends—don't assume.

the water took out my furnace mid winter-night. If you're puzzled by this, because you don't understand how a person so crippled could do what I did, think of the proverbial mother who lifts the car off her child. The story never says what her back feels like the next day. There are thousands of people with disabilities in the U. S. who lift that car constantly, because we have no choice. You do what needs to be done, and the stress it puts on the body might keep you from ever recovering from your disability. Society putting us in this situation is a crime and a sin, but there it is.

So, I'm playing home-owner-saves-the-day, and it takes an hour, maybe an hour and a half. Plenty of time to ruminate. I start thinking of a person I know whose basement doesn't flood. "*She* has money," starts the litany in my brain, "She *says* she cares about me, but where *is* she when I need her? The self-righteous, smug so-and-so!" Blah, blah, blah. On and on. "I'm gonna call her up and tell her I'm done with this fake friendship."

Okay, being without much money and unhealthy in America is a very bad pairing. I have a right to be upset, even terribly angry. And it's vital to feel, validate, and express the anger. Furthermore, my so-called friend isn't one at all. There's a lot to be healthily angry about *there*.

However, I was shrinking in that basement, contracting, becoming denser and harder each moment of my inner rant, until my monologue had reduced me to one tiny dried pea.

I am not suggesting I, or anyone, should ignore injustices or accept dubious friendship. But the moral superiority of a false ego is not the solution. As I said in part one of this piece, it isolates us and impedes the very acts that can stop unfairness, as well as creates a mindset in which it's hard to find *better* friends.

So, I studied the water surrounding my rubber boots, and told it, "Bubble. Bubble." I'm not sure what that meant, but it made me feel okay again.

Afterthoughts: It seems to me this piece needs more of an ending than what's above, except that it was really that simple. I a) recognized my shrinking state; b) said "Bubble. Bubble;" and c) was okay again.

Sometimes I demean the simple, effective solution. My false ego wants something more complex, more intellectual. My false ego wants something that seems deeper. But my false ego also wants me to avoid inner growth. Dubbing the straight-ahead solution "too simple" is a great excuse. There are times for complexity, intellect, and overt depth. But this does not seem one of those times.

In any case, I see one more part to fixing my problem. There was a d): I shared my solution in this little essay. Maybe the act of telling the experience also helped expansion start, a reaching out to others that reversed the implosion process. This implies that a solution to the shrinking state caused by false ego is, as I said previously, to run around hugging everyone. In other words, to reach out—reaching out is an expansive movement—and tell others, "Bubble. Bubble!" Here's one way to accomplish this: The next time you're imploding, point out this and the previous essay to someone, say, "These were good for me," and then request your companion read them.

Other ways to reach out:

◊ the hugging, of course
◊ telling the water, broken pipe, jammed CD drive, crashed computer, or broken window, "Bubble. Bubble!" (I mean it. Try it and see.)
◊ think of someone who needs help; help them.

I didn't call up my friend to tell her off. I did that years ago. We keep a tenuous connection—rarely in contact—which I maintain because I love her. I know that I can't have more with her, so I focus my friendships elsewhere. But I can, silently, right this minute, think to her, "Bubble. Bubble!"

"Encourage Everyone's Effervescent Egos" distinguishes between the hard to recognize false ego—which pulls you *inward* and isolates you in your "superiority"—and the healthy, effervescent ego, which pushes you *outward* and "runs around hugging everyone," thus encouraging self worth in them and yourself. "Encourage Everyone's Effervescent Egos, Part Two" is a story: I go on an unhealthy ego binge. Trying to deal with my flooded basement despite my disabilities, I plunge into a morass of moral superiority over America's treatment of the disabled, during which I also get on my ridiculous high horse about friends with dry basements.

I hope my personal solution in those two pieces illustrates methods through which we can honestly face social injustices, yet avoid the false superiority that both impedes effective action toward change and ruins friendships.

But there's a broader point in the essays. It is developed throughout this book, though often not dubbed as such. For a variety of reasons, many of us grew up having our self-esteem crushed. There are innumerable possible results. Here are a few. We might have been given the message that any sense of self was bad. Or that we should not feel good about our achievements. Or that we aren't worth self-care. Or that it is not okay to ask for what we need or want. Or that there is nothing special enough about us to make us worthwhile to a prospective mate, employer, or friend. Or that nothing we do is ever good enough. Part of healing any of these things is developing a *healthy* ego. In the process, or even after a healthy ego is gained, it is easy to misinterpret any message about humility or about forsaking *unhealthy* ego as a message to once more lack pride about who you are and what you do, and to be just a doormat once more. But until the unhealthy ego is addressed, only half the battle for self-worth is won. I hope this book helps you win the whole battle.

This false ego can greatly harm a person. For one thing, it wants us to avoid the inner growth needed for the *most* possible happiness. One way it does so is to mask our fears. E.g., I mentioned earlier that you might find yourself saying at some point in this book, "I already have done a lot of work on what Francesca is discussing, so her words aren't relevant to me." That *might* be the false ego saying, "Whoa, Francesca's words are touching on a fear that I don't want to admit, because if I do, I might get happier." It is healthy to be proud of what you've already accomplished, but the false ego will get all huffy, listing those same accomplishments as a way to sabotage you—stop you from achieving even *more*.

This book is both for newbies to the self-help process,

and for old hands. Please believe that I am aware that you may have overcome great obstacles to find yourself, to be enormously spiritual, to be very generous, or to be of immense service. I do not think you are pathetic damaged goods. Or that you have no self-perception or lack depth. Or that you have never worked on whatever issue is at hand in a subchapter. But there might be something left unresolved in an area where immense headway has been made—another step to take, without which the last nine yards cannot be conquered.

Then, My Child, the Bird Pecked the Little Girl's Eyes Out. Isn't That Cool?

Recently, my grown daughter said I traumatized her in her youth with a fairy tale I wrote especially for her. As a child, my little, beautiful, and dark Sicilian girl was thoroughly into the blue-eyed, blond, white-bread look. Therefore, I reversed it for her, composing a tale about a young, *blue*-eyed girl who wished for *brown* eyes. Next thing she knew, a bird came and pecked out her eyes, and the blood crusted over, leaving *brown* scabs.

What a terrible story! I hadn't realized it at the time. Oh, the awful, awful things we unwittingly do to our kids.

I had thought we were having a mother-daughter bonding experience. I wrote the words, she illustrated them. I'd considered it a tender moment. Oh. Dear.

I actually started laughing when I talked about all this with Stephie. She's also a mother, who's shared with me the ins and outs, ups and downs, of parenting. What a deep, throaty, and knowing chuckle she had that day! It absolved me. Ours was not a callous mirth but compassionate recognition of the awful mistakes we unknowingly make with our offspring. All you can *do* is laugh.

Here I had thought I had been so clever, finding a way to show my little girl her own beauty—a great mom! I still have the drawings, a memento until now. Yes, I even had her *draw* this. Oh. Lord.

When I looked back on that fairy tale, it just got worse and worse. The fable had continued with the girl blind, crawling through grass—sharp blades that cut open her skin. I was horrified at my invention. And laughing even harder because of it. Like I said, what else could I do? Laughter washes away the past. Not that I needn't take responsibility for harms done, but it's vital to find forgiveness for myself, my human—oh-so-human—failings. Dark humor is a rich, lush, and potent healing salve.

Stephie's and my ability to find actual hilarity, because I had been *so* off base and hurtful to my child, also opened the door to forgiveness of others:

When I was little, my brother Roger—who was nine years older—once shoved me into the oven, another time into the shower. (He only turned on the shower.) And once he put on a suit-jacket backwards to give himself Frankenstein shoulders and, holding his arms straight out shoulder height in front of his body, entered the room announcing, in a Boris Karloff drone, "I told you I'd be back." The day before, he had brought me to a horror film. He was quoting a line from the movie, which hadn't really scared me, but his imitation was terrifying. I had repeated nightmares from it.

I've always wondered how he could have been so cruel. Now I know. He probably thought we were just playing.

We try so hard, we fail so often. Our kids forgive us, or they don't. But one makes peace with the past. Not by rewriting it into more comfortable fairy tales, but by admitting if one was the evil queen or the vicious dragon, then letting understanding and forgiveness of others and self work its transformative magic. Sometimes, laughter helps this process along.

Since I did not hurt my daughter intentionally, there's also been another lesson for me in all this, a reminder to not assume a motive of evil or revenge or callousness when someone has hurt *me*. Instead, I need to remember that we're all in this mix together, stumbling along. So I make up another fairy tale that has nothing to do with my daughter. It is a fable I create here, now, as a way to discuss my foolishly assigning people negative motives: When the bad king in my tale hurt me, he was actually a commoner posing as royalty. He was afraid that any day his ruse would be seen, and he'd be sentenced to the dungeon. Fear made him clutch power too tightly, wield it unthinkingly. So he hurt me. If I think *this* way, I can forgive others their stumbles when they fall against me, knocking me down.

May our children forgive us—and themselves—the same clumsiness.

Afterthoughts: My granddaughter is now a teen. If she becomes a typical teenager, inflicting the typical woes, to which my daughter responds with typical parental mistakes, that may elicit more forgiveness from her.

And as I forgive myself, I more clearly see how both bad *and* good motivated me.

On the one hand, had I known better parenting skills, perhaps my daughter would have learned to say, "Mommy, this story is scary. Stop!" However, I too often silenced my daughter's outpourings.

And I was probably judgmental of her desire to be thoroughly all-American, after my own childhood of being told I was ugly because I wasn't Irish and snub-nosed. That critical edge might have leaked out in the fairy tale. Yes, the trauma she accuses me of was perhaps even more real than Stephie showed me.

On the other hand, I'd thought my writing okay because it was in the style of old-fashioned fairy tales. You know, the girl wishes for red shoes, puts them on, and can't ever stop dancing, 'til the woodsman cuts off her feet? Now I know why those horror stories were watered down into cute pabulum.

The story's happy ending? We learn, we grow, and I stop telling children old-fashioned fairy tales. Hm. The dancing girl received wooden feet. Stephie says they worked perfectly fine.

We survive. Stumbling on wooden feet, bumping up against each other. Oh, dear, I'm onto another gruesome tale here, aren't I?

And they say life's not a fairy tale! I give up.

Knowing Your *Full* Worth

Sept, 2008. Please read this even if you don't believe in Jesus, Buddha, Rumi, Lao Tzu, or . . . because they're not my point.

If Jesus returned today, no one would even notice. Christians would be too busy fighting "non-believers," or trying to convert them. New Agers would illogically reason, "Since God is in *all* of us, you can't be the real Jesus," as if *both* couldn't be true. Radicals would rebuke, "It is elitist to present yourself as special." Intellectuals would debate, "What is the nature of Jesus? Does it help an individual to identify as Jesus? Is that something none of us should do, or all of us should do?"

Do you think you are different—you would recognize Jesus, Buddha, Rumi, Lao Tzu, or the like (avatars, gods, prophets, etc.)? If so, *how* so? I mean, how exactly would you be able to recognize him or her? Figure that out, then apply that info, use it to spot the avatar.

The acknowledgement of avatars is not my real point. (That's good because, for example, you might consider a belief in avatars unhealthy.) I'm actually addressing a *larger* issue: In a commendable attempt to be egalitarian, some people have gone to an extreme by insisting *no one* has exceptional gifts. Whether it's as an artist, poet, chef, philosopher, or whatever else, we're supposedly able to feel better about ourselves by denying someone else's abilities.

But deep in the belly is a place that will not be fooled by this false position. This overly simplified solution ignores facts. And equality does not demand *same*-ness.

As long as one dwells in pseudo-egalitarianism, one

cannot *truly* feel equal. When we accept the extraordinary traits we see in others, it subtly shifts our cells so that we see our *own* amazing gifts. The inner transformation may take a while, and other actions may be required. But the act of honoring someone else in an honest way creates the capacity to do the same for oneself.

No one is better than you just because they're better at a specific endeavor or task. If someone in your childhood, family, school, workplace, community, church, or coven makes you feel you're less worthwhile because there is a skill you do not excel in or there is a type of undertaking you just can't do well, maybe it's time to let go of that worthlessness. Use the following as a prayer or affirmation.

May I Know My *Full* Worth

May I know my *full* worth. May I release any bitterness—known or hidden, great or small—because bitter feelings shrink my spirit and continue to keep me in the clutches of people who naysay, shame, or invalidate.

May I know my *full* worth. May I celebrate the specific abilities of people I meet or hear about, and thus embrace the wondrous possibilities in *all* humans. May I release all bitterness—known or hidden, great or small—about people who've successfully expressed immense talents. May I know my *full* worth.

~~~~~~

Also, I really want you to try the following exercise: Figure out how you'd spot talent in a person. Just pick one way you'd do it, even though in *itself* it may not be sufficient proof. Then apply what you come up with to spotting talent in those around you. If you can, do this with everyone in your vicinity for an hour or two, or a day or two. If you can't pull that off, do what you can. You are not doing this practice wrong if it does not always help you spot talent. But if it works only occasionally, it will enrich you tremendously. Now and then, return to this practice.

First of all, it'll help create the aforementioned recognition of your *own* specialness. But it's also a great way to identify possible friends. It can deepen a friendship you already have. And you get to enjoy the diversity around you, as well as become blessed by the subtle inner experience of acknowledging specialness over and over. I have many truly special days; recognizing the extraordinary in people around me is part of how it happens. Why, it helps turn this grumble-grim into Pollyanna sometimes (not a sickening Pollyanna either, but a sincerely happy person).

Also, I hope you do try to spot *avatars*. Again, pick just one way you'd know someone to be that progressed a spiritual being. Apply the guidelines that I've given in the talent recognition exercise. Use what you come up with, but know that the point is not to actually find an avatar. However, the practice can help us see spiritual integrity in those around us, and thus appreciate them better. Which helps when they're being typically human, AKA immensely exasperating dummies.

Off in Your Own World

The following involves me writing down some of my personal achievements. I hope you will understand that this is not bragging, but a necessary component of something I want to share with you: There are ideas I want to express that require I talk about a few of my accomplishments in an honest, straightforward manner. And so:

Been thinking a lot about how slow some of my projects have moved over the years. *Be a Goddess!* was published ten years after it was written. For one thing, it took *forever* to get a publisher. However, it went into thirteen printings and three languages. More important, I receive letter after letter telling me how much the book has helped.

Pick The Apple From The Tree, my music CD, also took ten years—lots of false starts, road blocks, and frustration. But I've been told by many people that they enjoy it and that it means a lot to them. It was a best seller and award winner, and is considered a classic in its genre.

My point in all this is that our society tends to equate success with speed. Do it fast or not at all. Nature, however, doesn't always work that way. And nature's the best role model there is. So here's my super-duper helpful hint: Trust your pace when it's slow. In fact, celebrate it! Maybe you're involved in something that only time can build. Nature's deliberate unhurried process can be a reassuring role model to help you believe in your *own* decelerated rate.

My other point is that I am so grateful to everyone who has supported me despite the appearance that, if I

wasn't finished with an undertaking *right now*, I wasn't ever
gonna be. When I was first teaching the material I create, I
never thought I was starting a spiritual movement that would
eventually be practiced all over the world. That was not my
intention, though I've since realized that I did everything
needed to do so: I created an extensive body of spiritual
practices that were of a piece, coupled it with moral constructs
and cosmology, etc. So, in retrospect, it only makes sense that
things moved at a snail's pace, given the nature of what I was
undertaking, with all the care, detail, and thoroughness that
implies. But mid-process, since we didn't know where it all was
headed, it was easy to assume a destination was non-existent.

Another reason it looked unimpressive was because
this mostly took place in my living room. Just a living room.
This was all way before *Be a Goddess!* came out. Hundreds
of people ended up traipsing through my home. I didn't know
that what I was teaching was spreading by word of mouth
nationally. My goal was just to teach the folks visiting in my
apartment. That's all I cared about.* And I am grateful for
each person who hung tight with me.

They took my classes, or read my little self-published
books, or helped fund projects, or even paid for groceries
when I needed the help. (Goddess knows, an alternative
priesthood as a profession doesn't always pay the bills.) Some
of my students started teaching my curriculum themselves,

---

* If God had decided that my visitors were the only people who ever
heard my words, that would have been enough for me, because I
would have expressed myself and been of service. Despite the previous
paragraph, I did not long for any "destination" except the one I had
arrived at: I wanted to share with my guests.

ignoring naysayers who debated its worth.

Thank you, thank you, thank you, every single one of you.

That brings me to my *second* super-duper helpful hint, which expands on this book's earlier notion of dreamers giving each other support to achieve their dreams. Innovative people often need to live in a world where time doesn't matter—because their work may have to develop for many years before there are visible results. The belittlement such folks are subject to means there is a real necessity for trust and mutual respect among people who are off in their own worlds, taking lengthy voyages.

The outcome of one's efforts may not even be seen in one's lifetime. Many an innovator whose art or science changed humankind was condemned as a slacker when they were alive. "Get a job . . . Be a man . . . You're such a frivolous woman . . . Stop wasting your time and do what's important." William Blake died a pauper. (Yes, there are many people who insist they're always busy with some great project, as an excuse to ignore their responsibilities to their family. I do not want this essay to support their false exemption of themselves from accountability.)

Moving on, and onto the third super-duper helpful hint: Even collectively, we are in a slow, painstaking journey, of learning to trust, support, and stick by fellow lunatics. I make the following prayer, right this minute, and hope you will join me (if you don't pray, the following can be used as an affirmation): May we continue this work for as long as it takes, not giving up because of loneliness, setbacks, false starts, or *incredibly* gradual improvement. May we not be waylaid by the fact that we all have our hands full with so many other things. May we learn the patience needed for a community that is built at nature's pace. We are part of nature, so its ways are often our own. This means that, like nature, we are sometime fast, sometimes not. May Gaia bless us with Her ability of slow but sure progress. And may She gift us with the capacity to move quickly when needed. May I have the patience and strength to build a community of wild hearts, not only for myself but also for others.

My own lengthy projects continue. Some of them have been in the works since the eighties, and seen *many* a false start. Bit by bit, they're happening. But it will take more time, some of them a lot more. I hope some finish in the next year, or at least in this decade. But right this minute I affirm the above prayer by repeating it. I know doing that will help me, so I hope you do the same, in case it also helps you.

Afterthoughts: It's harder to be patient with the slow pace of a family member than it is with someone not as close to you. Also, it's easier to miss your lack of tolerance if it happens at home. You may want to pay extra attention there, so that you give your family *all* the support you'd give someone else.

Generally speaking, respect for diversity is difficult at home. When someone's actions impact you in daily minute-to-minute ways *and* in major life-changing ways, thoughts of diversity can go out the window. Then we get the chance to apply our belief in honoring an individual's choices to one of its truest tests. It's a challenge, but it's worth it!

Read This, or Your Child May be Scarred for Life
Ten Things Never to Do to Your Offspring

I was maybe eight and felt absolutely gorgeous in my Halloween costume. Ooh, would everyone be impressed. Then, my mother told me I couldn't go out to trick or treat until I put a sweater on. This was preposterous! Cover my outfit? With a sweater, no less? A hand-me-down sweater that looked as bad as my clothes *always* looked? It was out of the question, no, I won't do it, and I climbed into my bed, deprived, bereft, and furious.

My mother, next, did one of those things that utterly humiliates her child. When my friends showed up to get their share of my household's Halloween candy, she paraded them into my room, so that they could talk me into going out. With a sweater on, of course.

I couldn't believe my mom would do that. I was mortified to find my privacy—my bedroom sanctuary where I lay fuming, grieving over the horrendous loss of my one-night chance for beauty—violated and invaded. My friends could see me, emotionally naked in my fury and stubbornness and sullen insistence that they go on without me.

Now, here's the thing. Why do I still remember this? More specifically, why have I thought of it three times in the past two days? Okay, I've been writing a piece (for this book) about a trauma I may have caused my own daughter, but that long-ago Halloween was hardly traumatic. I've also been thinking about how to write the essay you're reading, intending a humor piece subtitled "Ten Things Never to Do to Your Offspring." It was to be just a funny list. 1) Never insist they wear sweaters or coats over their costumes when they trick or treat. Ha, ha, a funny, cute little piece—nothing deep—providing a bit of laughter to help parents stay sane.

But something keeps bearing down on me, the Muse misdirects my pen.* There is something so poignant to me about that eight-year-old wanna-be beauty-queen, something new to the story. Suddenly, her situation seems less laughable, her outrage less feeble or silly. Her fury, as I write these words, becomes fully meaningful and right.

She was finally pretty. In a world, a time, where looks were everything. Finally pretty. And someone made her put a sweater on over it.

There's surely no trauma in my sad little tale. The title's jest about scarring your offspring was a set-up for jokes. You know, "Don't ever measure your kid's height in full view of him or her, then let them see you dig a hole in the yard to match the child's size."

Yet, despite no real trauma, that little girl seems so boundlessly pathetic to me that I need to redeem this whole tale. And I can't. The end.

---

* Yes, I often write by pen instead of computer. My disabilities radically limit my computer time. But there's another reason I use a pen (sometimes a brush-pen): I'm calligraphing these words as I compose them. It's a quick 'n' dirty calligraphy, done mindlessly and artlessly; it isn't at all good; but doing it helps me think clearly. It's not that I sit, grandiose, brush in hand, thinking, "I am *the great writer*, my words worthy of actual calligraphy." As I said, it's a sloppy, careless script. But a brush in hand relaxes me, allows me to say what I think instead of worrying about whether others might harshly judge my thoughts or writing style. I enter my own world, and what takes precedence is a longing to share that world honestly and clearly. You may want to try calligraphy, if you long to express yourself through the written word, but are stymied.

Crazy Sage teachings break down barriers that original thinkers have *even* with each other—inner blocks to the fun and support that friends, lovers, family, and community offer us. "Companions in Chaos" illustrates more ways we can help each other with both day-to-day and major problems.

Companions in Chaos

We wild spirits often walk alone far too much. As such, we might suffer loneliness, lack of support, and a sense of being too "out there" for other people to understand. In these pages, I try to address this, show this isolation is not necessary, and offer viable ways to change it. I believe that sharing my insanity helps you have an absolute cacophony of lunatics who'll "get" you and support your efforts to build your *divinely* mad, perfectly-tailored-to-you world.

Effectively dealing with chaos, and experiencing its beauty, powers, and goodness, are some major assets of your Inner Crazy Sage. Illuminated lunacy also includes trusting the chaos within those around us. It often holds wisdom, camaraderie, and other gifts that can help us with day-to-day coping as well as with major problems.

So let's explore these premises: The chaos within can cause miscommunication, which in turn can make us miss the depth of perception hidden in people we know. Then we're less likely to have companions in chaos, or be able to draw on the bounty in *their* chaos.

The following example is extreme, to make things clear. Think of the madly gibbering fool, the archetype in the movies whose melodramatically sad state causes others to shake

their heads in impotent dismay. Unfortunately, it's not just an
archetype. It represents real people, and they are not few.

Their words can seem no more than babble. But are
they? Sure, synapses misfire or psychological problems cause
incoherent talk. But in other instances, clinically insane people
are trying to explain connections (connect-the-dots): Jane's
father abused her. She told her mother, but the battered,
frightened spouse answered, "You're crazy!" As the abuse
continued, Jane kept trying to communicate what was going
on. Because her pleas for help were always met with the harsh
accusation of "You're crazy!," they became more and more
"coded;" her father often wore a blue suit, and when he came
home from work at night, she was terrified; her coded plea to
her mother became, "I'm afraid of the blue at night."

Since she was called crazy for revealing the truth, she
tried to not speak it. But she was equally desperate for help,
and therefore *had* to let someone know about her situation.
A "code" helped her both deliver and disguise her awful
message. She would convey it, sobbing, pleading, so frantic
to be both heard *and* ignored that she was in hysterics. The
words and her frenzied delivery of them make perfect sense if
you know the context and therefore all the *connections*. If not,
she just seems clinically crazy. And, of course, likely ends up
being exactly that.

This oversimplified, extreme example illustrates the
difficulty that many people have communicating important
connections. A person needn't be clinically insane for this to
occur. And it doesn't just happen in dire situations when we
need to tell someone about a trauma, as was the case with

Jane, but also when we try to share a precious belief about spirituality, or a fragile hope for our futures, or a technique that can improve someone else's life. You don't have to suffer from mental illness to code your message or otherwise make it unclear. Uncertainty about whether you want to risk exposing yourself might cause you to state your thoughts so vaguely or circuitously that they're indecipherable. Or nervousness about being judged for your ideas can make you jittery enough that you create a verbal mishmash.

As a result, two people whose minds are boldly coming at life from insightfully odd perspectives don't recognize each as such; they are left alone in their isolation.

Listen carefully to people. We need to learn from each other what useful connections we're missing. In addition, people need help they can't get if we aren't looking past their code, etc.

As you listen, realize that their emotional signals may be misleading, just like Jane's hysterics. For example, when someone's afraid of sharing a precious belief or hope, because in the past everyone called it stupid, their fear often looks like suspicion, dislike, superiority, and a lack of any reasonable trust. Try to watch for this.

There's an additional obstacle. If you have your own way of seeing life, it's likely been challenged a lot. Therefore, no matter how much you respect diversity, misdirected instinct might cause a knee-jerk shut-down in you about *other* people's own odd ways, as if by doing so you protect your own. Watch for that. (Really—*watch* for it. Don't automatically respond with "I don't need to. I am really open-minded." Twenty plus years working with amazingly innovative and open-minded folks has taught me that the shut-down can be incredibly subtle. It is one of many subtle ways we block camaraderie with like-minded lunatics. I hope you stay open when this book discusses any of them.)

The Cripple in the Corner
Connectivity, Service, Tribe, Arrogance, Humans with Names, and Humans as Ciphers

Years ago, an astrologer doing my chart told me I have a burning need for intense interactions as well as an equally strong desire for solitude. Spot on. It's been a lifelong balancing act. Even before illness made me housebound, I spent more time alone than anyone I've met. Luckily pastoral counseling—which I do albeit from an interfaith, earth-based mysticism perspective—as well as the small, personal-growth groups I lead, fulfill a lot of my need to be deeply involved with people, yet these situations also allow me to say, "Times up! Bye, bye!" and return to my cave.

One way that I've always felt connected to others is the act of serving them. It makes me part of the community and linked to something larger than my own, small, self-concerned obsessions. Luckily, my work has been *about* service.

Escaping an unhealthily constant and worried preoccupation with one's own concerns is not the only benefit of service. If you feel alienated and not part of community— whether that experience is rare, occasional, or constant— serving that community helps make you part of it. If this suggestion seems useless, flip to "Okay, So You May Never

Lecture to a Teenage Audience in China. But . . . " where I discuss what is and is not service. That might make the idea more useful.

There's another reward: Masks come off, we talk about our actual concerns, it is intimate, we share some time grounded in real life and in who we really are. I could not keep going without these precious moments of connection and authentic "being."

Now that I'm so ill, being homebound has me more alone than is even to *my* taste. I see humans a total of maybe five hours a week. The response to this is usually, "I don't see people much myself." But the speaker is not including time spent places like stores or the workplace. I have no human contact at all except a few hours a week. Though my disabilities cause this, they've also caused a new type of connection to others. Volunteers come over to do my dishes, bring in groceries, and otherwise keep my life going— literally—by taking care of its nuts 'n' bolts, since I can no longer do that.

It's an odd intimacy. These are often people I don't know well. (It's amazing who steps forward in times of need. But that's another topic.) They see me reduced, feeble, needing their charity. They also may see me unwashed, on the days my limited energy must go elsewhere. They're privy to these and other terribly private moments of a cripple's day-to-day life. When I'm unable or barely able to speak—this happens a fair amount—they don't obliviously demand speech from me, but move silently through my home, noiselessly accomplishing the chores needed for my survival. An odd intimacy, that would be humiliating were they condescending people.

Were they condescending, the intimacy would be more akin to that of domestic violence. For example, I have a relative who takes people in crisis into her home. She'll tell you, "I've got an unwed fifteen-year-old pregnant girl with me." (Good grief! What a way to introduce someone, even if only by mentioning her to me by phone.) I gently, calmly asked if this young woman had a name.

Another time, this paragon of virtue told me, "I have a homeless family staying here." My response was, first of all, to ask if they were in earshot to hear themselves reduced to pitiful charity cases, non-entities. They were! How humiliating for them. I said, "These people are guests. Call them by name. And call them *guests*."

I didn't speak in a nasty tone of voice, but gently and matter-of-factly. Nor were my remarks intrusive. She and I had an agreement to speak our mind when one of us felt the other was slipping up spiritually. I was wrong to think we had that sort of relationship.

It's a hopeless cause, talking to this woman, I discovered. She has a long history of smug superiority. She reinforces her self-importance by debasing others in act and word, and by telling lies about them that make them look small or evil. Therefore, when she became "born-again," her new-found religion with its home-based missionary undertakings was not an actual Christian experience but just a new showcase for her pathology. The above ways she spoke of the people she helps are two examples.

Here is another. She has offered to take me in. I'd rather die, truly die, than live stripped of dignity and name. Besides, my health wouldn't improve in an atmosphere like that. The emotional violence in a fundamentalist* household would be 24/7 traumatic.

I hang out with Christ, am not Christian, and also pray to a pantheon of other gods *and* goddesses. My life's been about serving others. I've helped a lot of people. These are all facts of my life, and she lies about them. In her home, I would be dubbed *Satanist* or, at best, *misled*, my whole life and the deities who have cared so tenderly for me invisible. I would just be the pitiful, loser cripple in the corner. I'd be half mad, clutching to my truths—the facts of my life and my gods—while she hammered away at my reality. That is not the only way I'd be constantly slammed and battered by this pseudo-Christian-but-in-fact-just-pathological nut job. Am I talking about her dogma? A bit. But more, it would be the often unspoken and accumulated small acts, some of which are so subtle that you might think you're paranoid. That degree of stress and secret sly abuse hardly allows healing. It is, of course, also a situation without moments of privacy.

In *addition*, I'd get sicker. (Hang in with me. This is a long litany of possible abuse, but you might find it relevant.) Past experience proves that she'd be sure to see I did not get the rest or care I need, because that is what happened when I was staying at her house once, way back when, and wasn't

---

* Christianity is a beautiful tradition. But all religions have their fundamentalists. Fundamentalism has nothing to do with spirituality; fundamentalism is a mental disorder that deserves compassion and possibly psychiatric counseling.

feeling well. Besides, she's told the family I am faking. Yes, one minute I would be her pitiful cripple—isn't she an angel to help me?—and the next minute I'd be a great big faker! Let's change reality minute to minute to suit our own egos, while everyone in the vicinity gets crazier and crazier because they can't outrun your ever-shifting, contradictory lies about them. ARGH! Goddess, help me!

I am violently opposed to good works done with a conversion agenda. They are, in fact, not good works, and usually abuse people who are so down on their luck that they have no one else to turn to.

I am blessed, oh so very lucky, that there are those who take care of me the way they do. They know I have a name and that I do my best to contribute to society. They know that my need for them embarrasses me. They don't degrade me by insisting that my situation came about through lack of motivation or spirituality on my part. It is an odd, precious, and true intimacy that celebrates the enormity of the human spirit, both theirs and mine.

And, in terms of my *specific* needs as a person with a name and unique desires, I am thus allowed both loving depth of contact and a solitude spent not fearful of the next pained assault on my human dignity but in, as that astrologer said, fulfilling an important function. My time alone is when I digest and relish my interactions. It is also when I do a great deal of my community service—preparing curriculum and writing books—yet another form of rich, gratifying human contact.

Some great lessons to take from this: Give humbly instead of becoming over-important from one's generosity.

We *should* feel really good about ourselves for giving to others, but that is not the same as becoming arrogant. How interesting that my caretakers' *humble* care is what *enlarges* them. Quite the paradox! And quite the opposite of the self-*aggrandizement* my relative attempts to gain by lording it over those she helps. My caretakers' acts enlarge *both* them and me. We needn't choose between one or the other. You know, I believe my relative is in a lot of pain, because deep down she cannot fool herself.

It would be easy to end the topic here, but I don't want to leave non-fundies with an excuse for smug self-congratulatory indictments of, well, people who aren't *us*. What's more difficult, and absolutely necessary if we're to create a caring society globally, nationally, and locally, is to see how we ourselves reduce others to ciphers.

It's so easy to do that that I condemn no one, not even the previously mentioned good-doer who, sure, I'm obviously angry at—I'm not a saint—but who I also understood is just another human being fumbling her way along like me (and you, if I may presume). And she's surely generous in her own way, that's for sure. And I *am* trying to release my anger at her.

I don't think that the diminishment of others to nonentities, whether in action or in one's own mind, is an easy trait to overcome. In fact, changing it may demand no less than a complete evolution of consciousness in our species. So it'll have to be a step-by-step process. Here's a step I'm going to apply *now*: For the next few days, I'll watch myself, and try to change my attitude when I realize I am thinking a person is "one of *them*." Maybe you can do this, too.

"One of *them*" might refer to a person with a political difference, or designate any one of a multitude of other things that I could use as an excuse to dehumanize and/or feel alienated from someone. Perhaps the person in question doesn't seem as authentic as *moi*. Or as "in the know." Or as selfless. Or as deep. Good grief, it's embarrassing to admit, but I *do* think these things. And they reduce people to caricatures in my mind—think about it!

However, I suspect I'm hardly unique. Most humans seem to skim the surface of people's being with glib judgments. Not all the time, but often. *And*, we can change this about ourselves, even if it's slowly. Again, we're probably talking about an evolution of consciousness of our entire species, but that may be the only thing that'll save us from annihilating ourselves.

Part of this evolution is coming to see humanity as one large tribe; otherwise humans may become extinct. Tribal sensibilities bind us, helping us treat each other humanely. Thinking someone "one of *them*" excludes them from tribe; we gain permission—however subtly—for ill treatment of them. The wars and other large scale wrongs of governments and big business continue. As do the wrongs *we* do as individuals *to other individuals in our daily lives*. Being banished from tribe was a death sentence in ancient times. It still is, even if it is the death of the *spirit*.

I think about a fundie's close-mindedness, and how it hurts society. I must also see that my own oblivious evaluation of others is no different. It's just as damaging and, if enough people can evolve past this in themselves, oh, la, we can more likely have a society where no one's nameless and thrust into a corner.

Afterthoughts

1) Dubbing a person "one of them" can be surprisingly easier, feel more acceptable, and readily slip by your notice, if the person in question is close to you, or is similar to you in a lot of ways. So this is something to watch for.

2) When we make a "one of them" judgment, we lose the chance for (deeper) intimacy with a person. And holding any attitude toward a person causes you to hold that attitude *period*. You will apply it to yourself. We can dehumanize no one without dehumanizing ourselves. The way I view my aforementioned relative will be how I view myself, even if subconsciously.

3) Perceiving humanity as a tribe helps us realize that everyone has a gift the tribe as a whole needs. Without each person's contribution, the tribe as a whole suffers.

Chapter Seven
Spiritual Fun–Making Wreaths with Bottle Caps

This section deals with God, wholeness of spirit, and dogma—including people who claim to be dogma-less. Though spirituality permeates the book, this chapter is more specifically focused.

Buddha Has Reincarnated as All the Black Cats in the World

A very wise religious leader, whose name I forget—does true wisdom often remain anonymous while clever ad slogans reap huge salaries?—believes that the next Buddha would not be a person but a community of good-hearted people.

I almost agree. Buddha has *already* returned. And it *is* in a community. Reincarnating as all the black cats in the world was much smarter than coming back as a community of humans.

First, let me explain how I discovered black cats = Buddha. I have long known that my own black furred feline, Teenie Bear, was Buddha. She puts up with me! Also, I have seen her calmly and lovingly play with a five-year-old and a one-year-old—simultaneously—for a full hour. Only a transcended being would not have run away and hid instead of being hugged, hauled about like a rag doll, and otherwise annoyed.

At one point, the little girl was about to lift Teenie Bear up and smoosh her into a basket—how pretty; smooshed kitty in a basket.

I quickly intervened, "Oh, you don't want to do that. You might hurt the kitty. Why don't you put her on the floor next to the basket and maybe she'll climb into it for you?"

Not! Any adult would have realized I was misguiding them! No chance that cat would climb in.

But the naive and hopeful child followed my instructions. And Teenie climbed into the basket, where she patiently remained as the girl patted and patted her.

Buddha, clearly.

And this is only one example. Teenie's like this 24-7.

Then one day, walking down the street, I saw a black cat who looked just like Teenie. Looking into her eyes, I saw the same spirit I see in Teenie's.

Though it *was* rather insightful of me to recognize Teenie as Buddha in the first place, clearly I hadn't the spiritual development to perceive the full picture. Buddha had put a piece of himself in each black cat.

Don't tell me other cats also have this blessing! My white and beige cat, Mud—if she's the incarnation of anyone, it's Satan.

Anyway, it was so wise of Buddha to do it this way instead of reincarnating as a bunch of humans. Because when I look in Teenie's eyes, when anyone looks into any Buddha-cat's eyes, they can see compassion. And, in seeing compassion we can realize that, right this minute, we can have compassion for ourselves, loving ourselves for who we are right this minute, mussed up hair, unbrushed teeth, forever short of making the cosmic breakthrough that we think will make us worthy of that love.

Compassion means loving the faulty, not the enlightened.

And maybe that *is* enlightenment.

All over the world, Buddha-cats are teaching this, to far more people than humans could get to. Plus it's easier to believe in, to actually see, kitty-compassion than a human's unconditional love, so the lesson is believable.

Smart Buddha.

By the way, my friend Edwina asked me, "Why *black* cats?" I don't know the answer. She wondered if it is because some people think black cats are evil. That makes sense: A disdained creature teaching compassion. Despite superstitious prejudice toward them, they continue to love fault-ridden humans; this definitely shows enlightened compassion. But, fact is, I have no more idea why *black* cats than I do why God made anteaters.

The above piece relates an oddball theory (that black cats continue Buddha's work of teaching compassion). I'm hoping that the amount of fun I have with my ideas supports you to enjoy *yours*! I also hope you *share* your personal beliefs, because doing so may help your listener trust hers, in turn.

Also honor your own spiritual *practices*. If constructing a wreath out of bottle caps tunes you into the Divine, do it! (Um, I made a wreath like that.) If sex is a way you connect with your spirituality, have a great time. If, like Lilo in *Lilo and Stitch,* you want to feed an ocean fish a peanut butter sandwich as a religious offering, because you believe the fish controls the weather, do it! Find, trust, and share your *own* outrageous, spirit-sustaining practices.

Now, onto more *fabulous* wisdom culled from the kitchen (oh, I love to mock myself): "Crisis Pie (When You Suddenly Discover Your Guest Is Allergic to Mincemeat)" offers an impromptu recipe I created with what was on hand during a Thanksgiving dessert emergency. Maybe sharing my process, which gave me both perspective on how I lose spiritual balance, and what to do about it, will help you as much as it did me.

Crisis Pie (When You Suddenly Discover Your Guest Is Allergic to Mincemeat)

A kitchen is a healthily sane place to be. Inner growth needn't always be hard work; pleasure heals! So here's more culinary self-help.

The evening before Thanksgiving, I foolishly phoned a guest to ask her if there's any kind of pie she hated. The answer was "I'm allergic to mincemeat."

"Damn," I thought, "I should have known better than to call her. Now that I think of it, the ingredients for anything but mincemeat pie aren't here!"

Housebound with my disabilities, I couldn't run to the store to pick up something last minute. And it didn't seem appropriate to ask one of my friends to do it, Thanksgiving guests included, because they all do plenty for me already because of my health-induced limits.

So I freaked out and, in a panic, improvised the following with what I had on hand.

Ingredients

◊   pie crust, in a 9 inch glass pie plate (If you want, use ground hazelnuts for part of the crust. Don't worry if that makes the crust fall apart when you're serving. There'll be hazelnuts in it, so no one'll care!)

◊   3 tablespoons melted butter

◊   1 cup unsweetened apple sauce

◊   1 cup walnuts that have been broken up a bit

◊   1 vanilla bean

◊   2 tablespoons Welch's frozen white grape juice concentrate (One of my test readers asked if I own stock in Welch's. I don't, but am grateful that I can use juice concentrate as a sweetener, since I'm allergic to sugar, honey, and the like.)

◊   cherry fruit spread or cherry jam

◊   1 egg

◊   pinch of salt

Step 1) Continue to freak out about the holiday menu, because it's just one of those stupid things we humans do at Thanksgiving.

2) Then bake the pie crust for about five minutes at 375°.

3) While the crust's cooling, and you ponder that this dessert issue isn't really a crisis—a heartless health-care system is a crisis—mix together the melted butter, apple sauce, and walnuts. Let that sit (because you

have other stuff to do. Maybe the mixture will gain something by waiting for you. However, if you have a co-chef, then she or he can mix the apple sauce blend while you do the following.)

4) Lower the oven to 350°.

5) Cut about two inches off the vanilla bean and cut it into tiny pieces. (I use scissors. As I snip, I let the pieces fall into the white grape juice concentrate, which should be in a microwave-safe bowl.)

6) Heat this mixture in the microwave for 35 seconds.

7) While the bean steeps in the warmed juice concentrate, spread a thin layer of cherry fruit spread or jam over the cooled crust. (It would have been apricot fruit spread, but I couldn't open the jar. I figure the apricot jar's lid being stuck was the way that God, who is all-knowing, implemented His fabulous decision of cherry instead, a better choice—it tasted wonderful!) The cherries in the fruit spread were not entirely mashed but marvelously whole or in pieces. If I had spread the jam evenly, so that it was all as thick as the cherries, my guests would've ended up eating cloying mouthfuls of jam. So I spread quite unevenly, transparent cherry smears between the actual cherries. Therefore, the whole bottom was covered, but delicately so between the fruit bits.

8) Beat the egg and salt.

9) Add the vanilla infusion—bits of vanilla bean and all—to the apple sauce mix.

10) *Right* before you stick the pie in the oven, add the egg (I was afraid the egg would curdle otherwise).

11) Bake at 350° for 35 minutes. (I accidentally had it up higher than 350° for a bit first, for what it's worth.)

12) Keep an eye on it. If the edge of the crust browns too quickly, cover the pie's edge with a strip of aluminum foil. I called my friend Alice, because I didn't want to get that icky thing that raw eggs give you. She promised me that 35 minutes at 350° would leave me icky-thing free. You may want to check that yourself. In any case, let the pie cool before eating. That way it can cook (and solidify) more.

"So," I mused after the pie had finished baking, "it doesn't matter how the pie turns out. Making it was fun, and that averted the crisis." The crisis, you see, wasn't what we had for dessert. My *panic* was the crisis, and it was solved by two things. The first was the calm feeling I got from a creative, relaxing playtime in the kitchen. The second was the sense of perspective brought on by the idea of a bad health-care system.

The lessons I got: Half of life's little ups and downs aren't crises. However our *reactions* to them can be. And sometimes changing our feelings can be hard work. But other times, you can simply do something that's nurturing to body and/or soul, the way culinary activities are for me. Garden, repot plants, make love, tap dance, write a plan to stop world hunger—do something that enriches you and perhaps others.

By the way—the pie was heaven.

I'd love to hear your ideas on how to make my instructions about this pie better, or ensure that it's egg-ickiness free, or other improvements. For one thing, it might have been nicer if the center was firmer, once it cooled.

Gentle Souls

I have a colleague whom a mutual friend recently defined as "marching to his own drum." But I'm not sure there's a beat there at *all*. The guy just seems lost.

He *surely* isn't conforming to common standards—like checking his calls, or tuning into others enough to follow half of what they say. Are these really acts of independent free-spiritedness, or just of passive aggression? And of, as I suspect, a drug problem?

The thing is: This guy is a lovely spirit. He's the sort of almost translucent being that you'd expect to come across in a fantasy forest. He's so gentle as to be permeable, he loves Mother Earth, and I get the idea that he has enormous creativity, hidden and squelched. There is a deep spirituality residing in him, though I am not sure whether he is in touch with it.

I worry about the people who, if they were somehow magically transformed into their animal counterparts, would become baby kittens, chipmunks, and field mice. What do we need changed in our culture to help them be more than food for an alpha higher on the food chain? What do we need different so that they aren't always dazed, puzzled, and frozen-in-their-tracks-because-the-world's-so-big-and-mean-and-complicated?

Okay, they *do* have a beat, perhaps that of the earth's very heart. Maybe, if we each slow down a bit, we'll hear it, instead of rushing so hard and fast to get our day "done" that we frighten these astounding humans into drug-stupors. And I mean street drugs *or* prescribed drugs. I'm not against psych meds, but they are often given when they do more harm than good.

Maybe we can learn from these gentle souls. It is easy to stomp on them, perhaps without even knowing it, in our haste to survive. But if survival is *all* we strive for, we lose life's meaning. Can we try to hear the quiet beat of the gentle soul instead? It would make us become more at one with Mama Gaia. As a result, we might find *ourselves* more, find more meaning—because nature would become more a part of each day, constantly helping to settle us into the priorities of earth and sky, a natural relaxed breath, a moment refraining from work so as to stretch a tight muscle, a sense of being part of something larger and grand and important.

If we are so focused on survival that it takes precedence above everything else, then we lose our belief in heroes, our ability to be "big." Because the hero fights not just for his or her own survival and dignity despite all obstacles, but also fights for the survival and dignity of the *weaker* despite all dominant powers to the contrary. These hero's obligations are *spiritual* concerns. Ignoring them, we lose sight of the spiritual path. I am not saying one is always in a position to fight the good fight. There are times when we don't have it in us, or our attention is *rightly* elsewhere. Perhaps on *self*-care. We also have to pick our fights. But to *never* try to be a hero kills something in you.

How, in fact, do those of us who *are* (so to speak) little furry beings protect *ourselves* and express our own rhythms? How do we create a society we can thrive in, under sunny skies, in warm meadows?

I think it's possible. You may remember that I identify as a rabbit in some ways. My motto is, "Never doubt that one wee creature can change the world." We can rectify this crazy-in-a-bad-way world! However, my adage alone prescribes too simple-minded a fix.

Right after creating my motto—and, I mean, *right* after—I went for a walk, during which I passed road kill.

I'm a *country* rabbit, so seeing road kill is not unusual, though obviously awful. And since I was musing on the motto, it was one of those days that a tiny, squashed being particularly hit home.

I continued my stroll and was immediately passed by a truck. In the back were three men, each with hunting rifles and day-glow orange vests. A daunting sight.

Road kill. Hunters. A message from the universe, for sure. Hence the following, improved, longer maxim:

"Never doubt that one wee creature can change the world. But be ready to run like hell, and avoid morons."

The second sentence is from a friend of mine. It might be misquoted, but she may have stolen it from Bugs Bunny anyway, since she pronounced "morons" as "maroons," accent on the second syllable. I so love Bugs.

I have two additional solutions for how gentle souls can help themselves. One: You may be akin to a gentle ladybug, but this is only one part of you. Somewhere in your ancestry were warriors. Their blood flows in your veins. A wholesome lunacy wakes that staunch blood, as part of *innately* nurturing all the potentials that run through you. Two: Though not always overtly, many tools in this book help overcome challenges that gentle spirits typically face. This paragraph adds up to: Go along for the ride that I keep asking of you (unless your gut tells you otherwise); you'll automatically feel the benefits, bit by bit.

My solutions aren't anywhere near enough in themselves, but they are important components.

Kind of an aside: I would be wealthy if the material I create wasn't so good. People always tell me that my work totally changed their lives. "You gave me the self-confidence to start singing in front of people. I am performing in shows every week now!" Or "Because of you, I trust my inner voice." Or "My soul is awake for the first time." Or "I was finally able to start my own business, doing what I love."

This is from a *single* book or class! If my material was not so effective, people would have to pay for a lot of books or classes to get the same result. Hence I would make better money. But, *no*, they get what they need, without giving me their whole bank account, dang it and *argh*!

That is not to say that I think this book solves all the problems it addresses. Often, in fact, its solutions to an issue are only a drop in the bucket. Which brings me to the immediate point: Even with exceptional methodologies, one book or class is never enough.* Not by a long shot! At *best*, there is always (or at least *eventually*) another step to a particular challenge one faces. Plus, there is always *another* challenge. And another height to achieve in your career or love life or community work. This is a good thing for me, joking aside, because it means that I *do* have long-term students and readers. Good thing for me that many people want to always keep growing, keep deepening, keep striving upward. And that they know when someone stops receiving spiritual lessons, his gains might evaporate from lack of attention. Ongoing clients, students, and readers are important to me for many reasons other than just financial. For one thing, they are strenuous seekers shoulder to shoulder with me in my own spiritual quest. I cannot succeed in this journey all on my own.

For another, I love to teach, it is what I was *built* to do. Unless I do it, my blood does not flow right. Every lesson I give adjusts my own spirit into health. And I have important things to say. So I am grateful to not be a voice crying in the desert, expounding my ideas bitterly because there is no one to listen to them.

One book is never enough. But you *can* continue the work. (If you choose to do so with *me*, my classes and other books are discussed in the resource guide. Classes provide personalized attention, wake up even more of your assets and aspects, help maintain headway gained, and nurture additional progress in areas you've already grown.)

---

* Okay, first I say that some people only need one book or class, then I say that one is never enough. Get over it.

Crazy Sage, Me. Crazy Sage, You.

A recap: Crazy Sage teachings are a multicultural form of traditional spiritual healing and lessons. This useful insanity—transmitted through personal tales, oddball perspectives, and humor—helps people find spiritual wholeness and mundane success.

   To help you find the Crazy Sage *within*—an inner guide who improves everything in your life—as well as help you become (or improve as) a Crazy Sage for others, I've been teaching you the aspects of the Crazy Sage tradition. I conveyed them in what I imagine is the traditional manner—bit by tiny bit, through inference and modeling behavior. Living a new modality by reading this book is more enlightening and useful than if you'd read explanations of that modality. There's no other way to receive what this book promises. We share a journey, and not just mentally. All you have to do is read (and use the tools herein) and your whole being—mind, body, and spirit—subtly goes along for the ride, gradually into a new way of being.

~~~~~~

Exercise

Find one thing in the book that helps *you* find your inner Crazy Sage, but that I did not mention was for that purpose. When you perceive a lesson on your own, instead of having it pointed out to you, it becomes part of you, which means you use it more effectively. When you name to yourself the power in something, you draw on that power better.

Finding or strengthening your mad wisdom needn't entail

boring lessons or didactic lectures but, instead, involves plain old fun. It'd be the antithesis of what I'm trying to convey if I got all pompous and theoretical! Let psychiatrists discuss, dissect, and define meandering minds. Let's you and I just enjoy ours! Too much theoretical discourse is mind-numbing, and I *like* my mind. I use it, bringing my lunacy to bear on important topics, like sex, career, and French fries. (Anyone who says they don't have a strong opinion about French fries is lying . . . I've made myself hungry.) I focus on practical application.

Both standard and new spirituality often work only in an ivory tower. They can be divorced from real life considerations, or suggest solutions you can't fit into your work day. No parent of a toddler has time to learn lengthy, complex practices! When I apply dubious insights to all sorts of topics, it might help you *easily* access your inner Crazy Sage in the kitchen, garden, or office, rather than just in rarefied situations like meditations. For example, one of my stories might spark your creativity, so you create and apply *your* style Crazy Sage wisdom while cooking, typing, or *whatever*'s next, today, right after you put down this book. Integration of spirituality into the activity at hand contributes to the Crazy Sage's holistic approach.

Another example of practical focus and of learning through traditional methods: When I gave a crazy answer to a student regarding a major crisis he had, he discovered that his sober thoughts came at this personal problem too straight on, and that a mind askew approaches things from such an odd angle that it provides vital understanding. He no longer automatically disregards his—or anyone else's—weird ideas without pondering their worth for at least a moment. He has found, developed, and come to trust his *own* brand of wacky, life-changing insights. We all have immense wisdom, if only we notice it.

Honestly share *your* "bizarre" life; some people *will* recognize it as their own. They'll feel validated, less alone, or otherwise benefit from your tales. And maybe share one back at you that *you* profit by.

My following background will become relevant. Until now, no one's taught trickster spirituality in print, neither my modern form nor the original tradition. I created a new system called *Crazy Sage* teachings. There *was* an ancient Sacred Trickster—a traditional wisdom teacher—but no one taught me how to be one. I took years to give it my own spin. The result is an in-depth development, providing an approach that's traditional on some level *and* relevant to modern times.

A Sacred Fool often carefully plans her manner of introducing chaos into everyone's life. I went through a rigorous seven-year shamanic training, done the old way: a full-time commitment, the way others attend college full time. Between my training and innate gifts, I've been made a spiritual healer. When told I was a guru, I protested. The response was, "A guru is not someone whom people mindlessly obey. A guru is someone who's tapped in and helps others do the same." I do that via the tools and theories I construct, as well as the way I teach them. (I consider my stories and jokes both tools *and* part of the *way* I teach.) I was blessed with an ability to construct an extensive, comprehensive system—practices coupled with a cosmology— that helps people, in turn, find their own type of power. One of those systems is Another Step (which Crazy Sage wisdom is part of).

Even when I'm a goofball, I'm using my linear, logical process. In the same vein, I "channel" many of the words I write, but the ability to analyze, edit, and rewrite, as well as the ability to consciously compose one's first draft, is just as divinely bestowed. I use them all. We're all channels of the Divine, whether "channeling" as mediums or using our left-brain, if we're tuned in to the Divine and self. Creative process—whether painting, parenting, math, computer-code creation, or my creating Crazy Sage teachings—is a second-by-second integration of a great many inner aspects. This constant ongoing integration of the whole self is a major goal of Crazy Sage teachings. And again, I can only convey it by *being* it during the lessons or, rather, by doing my best to be it both during lessons and the rest of my week.

Exercise

What do *you* want to convey to a particular person or group or to the whole world? For example, perhaps you want to offer hope to a friend in crisis, or bring calm to a troubled family. Maybe you want to teach trustworthiness to an irresponsible group. For the sake of this exercise, choose just one thing you want to convey. Then ask yourself how you can *be* that hope, calm, or trustworthiness—to use the same examples—model it, so that your presence teaches it instead of you ever saying a word about it. Using this exercise over and over is very helpful.

~~~~~~

Exercise

Going through a full-time training for years doesn't make one "better" at being of service spiritually. The training I had was required to accomplish what my Gods wanted *me* to do; and it honed my specific abilities. Ask your Gods how to nurture *your* innate gifts in order to accomplish what they ask of *you*. Don't rule out being self-taught. It is a legitimate training modality. Also, not all training is formal: growing a garden can strengthen an innate ability to draw on Nature's sacredness; and volunteering at a battered women's shelter can strengthen an already strong compassion. Repeat this exercise now and then.

~~~~~~

Crazy Sage wisdom is earth-based mysticism. My mother was a gifted psychic, so the mystical, otherworldly realities were never foreign to me. They were just a part of life. I'm a mystic. I make no apologies for this; I don't justify mysticism by saying it's only a psychological construct or a metaphor for women's power. While mysticism *is* a means to psychological health and gender empowerment, it's also something unto itself. Become too crazy to gloss over your wondrous inspirations.

My lessons don't provide the safety of a rigid dogma and prescribed set of actions. Instead, I provide lessons for people who take a frightening journey: They want to walk between the stars, achieve spiritual greatness—whatever that means to the individual—and find self-realization. Be foolish enough to believe in the wondrousness of self and cosmos.

Afraid of the dark? Maybe you're not crazy enough.

And why should you go into the dark alone? Even the darkness within. Part of this book's honoring of your illuminated lunacy, in all its power, is to celebrate your unique and undefined places—nameless states, some of which may terrify you, others of which can bathe you in beauty, satisfaction, and sumptuous revelry. Let's claim them all!

Sifting Sand Through Wiggling Toes

According to De Grandis's Dictionary for the Divinely Delirious, the definition of God is: everything. God is my big toe. And your big toe. Both of them. Both of mine. And all our other toes.

God is the sun, the rain, my joy, my anger, and whatever happens to be getting under my skin on any given day. God is my hopefulness and my despair; my powerful stubbornness; petty obsessions; and totally geeky fascination with the "Buffy, the Vampire Slayer" TV series. God is me, you, every person, tree, rock, and cat. Especially every cat.

God is also a distinct being unto Herself and unto Himself. I have no trouble with the seeming contradiction of this regarding gender. The universe is so marvelously chaotic, so whimsically illogical, so deep down right that anything—anything at all—is possible. Especially a God who is everything! In the same vein, I find no problem with God being both myself yet also God in the way the word's usually used. Nor do I get around this by believing that deity to be a metaphor. That's fine—don't get me wrong—if it's your belief. I support you. However, just for me, God is a real person.

And I don't solve the paradox of God being both inside

and outside a person by thinking self as God to be metaphor. When I say, "I am God, you are God," I mean it literally. It is not my way of stating that God's power is within us, or that She speaks to us in the quiet of our peaceful heart. These things, though true as part of the endless possible shapes reality can take, are not the point right this minute. When I say, "I am God," it is meant literally. So is the statement that God's a real person all on Her own.

Great hurt is caused by the idea that God is solely and completely a separate being. Mind you, this idea *can* be held in a beneficial way. But more often it manifests by being forced down people's throats to reinforce the message that, since God is separate from us, the material world, including humans, is *not* divine, but *innately* bad, in an *eradicable* way, therefore *always* suspect. This provides a heavy dose of shame about our human state, as if we are all born to forever be creeps, instead of born as God's beloved special miraculous children. Some people change this lack of self-worth by believing that God's in *all* things. For me, that's only half the battle. I need the "crazy paradox" that God can be all things, *as well as* an individual Deity unto Him/Her self.

I refuse to live in a world any less magical and wondrous and *fun* than one which can embrace this paradox. It also makes utter sense to me, though not the sort that words can explain. But it is rich with power, succulent with love, sensible as physics, down-to-earth as a mother's fretting, compassionate as a beach's warm, fine sand sifting through a child's wiggling toes, and liberating as the sweatiest, silliest, laugh-filled sex.

God is . . . everything.

Prayer *Can* Be a Four-Letter Word

While we're on the topic of spiritual health:

People argue too much about prayer. What it is, what it should be, when it should be. What it should be for, and why you should do it. If you think about it, isn't it terribly odd that there's so much dissension over prayer?

Maybe it's because when people talk to each other, they listen for details with which to disagree, instead of for signposts of commonality on which to build camaraderie. Maybe people feel special when they believe that no one understands spirituality but them.

For a long time, I thought I had the inside track with God. Then I became very ill, and my friends took care of me. They didn't preach at me, or leave me neglected while praying for me, as if the latter were sufficient. (I do understand that, often, your circumstances do not allow you to help a person on the mundane plane. In which case, your prayer is wonderful. The situation I was referring to is when someone—perhaps without even realizing it—hides behind prayer, forgetting that it's only part of the picture.)

They cooked my meals, washed my clothes, ran all my errands. Did everything for me. For months. Without a single spiritual theory or lecture issuing from their mouths.

Prayer is anything *you* want to call it, as long as your definition doesn't rule out any others.

It is important to trust whatever definition of prayer

you find powerful. Prayer is love, laundry-washing, diaper-changing, hand-holding. Beseeching God, accusing God, praising Her, or telling Her you hate Her.

I pray to you: Never tell anyone what prayer *isn't*. But, please—this is important—tell everyone what *your* prayer *is*. Teach everyone your prayer or prayers. We need to learn all the forms, so that everything we do becomes prayer. How else will we ever survive the conditions we have come to as a species?

Butterfly Barrette
May 2010, Writing Done in Trade for Gardening Work

Last week or so, my runaway cat sprinted up an oak. I stopped my chase. I thought, "There's nothing I can do to get her in." Studied the ground, avoiding poison ivy. And there was a moth, wing span almost as wide as my hand is long.

We spent the day together, while it dried its wings, freshly emerged from cocoon, its body white with orange and black polka dots, and as fat as my index finger. Legs were thick, orange, and furry. Crazy-looking thing.

Three days later, moving a small clay pot of catnip, I almost leapt—a dusty brown toad sat quietly and huge in the pot, in forbearance of my ministration to the greenery. Weird angel.

Today, Whitney came to help in my garden. And found a robin's nest in my thigh-high lawn, beneath the wrought-iron table where I eat meals. She generously insisted that I notice how perfectly the three eggs were arranged—precise visual balance.

Good stuff! My eyes teared.

Had I mowed my lawn last fall—which I'd desperately wanted to do, but couldn't—I would have killed the moth. The cocoon's spun in fall, then overwinters in the snow.

Tall grass, still unmowed, tempted robin, who gave me joy-inducing *perfect* three-way symmetry.

Gardening done, Whitney spins a tale: A crippled monarch had one wing so maimed that all she could do was clip it off.

Whitney gave it to young Deborah, whom I imagine tended the butterfly with a gentle care most adults think impossible in children. The monarch lived 2&1/2 more weeks, then flew up, not away, but onto Deborah—perched in her hair like a barrette. Flutter, flutter. It couldn't really fly. Deborah dubbed it *Flutter*.

When I doubt God's caring, or my own, what with my clipped wing, unclipped lawn, wallet too light, wheelchair too heavy to wheel myself (I need someone to push me in it), God sends me visitors: moth, frog, robin's nest, a gardener to tend the weedy wonders I live in, God sends a tale about Flutter.

We make beauty, we make Mother Earth, we make the universe, we make compromises and compassion (and compassionate compromises), we make exclamations over visitors in high grass, we make gifts for our friends, we make efforts for them, we make do. And God sends miracles (to add to those we make ourselves).

I should have no doubts of God or self, but being human I constantly forget there is a weave that sustains us, and that I sustain.

Flutter, flutter. The most imperfect being is a chalice for the sweet wine of God's love. Bestow it. Give freely. Know the gift you are.

     —because Whitney asked I "pay" her some writing
      the next time she gardens for me. The Weave!

Chapter Eight
The Way to Stay Sane in a Crazy World
Is to Be Crazier Still

Here are ways to make a difference in the world, whether through volunteer work, political efforts, or any other contribution. This includes the "little" things we can all manage to do, like being patient with a harried waitress who's become a sourpuss.

Sometimes the only service we need do—perhaps for years on end—is to take care of ourselves, until our emotional, spiritual, and/or situational factors allow us to serve others.

Don't forget that being your best with family and friends can change the world as much as efforts in the larger community: Both are needed!

Okay, So You May Never Lecture to a Teenage Audience in China But . . .

"Suicide is the main cause of death among young adults in China," says the *Weekly Guardian*. The article reported an estimated quarter of a million suicides in China each year.

I recently wrote a book for teens. While researching for it, I learned that, according to the U.S. Center for Disease Control, the third biggest cause of death for Americans between the ages 15 and 24 is suicide.

Mind-boggling statistics. As is the lack of resources

to support young adults in trouble. I can't imagine writing anything here, in a stand-alone, brief essay, that would amount to more than the outraged "Tsk, tsk!" and sad shake of the head we too often mistake for useful action. (Note the word "we." My finger's pointed at myself, not just at others.) But I have to try:

By writing the book for teens, I was in a position to talk to them about suicide as a lousy option, and show alternatives. Nevertheless, the book is not likely to be translated into Chinese.

And a single book was hardly a sufficient antidote to a suicidal *plague*. Also, it's about tools with which to meet the various aspects of teen life. Since suicide is one of many, I had a limited number of pages with which to focus on it.

As I researched services that my book might refer troubled youth to, I met the nightmarish lack of resources you might expect. I would break down in tears trying to make a difference. And kept meeting caretakers who work with teens and are just as frustrated. Lack of funding, paperwork taking priority over teen-rescue, and politicians' disinterest leave those who are on the front lines with young adults limited as to what they can accomplish.

However, I also believe in the power of one, and know that small acts make a difference. Yes, this may seem a contradiction of the impotence delineated in the previous paragraph, but in optimistic paradox—a domain joyfully occupied by the crazy dreamer—we often find our solutions. So, it's important to try to help, despite the odds.

If your efforts save even one person's life, that's a

person's *life*. Also, there is no "they" to take care of individual community members; there is only us. If you espouse a free lifestyle, in which no one dictates to you, then, by that measure, you must also take responsibility for yourself and your community. Otherwise, your free lifestyle is the sullen, impotent rebellion of, well, adolescents—"You can't tell me what to do! Na, na, na, na, na, na," while you sulk in your apartment, rant on-line, or take your clothes off at a concert. (*Do* strip if you want. But also know that being truly free of societal shackles involves stepping up to the societal plate to fill the void.)

If you despair because your work schedule leaves you little time for community service, don't give up. Do what you can, no matter how small. I promise you, it'll make a difference. Sulk, rant, strip to the music—statements of personal freedom are our lifeblood. Nevertheless, they only get you halfway there. The other half is about reaching past your own rebellion and self-expression to help others do the same. (And if they aren't fed and clothed, they can't dance to the music.) Going to hip concerts during which the spirit soars, convincing you that anything is possible, isn't sufficient. One must return from them and do one's part; this will *keep* the heart in flight, your wild, crazy heart.

I'm not saying we each have to take on every existing cause and problem. If the Right has taught us anything, it's the power of focus. Spread yourself thin, you might accomplish nothing. (This from the queen of twenty disparate projects. However, I'm truly attempting to learn from my own words.)

So, if it's not teens, make it something else. And, if all you can do is send an environmental group fifteen bucks, don't refrain out of doubt.

A lot of people's combined efforts, including small, wee ones, can kick ass. As long as after we "Tsk, tsk. What an outrage!" we act.

Afterthoughts: Some people sit in rebellious apathy because it falsely promises what community service actually delivers—freedom. Helping others sets your heart soaring. This benefit may seem unlikely. You have to serve to find its merit.

Maybe this suggestion about service seems irrelevant, because you already help others a lot, and it drains you. You might be right, but you may be serving with the wrong attitude. Service is a state of mind. Service means thinking about what the other person (or people) in the room needs, instead of a focus on yourself. Examples of *not* service:

◊ helping someone with a secret agenda of getting something in return
◊ being so worried about your performance when you aid someone that you're in an emotional knot
◊ lending a hand when you know your attention belongs elsewhere, perhaps on self-care
◊ helping someone out of a sense of worthlessness or because you're afraid you'll otherwise lose their love
◊ giving so much that your health fails
◊ assisting someone while obsessed about what it will cost you in time, money, or energy

Mind you, a *healthy* sense of self while helping someone is, of course, fine. For example, one only has just so much energy to give, so checking in after an hour (or after two minutes!) to see if one is too tired to continue is a good idea.

As I said, service is an attitude, a state of mind. And I find it to be an *impossible* spiritual discipline. I forget to apply it constantly. But it comes down to asking myself, "What do others present need?" Anything can be done in the attitude of service. We can be of service to our community, family, and friends.

One of the most neglected steps of the modern emotional-healing process is service. I have seen people spend years in unnecessary pain, unable to go the last nine yards healing their soul wounds, because no one ever told them that certain final stages cannot heal without the balm of a service attitude. Some blessings only flow to us if they are flowing *through* us to another being, and their channel is a service attitude.

It can be learned, bit by bit. Part of doing so is to try on an attitude of service. Over and over, as a spiritual discipline, an exercise, until we get "service muscle."

Be a Crazy Sage: don't pontificate about healthy insanity; apply it to real life issues. Don't talk about your insane worldview. Live it! (If this book includes visions and wild hopes that aren't *about* healthy insanity, they may be *embodying* it.) You'll know your beauty, be free, and fulfill your daring fantasies.

How to Save the World

I've spent my life alternately trying to be, on the one hand: ethical, useful, cool, fulfilled, desirable, authentic, healthy, spiritual, sexy, educated and, on the other hand: numb. (Lots of time focused on numb.)

Despite how much numb that adds up to, I want *more* lately! I work my butt off trying to write material to change the world, save someone's life, or otherwise "make a difference." Most of my 9-5 is equally challenging. For example, I counsel trauma survivors and deal with many other tremendously hard-core "real life" issues. Don't get me wrong; I know I'm blessed, and love *every* part of my work. To do what I feel I was put on this planet to do is fulfilling and a true privilege. But I need low-stress pastimes, to balance my day.

So I read a lot of fantasy, murder mysteries, and romance novels. Light-lit* keeps me sane. And I've needed even *more* of an escape lately. There's heavy stuff going on in my personal life. I'm also waiting to see if a no-holds-barred book of mine will get picked up by a publisher. Spent ages on the project, and am getting nothing but rejections. It's hard to keep going on it.† There are also an exceptional number of other blocks to my community work. I'm taking measures to overcome the various current challenges, but they're uber-painful; since my efforts aren't resolving anything (*yet*), I at least need to run away from the pain for a while each day.

---

* I don't consider *all* fantasy, murder mysteries, and romance novels light or trash. I think some of the deepest, most thought provoking material *available* happens in pop culture. So just bear with the *gist* of this tale.
† You hold the book in your hands.

So to achieve the aforementioned *more* of an escape, I've started *writing* escapist stuff, instead of just reading it. Recently, in addition to my "real" writing, I've been composing a "trash" novel and have finished the first 100 pages, plus lotsa notes. Staying up til 4 a.m., scaring myself silly penning its horror scenes or otherwise numbing myself with the story, has been the perfect distraction.

I get to spend time every day living in an entirely other world, as I construct an alternative universe in my doesn't-need-to-be-deep novel.

Here's to escapism—without it, I'd go around the bend. Then, I'd never get to save the world. What do *you* need to take care of *yourself*? Whatever it is, do it. It is necessary if you're to be fit 'n' happy enough to do a good job of caring for others.

Afterthoughts: The novel's done. I kept at it while I was waiting for yet another publisher's rejection of *Share My Insanity*, or was otherwise held up on it. Writing it was truly an escape, but it wasn't relaxing, except for the first few hours. It was an immense amount of work, stress, focus, and other non-numb stuff. I'm not complaining; I loved writing it. But remember that I am so exhausted all the time that I have medical problems, and that I'm not good at taking it easy. The novel was yet another way I kept myself from resting, and became yet another project from which I needed to escape!

No matter what I am attempting, I fail every 10 seconds. Luckily, my Gods ask only that I try my best. My best efforts result in falling on my face every 10 seconds.

People are giving my fantasy novel a classier name—*speculative fiction*—and saying it has an important message and is on the cutting edge of literary style. (So much for pulp fiction being shallow.) I am telling you that to brag. But mostly I'm saying it because their appraisal affirmed there's something wrong with me; I'm so bad at giving myself the rest I need that, even when I try to be shallow, I'm deep! Deep is not always good: My idea of taking a break was to exhaust myself writing a novel, subconsciously breaking new ground! Time and again, I see "deep" defeat people when they need lighthearted fun, lackadaisical relaxation, or simple hope.

People's response also had me worriedly asking myself, "Is my mega-weirdness so innate that it comes through in *everything* I do, without my knowing it? Is my eccentricity what's being called innovative?" I don't know; I *do* know that, no matter how hard I try, I've never been able to pass for "normal" for more than five minutes.

Self-Help Loop
Written when the media was covering the first week of hurricane Katrina's devastation of New Orleans

September 1, 2005. What a day. My first one back at work after a vacation. At 5:30 p.m., my best bud and I made frustrated noises together. She growled loudly, while I mumbled and made Jim Carrey faces, since my physical disabilities allow facial expressions but not volume.

The President is still lying (hardly newsworthy), people are dying in the streets—never less than a tragic horror—and, typical of many people when they return to work, I'm swamped by an abundance of idiotic business procedures. However, my problems pale by comparison.

Nevertheless, they seem tied in to world events at a deep level that I hope I can figure out, because there seems an epiphany involved:

Ah, I get it: The world's crazy.

That gave me great satisfaction to write. It also made me laugh. But it's hardly a sufficient analysis, there must be a deeper relationship between my day and the world news, I must be sensing more than "The entire world is nuts."

No, actually, that's a deep link. Since September 11, I can't tell you the number of clients, students, and friends who have told me that their lives have gone to hell. And they're all trying to figure out what they did to cause it.

However, once I explain that it's not *them*, it's that the world's crazy right now and, therefore, of course their lives are rough, the relief and empowerment I see is huge. This has happened so many times—with so many people—that I think I should relay the same message here for readers who feel the way all these other folks do. So, let me tell you the rest of what I say to them:

In a country where a great many of our government officials are acting insane, everyone's lives become odd, exhausting, and stupid.* But people don't see that connection. For one thing, Americans tend to view themselves as self-made, rather than as part of a society that shapes their inner and outer lives. I'm not suggesting that environment is all—we each need to take responsibility for our lives. But that can go

---

* Reminder: I'm a spiritual counselor *renegade* style.

too far. A crazy government, a selfish government, affects things, c'mon!*

For example, a lot of my clients, students, and friends are traumatized—I use that word literally—by the financial stresses that are more common now. Many are equally devastated by the betrayal of what they believe in as Americans. This trauma also serves as another illustration; it's yet one more reason folks wrongly think themselves the root of their problems right now. Amidst their mental dizziness and emotional distress, they lack the clarity to discern exactly whom they should point a finger at. (Let me repeat: there *are* times when you have to face up to your own undoing. I'm not referring to them.)

There's also another reason folks blame themselves too much lately. Each person's problems play out with such unique details that it's hard for that person to recognize his or her dilemmas as part of the aforementioned larger societal picture. For example, when you're pushed to the wall, your less desirable traits might emerge. They're different for everyone. In that difference, it's easy to blame your reaction rather than the wall. In the same vein, the trickle-down of insanity might cause different walls for you than for me. More reason to not see the commonality.

---

* One might argue that the government's a bit better since I wrote this, but the corporate world is far worse. And its equally intense greed has equal impact on the collective psyche and people's lives. On the other hand, there was a five-year span between writing this piece and adding this little note. If it takes as long to get this book into print, the government and business sector may be something else altogether. We can hope and work toward that!

All this is not theory on my part. As I said, I've watched anguished person after person beat themselves up. As I did to myself today (forgetting everything I'd told upset members of my community, until I had my epiphany—again). For the past few years, what with the U.S.'s current political, societal, and economic dilemmas, every step forward of the work I try to accomplish is so frustrating that my teeth hurt. And this work not only pays my bills—kind of—but is also focused on community service. So I'm complaining about how hard it is to keep a roof over my head *and* about how hard it is to help others live happy lives.

Therefore, I'm going to do what I've kept suggesting to everyone who's felt ravaged by our national situation. I hope you try it also. Tomorrow, when I hit the zillionth road block, and the day after when I'm trying to figure out where I'm going to get the money for the gas bill or the phone bill or the . . . [insert frustrated scream], I'll pause for a moment. In that pause, I will not try to calm myself. Nor will I ask what I can do to be more proactive about earning money. I'll ask that later. Right then, though, I'll pull my anger and frustration close to me, like a little kitten. I'll pet it. I'll celebrate it. I'll announce, "I'm insane! Anything else would be an indication that I'm on drugs."

In other words, I will affirm my madness as fabulous. The result will be that I won't waste my time in a self-help loop, the endless cycle of self-recrimination that I've come to see is so useless in those I counsel. I can instead use my energy— and healthy madness—to change the national picture. I'm not disavowing self-help. What you're holding is a self-help book, however odd a transmutation thereof. But, like anything, self-help can be a trap.

Now, go let yourself feel frustrated. Then, go change the world.

Anti- Self-Help Loop Affirmation

"I will not try to forcibly calm myself. I breathe into my upset, letting it gently flow, without rage. I breathe into my upset, letting it be. My anger and frustration breathe. My anger and frustration relax in my belly, and just be. My anger and frustration become a *kind* of calm, without my trying to make it so. It is a gentle unforced calm. It is easy. I do not steel myself. I do not explode in destructive behavior, hurting myself or others. Nor do I clench myself into shameful knots. I breathe into my upset, letting it gently flow, I breathe into my upset, letting it be. My anger and frustration breathe. My anger and frustration relax in my belly, and just be. My anger and frustration become a *kind* of calm, without my trying to make it so."

If, while you are trying to change the world, and still find yourself blaming yourself when you didn't cause your problems, if this launches you into an endless cycle of self-recrimination that leaves you without the power and energy to address the actual source of your difficulties, pause for a moment. Then say the affirmation once or repeatedly. It might help you focus your energy to change the political climate, social norm, or personal situation that *is* causing the problem.

Why This Anarchist Votes

To explain why this anarchist votes, I'll give four reasons I voted in the last presidential election:

Reason 1) I'll admit that just about the only difference between a Republican and a Democrat is that the latter dresses better. However, my insightful cynicism stops dead in its tracks when I realize another difference: A Democrat in power would help prevent endless numbers of women dying from illegal butcher-job abortions. My anarchist ideology is something to be ashamed of, if I allow a single person to needlessly die just for my rhetoric.

Life before legal abortion was ugly. Finally changing the law banning abortion took an incredibly difficult struggle. Once that hard-won headway is lost, it will take a long time to regain. During that time, many will die.

Reason 2) I'm *really* an anarchist. So I don't let ideology (even anarchist ideology!) limit me. Instead, I embrace the power of chaos, which entails using any legal, moral tool that'll get a job done. Voting is such a tool. To let the endless war continue in the name of anarchy makes a parody of anarchy. I want to *live* my rhetoric, not just spout it.

Remember earlier, my saying chaos is moral, chaos is God's hard-to-understand but beneficent plan? So a *real* anarchist would end up middle management for the Chaos Gods!

Reason 3) I want the power to make a difference. I won't fall into the trap of thinking, "Since all politicians suck (the government structure sucks, America sucks, the Electoral College idea sucks . . .), I'll take a stand by not voting." That won't actually give me power. That's rejecting a power I actually *do* have. It's kind of like being four years old and getting so angry and infantile that you pack up your marbles and go home. If I don't stay in the game, I can't win. Then Mother Earth dies. Voilá: no home.

Our anger needn't immobilize us. Healthy, but misapplied, anger can keep people from creating social change. The above is an example: Some Americans, upset by political corruption, feel that not voting is a way to take a stand, a way to say something. As a result, they forsake what power they *do* have. Unscrupulous politicians are then more likely to win elections and make damaging decisions.

Reason 4) I figured, "Sure, Bush will probably declare some sort of emergency that will necessitate him seated at the oval office desk until his 24-year-old nephew Jeb Bush, Jr. is old enough for the job. Can you say MONARCHY?" However, acting against all odds is the only way any *real* change has ever happened. Believing in the impossible is a prerequisite for ground-breaking revitalization of a society.

I also felt that I couldn't risk another president as bad as him just because the odds were good that they'd once again disregard the voters' choice. We can't afford to ignore the long shots available. They may be all we *have.*

And I'll use *any* legal, ethical recourse we have—

because doing so is the difference between people who just whine and people who save lives.

I cling, for all I am worth, to my idealism, individuality, and personal freedom. But they often wrongly motivate a person to remain inactive, when these traits could help someone effectively address community issues. The solution is madly, foolishly keeping my heart open despite the endless wrongdoing I see in the world. Being a crazy, open-hearted dreamer. Use your admirable ideals to motivate action instead of stifling it—that's a *real* anarchist.

Moving on to the next piece: What if you *do* decide to be crazy and step up to the plate?

Be Yourself?

"Be yourself," we're told. However, that advice is almost inevitably served up with a side of guidelines mandating exactly who you should be, as if there is only one specific way a unique and fully expressed individual thinks and acts. A conservative, for example, might insist that being yourself always means a "Me first, yahoo! I'm a cowboy!" selfishness in business. While a radical, like many a teenager, may get caught in the dogma of the alternative community. (For example, "We're all individuals. Leadership shows oppressive hierarchy. So I dare not take initiative and point out the exits, even when the building we're in is burning down.")

The building is burning.

Be yourself. That's a terrifying proposition if you are, in fact, going to be your own role model. What if you point out the exit, and you're so nervous you point the wrong way? What if your mother sees you stepping up to the plate and tells you to behave? Or they—the big "they"—come for you in the night because now they have to set another fire and don't want you to interfere a second time? What if you're embarrassed in front of everyone—really, really everyone— because you misspeak, and now everyone—really everyone— thinks you're a big, stupid, neurotic, uninformed, misled, useless, paranoid nothing? What if exits are irrelevant to you, so now you have to figure out what else to do in the fire? There's no denying the importance of marching to your own drummer (or saxophonist, if you prefer), if you want to serve the community or your family.

How do we overcome the fears that accompany truly being oneself?

For one thing, practice rebelling against the rebel's dogma. Imagine yourself saying unhip things. For example: "The exit is over there." Or, to use an example of what people go through in a more personal arena, "There is *too* a vaginal orgasm. Sure, it was given an absurd, sexist priority that denied many women sexual satisfaction. But that doesn't mean the solution is to now block yet *other* women's orgasms by brain-washing them into denying what *their* own bodies tell them. Hell, there are *big-toe* orgasms."

There's an exit, look, I see it right over there. Where in your unique body is your unique orgasm? Personal pleasure and the power to make a difference in the world—long a necessary pairing. And, please, if you know different exits than the ones I see, tell me! If you think we need to stay in the fire, tell me why! I need the info.

Let yourself happen. Let yourself be.

P.S. I do not mean to imply that self-expression eventually means you try to become a leader. That would be yet another dictate disguised in the name of individuality. For example, some people's uniqueness is expressed by silence. Social change needs everyone's own, special contribution.

"You Don't Matter"

Living in a rural area, I put my missives in a mailbox across the road, where the mail carrier can more easily pick them up. This morning, I put on my boots, grabbed the letters I needed to send, and went out into the foot of snow that had fallen the last day or so. When I reached the end of my driveway, its end was blocked by a huge, high pile of snow, packed hard.

When snowplows go by, they shove all the snow on the road to the side, along everyone's property. Not a problem if you're able-bodied or have the money to hire someone to do your work *for* you. But now, a snowfall I could have managed without further ado became a problem—no one could get to my house over that hump of hard-packed snow.

I asked myself why anyone would create snowplows like this when, with the enormous inventiveness humans have, there was probably a way around it. I heard, clear as a bell in my mind, the proverbial "It's a good solution that will inconvenience only a handful of people."

Variations of that line are constantly used by government, big business, and others who shirk their responsibility as members of a large community—as opposed to only a member of their country club. But a lot of us know: It's *not* only a handful—it's the poor, the elderly, the handicapped. All these inconveniences aren't usually little, especially when they're added up.

Some people reading this will, hopefully, be cheering me on, relieved that someone's saying this, and others might think I'm whining. My thoughts in this piece, according to the dictates of our society, would be more believable and dignified if I, myself, wasn't impacted by the issues raised here. Great!—if you're treated badly, you're supposed to wait until someone else will fight for you. Talk about losing human dignity, talk about a norm designed to keep you from getting your needs met. Talk about revictimizing the victim, insisting that your only solution is to be rescued, you poor dear you, so sad. But isn't it great that someone is helping poor pitiful useless you?

Hah, good thing I'm too crazy to honor those norms!

In any case, it's not the snow. If it was an isolated event, that would be one thing. It is the constant dismissal of your needs, as if your lives don't matter. It is, as I said, the *accumulative* effect of one's needs being ignored, making one's life extraordinarily, unnecessarily, difficult over and over.

So, next time you hear some version of, "Only a handful of people will be inconvenienced," recognize the real message: "They don't matter." Then write or call the politician, businessman, or whoever else said it. Tell them, "It's not an inconvenience, it's a real problem, and we're *not* a minority." Then, pull your funding out from under their ass—make sure you let them know why.

Stop the powers-that-be from using blithe rhetoric to cover up their misdeeds.

If you speak passionately about injustice, you're considered crazy. So call *yourself* crazy. Then you can address issues that may otherwise be ignored.

Let's go from à la Crazy Sage wisdom about human needs and the powers-that-be, to another pairing—world peace and advertising.

How Do We Market Peace?

You have to be a little crazy to be a healer in this culture. Ditto someone who brings *any* kind of healthy change.

I mean, how do we market peace? Why, every time I want to save someone's life, do I have to come up with a marketing plan? I have to *sell* happiness—you'd think people would just *want* it—not just when I pitch a book idea to a publisher. The classes and counseling I give cause nothing short of miracles in people's lives. But damned if I don't have to practically run alongside people's cars waving my arms, yelling, "Help! Someone! Someone! Help! Someone, let me *help* you!"

Then, because I tell people about my amazing ability to create happiness, I'm accused of commercialism—in it "for the money." Lawdy, lawdy, lawdy, if I was in it for the money, I wouldn't be in it. There's no money! I can't afford health insurance. I do this work because I'm crazy!

Sometimes, I think about becoming a copywriter,

making fabulous bucks creating advertising slogans. "Raid kills bugs dead."* People's opinion of me would not sink.

Sometimes, I want to lose all my cool—okay, I have none, I don't have one mellow or hip cell in my body, but bear with me—and say to people, "Why are you such an idiot? You keep saying you're struggling with things that you know I can help you with. So *call me!*"

Maybe, I'll try it. Without the "You're such an idiot!" part.

Hip. Cool. I wasted years of my life trying to be cool. I caused immeasurable damage to myself and others. My left shoulder's permanently hitched upward because of my attempts, from ages 14 to 31, to carelessly hunch while sucking on a cigarette. Now, though, all you have to do to be hip is wear the right jeans, make-up, and hair styling products.

Hip used to have something to do with a lifestyle. When hippies wore blue jeans, it meant something. Or at least so we hippies thought. Then blue jeans became a fashion statement.

There are incredibly fine minds in advertising, people using their amazing talents to bastardize innovative political and social movements into "If you want to be *free* and *express* yourself, buy this dress that everyone else will also wear!" I wish these people, with all their mental prowess, could get paid to market peace. Otherwise, that just leaves us crazies trying to change the world.

---

* Lou Welch was a major American poet of extraordinary talent. But his best known legacy consists not of his poems but of four words—"Raid kills bugs dead"—written when he was in advertising. Sigh.

Chapter Nine
Whipped Cream Brain–Miscellaneous, Meaningful, Mental Meanderings

This final chapter applies useful insanity to topics not addressed in other chapters, and further develops earlier material.

Creating Peace Instead of War by Creating a New Culture

No means, just being.

You can be an agent of change by living within a culture that you believe in. You live it (note the shift from *living in it* to *living it*), even if it is just in your living room, office, grocery store, gym. No means, just being. I know this principle works: When I did it in my living room, the result was something I mentioned earlier—hundreds of people came to my home to sit with me; unbeknownst to me, the material I created and conveyed there went national before I ever published a book. (But hundreds needn't encounter you personally for you to create mega-shifts through the way you live.)

Part of *my* inner and innate culture is that one lives in service. Maybe better wording would be "in a state of service." Service is not a moment, it's an inherent state. I enter the non-living-room professional realm with my focus on service.* Initially, I was—and still am sometimes—stunned by how often other players try to block me because they're jockeying for power. (It's been a real shock to me.) In some ways, they are in a culture of war: A paradigm of war is the need to have "the power," though "the power" is an absurd idea if applied certain ways.

I mean, yes, power is a good thing, and I like power but . . . well, there are many obvious ways a quest for power can go wrong, so I won't explore that here. We have a lot of ground to cover in this subchapter, so I need to ignore anything I can.

What I am discussing here is creating peace through a *cultural* shift from power emphasis to service emphasis. Something experience has taught me about this shift: The better I live within my service-oriented culture, the more it's opposed. In other words, the stronger an agent of healing I become, the nastier and more dangerous to me is the opposition. But I don't want to live in their culture by fighting on their grounds; if I fight for "the power," I can't win. Even if I "win the power," I have lost: I've bowed to their culture, been subsumed by it, which obliterates my freedom to live as I choose, do the work I want.

An *over*-emphasis on power is so structured into our DNA (I am committed to shifting human DNA) and into our social structures, that even thoughtful, honorable, alternative groups often buy into war culture by fighting for "the power."

---

* On a *good* day! Heaven help me, I fail a lot, despite my efforts. Sometimes I can maintain the state by and large for an hour or more, sometimes only ten seconds, and sometimes I forget completely.

There are various ways this happens, but let's look at one: the *structure* of their organizations.

An organizational structure for one's business or non-profit is not a bad thing.* However, most alternative groups unwittingly fall into "the power" paradigm because of the *way* they structure their organization. The group may still do a lot of good, but that doesn't mean there isn't a better way, a way that creates a cultural shift in and of itself, and that also makes them more effective.

Through a focus on service, I have managed to have a business that is both extraordinarily effective and streamlined. Mind you, I do honor important structures (e.g., teaching methodologies, monthly e-newsletters, guidelines for staff, etc.). I even have some *rigid* structures.†

But I didn't stall classes until I could afford to rent a space for classes or until my living room looked good 'nuf. In fact, I started teaching in my shabby studio apartment on the edge of S.F.'s Tenderloin. I didn't wait til I had funding or prestige. Waiting until you have these things creates a culture in which service is only a moment. Service can be a given, even if service is simply getting a good night's sleep so you're in decent shape *to* serve. No means, just being.

But org after org will start out by spending two years to raise the money to buy a building, then they will delay

---

* To use *The Art of War* as a reference point (if you're a fan of Taoism), organizational structure is the direct (or "common," depending on your translation) action suggested in *The Art of War*, chapter five. (I'm applying the principle not for war, but as strategy for its opposite—left-brain analysis used to create a way of life that *opposes* war.)
† All these structures are the "direct/common" part of *The Art of War*.

operations until they paint their building, then network to position themselves, then . . . (the following is a kingpin of what I am hoping to convey) all of this done to *acquire the power to serve*. The shift is subtle but has a huge impact. *They are in the power shuffle!* They are playing by the rules of war.

Sure, preparation is important, and often must be lengthy, but enough is enough. For one thing, their structure might become unnecessarily complex, towering precariously, until the organization as an entity could easily be destroyed. Then vigilance is required to protect the organization instead of time being spent serving community (AKA an *over*-emphasis on structure and power to keep the structure/org going). *All* means, *no* being.

Do I think that working to get power to be better able to serve is entirely wrong? Of course not. Instead, I'm talking about an *overemphasis* on it creating a self-defeating culture. Throughout this essay, I over-generalize, am one-sided, make black and white statements, and simplify.* But to get back to an org becoming too complex: I have found that business structures that best support service are bendable, elusive, and often use invisible instead of written policies. They are minimalistic in the sense of simple if possible, complex or large only if needed.

Such modalities do the following:

1) They allow me to move swiftly = I can be of service

---

* The book as a whole tackles complexities and fine gradations that I ignore in this subchapter. Again, my writing may not deal with these things intellectually, because I try to experientially immerse you in the *culture* of what I address in this essay (and in the culture of other things that I hope to convey).

to someone who has time-sensitive needs instead of finding myself stuck in a committee meeting, getting delayed for months. (I don't know who it is that said that governments and businesses work slowly, but people can act swiftly.) No means, just being.

2) I don't have a kingdom to defend. Yay! When opposed, I can move into a new moment. No means, just being.

3) Service-oriented structures allow me to see the overall gestalt of a moment. Amidst the seemingly random chaos of a situation, I can see its beauty and goodness, I can see it as a Divine plan, I can analyze it, use it, move adroitly within it, as part of it. Hence, a structure that focuses on service actually tunes me into *tremendous* power.

4) I can see the various patterns, note which is/are best to ride (Taoism again*), am free to then ride it/them, am well *positioned* to ride it/them, can see how all the patterns of the moment weave as a larger pattern that I am part of, and how to ride it all, as part of it. It repeatedly becomes ecstatic. A service focus has been a way to be a truly integrative *being* as opposed to just talking about it.

This essay delineates how I've run my business all these years, so I've seen its effectiveness as a business model. I believe it's an effective model for a better culture. I started playing music in clubs when I was 14 years old, instinctively using this self-made model, producing my own shows. Without this approach, I wouldn't have had the resources to function as the producer of my shows at such an early age, particularly

---

* It is a Taoist principle to ride the currents.

since my folks had no money and were unable to even come to auditions with me.

Unfortunately, no one taught me this model, and I've almost never been able to teach people how to use it. Perhaps, it only works for a few people with a specific temperament, and they do it automatically. What success I *have* had conveying it has not been by just explaining it, the way I've tried to do in this essay, but by conveying it experientially and through a process that evolves the students' being (note we're at the word *being* again) until they don't feel the *need* to over-prepare, etc. Or at least they become able to resist that need a good deal of the time. Shifting human DNA!* In fact, I've never felt merit in spelling it all out to anyone the way I have above. This is an exception and experiment; as such, I don't know if it worked, don't know if it does convey my thoughts, don't know if it's useful in the sense of actually helping anyone change their being. This essay is an oversimplification in part because it's neither experiential nor contextual.†

Another element needed to convey all this usefully is a process that is both right-brain and left-brain. For example, as someone who taught ballet, I actually believe in vigorous preparation. In that spirit, I think people have to work long

---

* Maybe part of that shift is happening experientially for you by reading this book, the total of its parts perhaps shifting you as a *whole* person, which in turn shifts all your parts.

† But I'm giving it a shot. I could, BTW, easily develop this piece into 200 pages. But then you'd have 200 pages instead of a new culture. Also, there are some topics about which words inherently fib, especially if you use too *many* words. So enough is enough.

Though I tend to avoid (and condemn) theory in my writing, I have spent decades vigorously developing the theories that underpin the methodologies I have created. Yay!

and hard to make the inner shifts needed to live a new culture. In addition, to help people make these inner changes, I spent years creating very defined methodologies, which I structured into a coherent comprehensive system. And I tell students to not adapt this training.

However, it's beyond just right/left-brain. It's about integrative *being*. (When people use the term "integrative *vision*," they're contradicting the very thing they're trying to promulgate. However, the concept of integrative vision is a commendable, brave, worthwhile effort that should be supported.) The training I give can only be conveyed with my students and I living the new culture together (as happened, and still happens, in my living room. But now I sit there, having moved to an isolated area, being with students through group *phone* calls; that's how we do classes despite their or my locale.).

Perhaps, if nothing else, this essay will compel you to join me in my culture some time, in ways other than this book. At book's end is a resource guide with info about my classes.

No means, just being = Don't wait to serve. Instead, serve with what inner and outer resources you already have, no matter how small, unkempt, or humbling.*

The Modern Renaissance Person, Take Two

Let's look at the modern Renaissance person from an entirely different angle than the first essay about the issue, continuing the theme of being everything you can.

---

* The essay's a drop in the bucket when it comes to explaining most of its points, but I felt compelled to include what I could.

Becoming a Renaissance person—someone who has a
wide range of highly-developed, disparate skills—is difficult
nowadays. However, it's possible. All you have to do is be
poor.

In today's world, there aren't a lot of other options. But
poverty's *not* the only way. For example, you might acquire
enough wealth that you're free to spend the rest of your life
cultivating skill sets (for example, taking painting classes or
studying carpentry). But, more likely, once you had the money,
you'd spend your entire existence pursuing more of it, or
ensuring its flow. Or shopping. (C'mon, can you really say for
sure it wouldn't be like that? Or, at least that shopping, dress-
up, and luxury vacations wouldn't eat up enough time that you
hadn't sufficient left to master a handful of different talents?)

Besides, there's not that much difference between
poor folk and the rich. We both eat strange foods—albeit for
different reasons. We're both obsessed with money (um, also
for different reasons), and . . . forget it. Being poor is not like
being rich.

But it is a way to do what you want. If you decide
you're willing to live your life on the edge, you can spend
the majority of your time developing a multifaceted self.
Funny thing is, the universe will support you. Next thing that
happens, someone offers you a free trip to Europe—I mean
for *free*, no hanky-panky expected in payment. And a trip like
that stirs the creative juices tremendously. Or you'll "happen"
to stumble across a retired scientist whose specialty is the field
you want to explore, and who's eager to teach you, what with
all his free time.

I know this sort of cooperation from the universe might not be believable. I hope you'll try to take my word.

And remember: Throughout history, artists and scientists who commit to their work have had sponsors and mentors. There are many ways to commit to art, but the one relevant here is the mad drive to put one's work before money, prestige, or even survival. This wonderfully insane commitment has won many a creative person benefactors.

There's another reason being broke all the time helps you polish a lot of different skills—you can't afford to hire someone else to do things for you. Want a nice garden, it's up to you. Heck, want the kitchen drain to ever be usable again, you'd better get on it. Whether your sewing skills end up ranging from mending clothes to constructing innovative ones, or your carpentry eventually moves well past stabilizing an old shelf by hammering nails into it, expertise will abound.

The next time you wish you had the time to be innovative, consider a lifestyle change. Or, if you don't want that but are envious of a creative friend, remember they might pay dearly. It's a trade-off for most people. If you keep that in mind—this also holds true for the starving artist green with envy over a pal's posh home—it can be easier to honor your own choice.

Afterthoughts: Okay, I jokingly posited poverty as an actual technique—one of few nowadays—through which you can fully develop yourself. But it is not jest alone. Individuality involves risks and might even leave you poor. But the universe will support you; all in all you'll manage financially while you also get to express yourself 100%. This is not cheap talk on my part. I didn't come from money and never had money. And poor finances have caused immense, dangerous, and emotionally battering challenges since my health failed in 2001. But I don't regret the risks I've taken. I am grateful that I was given the inner resolve to take them. I have seen so much loss of self in some of my friends, the inner spark eroding bit by bit, from actions ostensibly based in survival, until the light was snuffed and, then, what is the point of surviving at all?

Utter Indulgence Is Important if You Want a Healthy Body and Happy Spirit

Pleasure is a vital component of the spiritual life and one's healing process. The mystic's deep, ecstatic union with all of nature—and the cosmos!—is an underlying premise of this book's *wholly* holistic theme. Such moments of connection to *everything* in existence are an ideal that few people can attain, but one can develop *some* ability to enter into "one-with-all" mystical states, any degree of which—even the most minimal—is healing to body and empowering. And it can be joyfully fulfilling.

Though I've not discussed it as such, reading this book's pages and using their suggestions constitute steps along an ecstatic path. Here are a few reasons:

◊ Crazy Sage wisdom helps more parts of your inner being come forward. Thus more of you engages in your experience of what's around you.

◊ The book nurtures your ability to connect with more and more "dots." *That* is one of the very unions the ecstatic mystic strives toward.

There's more to ecstatic spirituality than one book can cover. But the trickster element reveals and develops parts that are hard to otherwise even touch on.

This essay is a cursory look at ecstatic practices. Buddha wouldn't discuss theory or cosmology with students; he felt there wasn't time to do that *and walk* one's path. I *almost* agree. I *do* like head stuff, so I indulge in it. (Note essay's title!) My mind is part of the holistic whole, every second of the day. But I don't let it take over in typical modern ways that take time or other necessary focus from actually walking my talk or doing my spiritual practices. The book as a whole *well* represents the ecstatic path, not by theory but by embodiment and relevant suggestions.

Although this subchapter is not discussing *only* the pleasure of *material* fulfillment, it's definitely included. So it's important to address how difficult it is for some people to pair material pleasure with spirituality. Perhaps they were taught that "good" people ignore their own needs, and only think of others, as if giving freely meant always denying the self. Blech! Sometimes, yes, it is right to put others' needs before our own. But not all the time!

Or perhaps someone was taught they were "bad" to want abundance. The Divine loves us and, like all good parents, wants us to enjoy our lives.

Or maybe someone's church shamed them about sex, insisting that it's evil. Sex is holy; it is part of being human; it is a gift from God; it is a way to express love; it is a way to express joy. I hang out with and pray to sexy Gods!

Utter indulgence is only wrong when it harms you or someone else. Example: I don't eat sugar. It makes me so ill I'd end up at the hospital. Eating sugar is not indulgent for me; it would be self-abuse. But I could use the sacredness of self-indulgence as an excuse to not take care of myself. Or to hurt someone else through neglect or selfishness.

However, the rest of the time, utter indulgence honors the magnificent gift of life that the Divine has given us. So enjoy yourself, say "Thank you" to God (by the way, doing so helps you experience more pleasure in what you do. Words can't explain why, so try it and see how it goes for *you*), and know that maximum permission to enjoy the world around you is good for you and oh-so-spiritual.

Everyone Should Take at Least One Cross-Country Road Trip

I decided that, instead of flying to my new home in Pennsylvania, we should drive. Medically speaking, I wasn't up to *either* option, but an airplane might have been "saner." Quicker, less physical wear and tear.

So let me explain why I chose what I did.

As I said to Thom and Brian, when trying to talk them into doing the trip with me, everyone should take at least one cross-country road trip (they'd never done one). And, though I'd already made about four, I wanted one last on-the-road, stupid-thing-to-do adventure. With what was going on physically, I knew I might only live a few more years. It *could* turn out to be another fifty. But it could *not*. (Later note:

Dear reader, it's been quite a while since I wrote this road-trip story. Not to worry. Things have changed. I have another ten, twenty, thirty years. But at the time I wrote this, odds were toward me surviving only a few years.) I couldn't let that stop me. I'm not trying to sound all heroic, I'm just talking about my life, and saying what happened in it, you know?

Cross-country road trips are insane. For one thing, you end up so exhausted that, as a friend said years ago, only the very young should attempt it. But that insanity is part of what appealed to me—the freedom of moving past my body's limits and saying, "What the hell!" We had a great time.

It was mostly driving and stopping to sleep at night. Sight-seeing wasn't an option if I had any chance of surviving the expedition. We had to keep the trip as short as possible. Just drive, eat, sleep. For seven days. Thom drove my stuff in a truck, Brian drove me in a car. We rented the widest one we could find so I could lie down in the back seat. There was no way I could sit up the whole trip. I mean, understand, most folks with what I'd gone through never get out of bed. So most of what I do when up and about is a cross between an intricately-planned, mega-detailed, military operation and a maneuver the delicacy of which is on par with surgery.

Though we didn't stop except to eat and rest, I had a blast. I found the sense of freedom I wanted. And I was "on the road again," to quote the song, knowing that if I were dying I would nevertheless live 'til the last as a vagabond mystic.

My whole life I've heard, "You can't." Nevertheless, my whole life I *have*. Often, the naysaying speaker was truly being sensible. Thank Goddess, I'm not.

Piss Artist

My British friend, Chloe, listening one day to my complaints about a colleague, responded with "He's a real piss artist, eh?"

I discovered, once I asked her to explain, that *piss artist* is used in England to denote a person who's a flake. Chloe said that the term also might be used as synonymous with *drunkard*, but not usually.

Never, ever, ever say anything like all this to a writer. He will have a field day playing word games. For example, a piss artist is not, Chloe confirmed, a bullshit artist (a wordsmith who uses language creatively for purposes of deception).

This leads me to the question: Why is urine the artistic medium with which to express flakiness, and bovine feces the artist's choice for bold lies? And if *piss artist*, in a specific instance, refers to an alcoholic, wouldn't it likely, at such a time, be synonymous with *bullshit artist*? I mean, if you've ever asked a drunk why he hasn't made it to work a single day this month, you know that his response is where the two artistries collide. (You also know that, once your alcoholic has used their excuses with you enough times, they're "pissing in the wind"—an expression meaning to speak to no purpose; making useless statements.)

What has this literary exercise done for me? A lot, actually. It was three in the afternoon, and I'd spent the day on the insanity-producing, trivial tasks that must be done in order to accomplish things that actually count. Amidst that insanity, I forgot to be happy, forgot that life is good. Sitting in my sunny backyard, calligraphing* these words—you'll see them typed, but it slows my mind and breathing down when I calligraph— and enjoying some word play, gave me enough of a respite to remember that the day's mind-numbing efforts had a purpose: It takes a lot of bean-counting, office-supply ordering, phone-message answering, etc. for the things that matter to me— writing books, counseling people who need support, teaching classes, etc.—to happen. I'm going to go eat a salad now, picked out of my garden. It's far too late in the day to have not eaten lunch. Then, my spirit and body nourished, I'll be ready to re-enter the fray.

The Mysteries of Rural Life Explained

Now that I've been in rural Pennsylvania a year, I understand a lot about the country. To save you some of the time I spent learning my way—or, more honestly, stumbling through my new life with a suddenly irrelevant citified perspective—here's what I've learned:

---

* To expand on my earlier suggestion about calligraphy: It can easily be yet another helpful inner resource. Even if you suck at it, it frees the mind from the modern onslaught of media, digital info, and financial stress. This applies to many situations. For example, an unexpected onslaught of home repair bills had me terribly upset. How the heck was I going to come up with that much money? Adding up the sum and making other related notes, I found myself calligraphing it all—including calligraphic décor in the margins—without any intention or forethought of doing so! Nevertheless, doing calligraphy almost *immediately* freed me from a large part of my immense and dreadful anxiety! Gone! And as I said earlier, the quality of pen-work was irrelevant; it was not done carefully, thoroughly, or precisely; the *process* is what helped me.

Don't even bother to take calligraphy lessons; when you need to put words to paper, use your everyday, ordinary pen and just play. As to calligraphic decorations, make doodles! If you eventually find you want to develop the art of calligraphy more, *then* take lessons.

♦ When it comes to plant identification, for some bizarre reason, everything's in the mint family.

♦ This would be more useful information if the family wasn't so diverse. Some of its members not only taste nasty on lamb but could also poison you.

♦ My friend Dixie is right, there's no fresh air out here. Everyone burns old tires, vinyl shingles, and plastic wrap in their backyards. Okay, not *everyone*. But enough folks to consistently require that you bring your patio brunch indoors or put on a gas mask!

♦ The dream of going to an untouched place is just that—a dream. Neighbor-induced air pollution is only one example. Here's another: Before there was curbside pick-up, the back lots of many houses were used as the owner's personal dumpsite. Since this often went on for years, I shudder to think what's under my vegetable garden.

♦ The implausibility of retreating to a serenely undefiled place is even clearer when I walk in my local woods. Though they're utterly fabulous to be in, an absolute gift from the Divine, there's nevertheless something wrong with them, a lethargy, a weakness, even a sadness. I can't explain why this is so, or how I know it. I'm no scientist. But I'm convinced my subconscious mind is picking up visual cues; and I'm *surely* feeling the problem *energetically*—a stroll through nature doesn't feel nearly as good as it once did.

♦ This reinforces two things for me. The first is the extent to which we've hurt our planet. This is a motivating realization, fueling my commitment to a healthy environment.

♦ The second reminder is—as I've said elsewhere herein— that problems are inevitable no matter how you handle your affairs. That includes choosing a new location. Not that I regret leaving the city; it was one of the best things I ever did for myself. But we can't run away from life with its ups and downs; we *have* to come to grips—and even accept—difficult circumstances.* And with that, onto other aspects of the country life:

♦ Despite media's portrayal, people aren't stupid here. They only pretend to be. They're very savvy to take advantage of a cliché like that, which makes them very dangerous. Or a lot of fun, depending on whether they're your pals or not. If you are, they let you in on a lot of jokes.

♦ The gorgeous flowers by the roadside are not for picking. They're growing on the edge of someone's property. Everyone here has guns.

♦ This is not to say they're all yokels. Only some of them are. Probably the same percentage as are comparably unbearable in the city.

♦ To quote a pal, everyone in Pennsylvania hunts. It's actually necessary, because otherwise the deer population will become insanely huge. We need to issue birth control to all those soon-to-be-mothers of Bambis. Until then, we need to issue hunting licenses.

---

* This is not a suggestion that you surrender to limitations in *unhealthy* ways.

◆ Besides, as long as you eat what you kill, good for you. (Don't argue by proposing the kindness of vegetarianism to me. Carrots scream when you pull them out of the ground. *No* one wants to be eaten. And eat we must.)

◆ However, it's really weird to look out your front window one day, and see a guy walking past in full camouflage costume, with a rifle slung over his shoulder. "La, la, la, I'm off to kill Bambi," being all casual about it—and, understand, *here* this is a run-of-the-mill scene, on par with someone strolling out of a 7-11 sipping on a Coke in the city.

◆ It's important to own a bright orange vest, hat, or other article of clothing that identifies you as not deer.

◆ It's also good when first moving in to ask your next-door neighbor if anyone ever hunts in the woods on your own lot.

   "No, except my son might go over with his bow and arrow."

◆ Do I need to add that one should respond, "Oh. Well, um, please tell him not to do that anymore. I like hanging out in my woods, and I don't want to be hit by an arrow"?

◆ Also, don't believe the neighbors who say, "No one uses a gun to hunt deer that are close to our houses. That would be illegal." Yes, they're telling the truth about the law. But one of them is bound to be lying about the rest, and all it takes is one shot.

◆ Speaking of bad eggs: When you're hanging out on your rural porch, watching the bunnies, butterflies, and bumblebees, you might have a neighbor across the road. If, sitting in your wicker chair, you eventually notice that it's a house filled only with dudes, single cars seem to constantly arrive then depart shortly thereafter, and weeknights there's a whole *bevy* of vehicles parked out front 'til dawn, yes, drug dealers live in the country, too. (In fact, it is a major rural problem.)

♦ I've also learned the ramifications of there not being as many people here. The U.P.S. deliveryman, who sees you at nine a.m. with your makeup smeared because you didn't wash it off the night before, may be the only single male you'll meet in a month. He also is the brother of the postal carrier you luckily refrained from blowing up at yesterday. Otherwise, both your mail and U.P.S. packages would never arrive. At least not intact.

And with this small a community, everyone takes care of you. In San Francisco, I was locked out of my apartment one night. A neighbor three doors down refused to let me in to call a locksmith. Here, the guy at the vacuum cleaner store lets you borrow merchandise to see if you like it enough to buy it, and doesn't want a credit card number or address for collateral. You hear a lawnmower in your front yard and look out to see a neighbor mowing unasked, because he knows you're too sick to do it yourself.

Just don't sleep with anyone married. The postal carrier'll know.

♦ Country life hasn't dulled my edge but sharpened it; solitude provides new creativity, greater awareness of global issues, and more effectiveness in community efforts. As a result, my work even has new *international* impact.

It's hard to stay on course living in the local conservative milieu. I'm constantly looked down on for being enthusiastic, thinking big, or having priorities that don't keep me small and fearful. I get lonely from this, too. But my global community and few good friends here keep me sane and on track. And when you tune into *yourself*, mad hatter though you may be, you discover the entire world. I was right to believe in the importance of "going nowhere" and to allay my fear that leaving the city would mean no longer being in the mix.

♦ Finally, this move has convinced me that, whatever your crazy dream, whether moving to a penthouse or an igloo, opening a health food store or a sex toy store, starting a novel or a revolution, you should do it. Sure, you need to plan first. Sure, you don't want to go off half-cocked. But, then, do it! It's worth the risks, it's worth the risks.

Environment as Affirmation

This book uses affirmations. I love them. They truly can shift one's being for the better. But one's environment can be an even more powerful affirmation.

For example, the words "I'm worth a nice home" can help some people feel better about themselves, but saying it by cleaning your kitchen can impact you even more. (This may not seem true until you try it. The effectiveness of many practices becomes evident only when you use them. Yes, I've said this earlier. I can't stop myself from making a few last repetitions, as we near the final pages.) Ask yourself what you can change in your home to mirror your self-worth back to you. A clean kitchen does that for *me*, but what works for you might be different. Another example: Does each room of your home have one thing that reflects your values, affirming them to you by reminding you of them?

When trying to make your environment an affirmation, don't expect too much of yourself. And don't be all or nothing. E.g., cleaning a whole kitchen's a big chore. It can be too intimidating. For me, it's more than I should even *do*, what with my disabilities. But if I clear off and clean just the kitchen counter, and maybe light a pretty candle on it, it looks so nice that I feel great. And that may also motivate me to do a bit more environment affirmations over the next few days or so. Every bit helps me feel better.

Environment is not just physical surroundings. We are who we hang out with. A successful, happy person has a vibe that rubs off on you. It's like being in the company of a walking, talking, good-luck charm.

Place is usually more powerful than any words, when it comes to changing us for the better or the worse. One of the few times remarks are as strong as place is when they *create* environment. Snide or cruel comments build a disdainful unsafe surrounding that can make you shrink into yourself. Declarations of praise surround you with nurturing warmth. When trying to support loved ones or build community, think about what environment your words—*and the tone in which you say them*—create.

I've tried to make this book an environment of health

and change for the better, in which you could reside simply
by reading. In other words, I've tried to craft words the way a
landscape painter carefully applies paint to construct a terrain.
It is where I live my crazy life so successfully.

    While you've read, you've done more than read about
that terrain or that insanity. You've been sharing both. I so
hope you've enjoyed traveling this terrain with me. I can't think
of a way to thank you enough—really, for *once* words fail
me—for your visit with me. My goal has been, and still is, for
you to thoroughly thoroughly *thoroughly*: Know your beauty,
be free, and fulfill your daring fantasies.

Middle management for chaos gods, mystic genius, and your
grateful servant,

Francesca De Grandis

Appendix

Resources for Illuminated Lunatics

I've made a life's work of creating services and goods tailored to people who want to be on the leading edge of the leading edge. So this guide starts with what I offer, then moves onto other resources. I cannot be held personally responsible for the results of using any goods or services below, blah, blah, blah, etc., etc.

♦ **The *Share My Insanity* Guide is free**. It includes a Study Group Guide and a Play Group Guide: You can benefit others and yourself by sharing the book through either an event that meets for several weeks or through a one-time playtime. For a book discussion group, class, church, coven, night off from the children, mid-workday lunch, pajama party, salon, or other gathering. It needn't be an "official" group. Email me for the guide.

♦ **Embrace ecstatic union with nature and cosmos.** Another Step is nature spirituality without dogma: earthy, wild mysticism. This curriculum is for people of any faith (or happy lack thereof). Or study the equally passionate Third Road—a Goddess tradition of Faerie shamanism. Both curriculums evolve your spirit and DNA, light years past both mainstream and alternative lifestyles. They help you find and embody your unique truths and core desires 100%. Third Road or Another Step = sacred madness helps hearts soar.

◆ **Founded 1986, Another Step is a body of mystical teachings** and tools that supports the wild soul you are—or would like to be. Lessons address challenges that independent thinkers face. Drawing on ancient transformative practices and wisdoms, as well as on my inner resources, I developed Another Step's innovative modalities and theories. I've taken alternative methods of spiritual healing and empowerment *another step*, so we can go the last nine yards to our personal dreams, human rights, and Gaia's well-being.

◆ **Third Road classes and books are Wiccan.** My style of Wicca embodies the following philosophy and provides tools to implement it: We need no priest to tell us how to act. Anyone can talk directly to Deity; hierarchical dogma can be replaced with connectivity and personal revelation, through which one finds Goddess, self, and wholeness.

◆ **I love Wicca, so am heartbroken** that it's become one more organized religion with large sectors that insist on set beliefs and liturgies, invalidating thousands of sincere seekers. The word *Wicca* has come to represent an oppressive approach to many people. I don't renege on my Wiccan teachings; I just call them *pagan* sometimes or explain that they're my *own* teachings, and I stand by them.

   Like Another Step, Third Road is earth-based mysticism and an ecstatic path. It's also magical practices for the Goddess's children. But, *nowadays*, calling it *Wicca* confuses some folks about what I teach. I will use the word, though. The Goddess frees us from oppression: It is important for non-fundie Wiccan traditions to remain.

   My Wiccan books are *Goddess Initiation* (HarperSanFrancisco) and *Be a Goddess!* (HarperSanFrancisco).

And ***Be a Teen Goddess! Magical Charms,
Spells, and Wiccan Wisdom for the Wild Ride of Life***
(Citadel) provides power steering. No talking down to the reader,
no lies. Adults find this book as useful as teens. ***The Ecstatic
Goddess! Wild Meditations, Lyrical Rituals, and Earth
Sexuality for the Pagan Heart*** has poetry in the ancient
Faerie Faith tradition. Each poem is a rite: an invocation that helps
you feel the Goddess beside you right *now;* ceremonies that tune
you into Gaia's beauty and bounty; or something extra to add to a
ritual you're creating.

♦ ***Any of my books add elements to the work you've
done in Share My Insanity,*** to maintain and further spiritual
and material abundance.

♦ Moving on: **I have taught creative process** to newbies
and pros in a variety of artistic fields for over two decades. Some
classes focus specifically on this. Private sessions available.

♦ **Study where you live.** Almost all my classes—Goddess
Spirituality, interfaith earth-mysticism, and creative process—are
teleseminars: **classes by telephone.** No computer or special
equipment needed. Participate simply by dialing the phone. (See
below for how to get info about upcoming classes.) I've set up
a lifestyle that allows me authentic relationship with clients and
students. Be in now with me. Get in on the ground level of the
cosmos' moment to moment.

♦ **Contact me at outlawbunny@outlawbunny.com
or via The Wiccan & Faerie Grimoire of Francesca De
Grandis,** at www.well.com/user/zthirdrd/WiccanMiscellany.html,
where you'll also find Goddess poetry, rituals, and articles. There's
detailed info about The Third Road there, too, and **instructions**

for how to be on my emailing list to receive my free e-newsletters, helpful spiritual hints, and news of upcoming books, classes, and other events. I created this grassroots website to provide free educational material and nurture high standards of Wiccan training and ethics.

♦ **Or contact me via www.outlawbunny.com**, my site where pagans and other free spirits explore everything-under-the-sun. It's an interfaith, interdisciplinary intertwining of newly evolving DNA. Topics range from personal growth to environmental issues to art to cooking. The site is for the *whole* you. Blogs, a detailed description of Another Step classes, and more. All sorts of people visit me there, which I love. **Instructions for how to be on my aforementioned emailing list are also at this site.**

♦ My mega-many projects mean that I could not possibly do enough website revisions, tweets, and blogs to cover everything I'm doing.

But **anyone can stay current re my classes, brilliant insights, books, music, life's synchronicities, and all the other stuff that drives me: Sign up for my emailing list.** I only send a few emails a month.

♦ **To be even *more* current, move into oral tradition** with me. Nothing can replace it. We can progress faster and to greater depths, in ways written words and social media can't facilitate and can never catch up with. A significant portion of my forward-thinking work happens only within oral tradition. We can go places that no book or website can bring us. I can't explain how or why. Words fail.

Oral tradition can't be explained, only experienced. Descriptions of my classes can't convey the methodologies used in them. My books can't represent oral teachings.

Oral transmissions have no contemporary reference point. So *any* way I describe them might elicit the response, "Social media (psychological counseling, a class, a support group, a discussion group, <u>fill in the blank</u>) does *that*." Oral tradition can happen *in* a class, and might involve a support or discussion group, but it is something unto itself.

And stating its incredibly immense benefits sounds like hype!

Since words can't explain it, the important thing here is to invite you to join me in it. And to say I want you to have it because I honestly care about you. Please check it out. It's the most powerful tool for inner transformation I've personally experienced or used to help others. I'm *thoroughly* embedded in it. As devoted as I am to the *written* word, I'm equally if not more devoted to oral transmission. They each have their place.

I use books and social media to connect with a lot of people, as well as to try to create an all-encompassing weave around them—surround them with a blanket of beauty, love, and power. But books and social media weave *part* of the cloth, something different from what oral tradition weaves. Oral transmission's loom is the moment of our togetherness. It is a living, breathing now and experience. It's *being*.

It's an all-encompassing weave of the moment of our togetherness and is being, *being*, being together with people within an all-embracing cosmos.

It is about presence and being.

And phone can be its vehicle, so I teach and counsel by phone.

♦ **The doorway into my oral teachings** is to sign up for my emailing list. From there, a lot of options show themselves, like classes and free global rites that meet via group phone calls; the newsletters announce their dates. **Or call me for *yet* more info: 814-337-2490.** Yes, you can call me. My spirituality's about connectivity. And spiritual "leaders" need to be available.

Using the phone is one more thing that makes me a weirdo *nowadays*, but I'm to the point, not wasting your time. Email me your phone #; I'm happy to call *you* to save you the expense, as long as you're in the U.S.

If you felt this book deeply, but are phone shy or don't think phone-classes can go deep: If a *book* helped you, imagine how much we can accomplish when we're actually together, even by phone! As to shy: Come lurk at one of the global rites to feel it out.

Call me to ask how my counseling or classes flesh out, maintain, or add to benefits gained through *Share My Insanity*. We can get happier and happier.

♦ **Another way we can connect: I twitter as @outlawbunny**. I follow back (unless you tweet more than I can manage).

♦ **Down-to-earth, professional, spiritual guidance by phone. Pastoral counseling—renegade style by crazy shaman**, me. For pagans and other wild hearts, to help you live fully and make a difference. Celebrate your inner diversity. Be supported as an individual with your own style, needs, and goals. I work with people all over the world. My sites have further info. If that's not enough info about counseling, or you're ready to make an appointment, **call 814-337-2490**.

♦ *The Modern Goddess' Guide to Life: How to Be Absolutely Divine on a Daily Basis*, which I wrote for women, is an easy-read insane guide to *many* aspects of life, is a humor self-help book, and is interfaith (though *Goddess* in the title may imply otherwise).

♦ **Faerie Nation is a global village of happily mad folks**. Learn more at www.outlawbunny.com and go to our online group at http://groups.yahoo.com/group/faerienation to make illuminating jokes about social change, dialog about spiritual concerns, or hang out on-line with like-minded lunatics.

♦ **Imagine how Faeries adorn themselves and their tree houses.** Elvin décor for your enchanted cottage and secret retreat. Wearable talismanic art. Fantasies. Indie culture. Busy bunny. Check out www.outlawbunny.etsy.com. (Talismanic visual art is a way to serve community despite being housebound. Service makes me whole. Illness keeps me home, but my spirit travels; my art connects me to people everywhere, and I get to add beauty to their lives.)

Also available in my online shop: I indie-produced an award-winning album, *Pick the Apple from the Tree*—original Goddess Spirituality music by a shamanic-bard: me. There's also a spoken word album, *Bardic Alchemy: Enchanted Tales about the Quest for God/dess and Self*. The search for Divinity and self can feel like a solitary struggle. The stories create a richly mythic matrix—real and palpable—in which you can thrive, celebrate life, overcome challenges, and center into your truths.

♦ **For advice** about the mystic's realms or your specific life situation, networking help, or referrals, I hope you'll think that my books, websites, classes, professional counseling sessions, and online Faerie Nation group (see above) are great.

By the time I'm done with them, and related correspondence, I can't answer letters, emails, or phone requests asking for advice about the mystic's realms or your specific life situation . . .

♦ **I regret that I can't answer email asking me for free advice**. I hate that you can't be an exception even if you're clever, in crisis, or unusual. I'm already swamped with gratis work for the clever, in crisis, and unusual. To serve you well, maintain my dubious sanity working full-time at a grassroots level, and protect my health, I need these boundaries. I'm here to serve you—really want to—and hope you understand the limits of my abilities. Thank you *bunches*.

♦ **It is an honor for me to hear from you. Please write just to say "Hi,"** tell me how this book went for you, what you think of the web sites, or what you'd like to see in another book. Even if it takes six months, I'll find the time to answer.

♦ **Below are more resources for the healthily mad.** Some represent folks on the leading edge of *their* field, with work so good I have to turn you onto it.

♦ **Yoficosmetics.com rocks!** They've an unbelievable range of glitter. **Important**: Some glitter can't be used near eyes; if it gets *in* an eye, you're off to the hospital, big time. Certain Yofi glitters are specifically made for use around eyes, thank goodness! Pink glitter on the eyelid is God, and God is key!

♦ **The innovative Annie M. Sprinkle, Ph. D.** describes herself an artist, sexecologist, author, lecturer, educator, faculty wife, thespian, pioneering film director and performer, former sex worker. She says that she's "all about ecosex now, and making love with the earth . . . ecosex walking tours, ecosex weddings, ecosex symposiums." Elizabeth Stephens is her partner in all this. http://loveartlab.org/

♦ **Susun Weed's work is the epitome of herbal medicine.** I probably say that because, independently of each other, we developed similar theories underpinning our bodies of work. (Have I *no* shame?) But if you like my work, you might enjoy Susun's books, workshops, correspondence courses, free on-line herbal info, and other offerings. She also publishes cool books besides her own. www.susunweed.com

♦ **Candace Savage of Gypsy Moon clothing** committed to the mad dream of making a profession out of her artistry. Her *gorgeous* designs could dress you for *any* escapade. She says it's "about women, not fashion . . . creating clothing that goes beyond age, size, or outward appearance. Our creations . . . stir the imagination. We're driven by the savage rhythm of adventure." www.gypsymoon.com

♦ **Check out books from White River Press.** I'm putting White River Press in this guide not because it's my publisher. It's my publisher because I think it's cutting edge. I love that Linda Roghaar, who owns the house, spots gemlike books and decides to publish them *years* before other publishers recognize or act on them. (Okay, of *course* I'd think that, since she published this book, but I also can be objective, guys!) Linda says the press is "for experienced, published authors who cannot currently find a home in traditional publishing." Some of these are bestselling or award winning writers. Also, her innovative business model rocks, empowering authors without giving up good book distribution or losing high editorial and production standards. www.whiteriverpress.com

♦ **If your wild fantasy is homesteading,** you may be inspired by "one couple's dream to live a more self-sufficient life through homesteading in Northern Vermont. Through learning to garden organically, raise livestock, hunt . . . [they are] walking the path of their ancestors, who also raised sheep and goats . . . and trying to find [their] place in the natural world, with the land and with the animals that bring so much joy." http://www.gotgoats. com/

♦ **Paul B. Rucker's visionary paintings** are lush, dynamic, and accessible. He sums up his work as "Gods, Goddesses, Faeries, Angels, Body Art, and More," adding, "For me, making art nurtures a sense of the world as alive and full of meaning . . . I seek to open windows that offer [transcendental connections]." http:// paulruckerart.com

♦ **The Unitarian Universalist Church** honors diversity and has over 1,000 congregations. They tend to be places where freethinkers gather. Your local Unitarian Universalist (U.U.) Church may have members who walk Wiccan or other atypical paths. U.U. educational programs for children and young adults can be excellent. Check out www.uua.org for more info.

Acknowledgements

With my whole heart, I am grateful to the following people. My dear and irreplaceable friends, Kush and Vanna Z. Red, help me trust that what I long to express has value. Everyone else listed below has helped do the same. A whole slew of test readers—Kat Anderson, Rev. Steve Aschmann, Angie, and Kestril Trueseeker among them—generously and boldly pointed out where my manuscript was obnoxious, harmful, boring, etc. Kathi Somers' layout was pivotal, because layout was going to make or break this book. She also listens to my woes, without judgment. Ade Conway's copyediting was so necessary! Linda Roghaar is an extraordinary publisher. Adrienne Amundsen, Ph.D. and clinical psychologist, and others in the mental health community—some are caretakers, some suffer from mental disabilities, and some fall into both those categories—gave this project tremendous support. Kaitlin Hilinski is my enthusiastic and brilliant social media aid. The fabulous Kathleen Marshall did the tech work on the book's promotional vids. Through an Allegheny College publishing internship, Katie Selby did everything from type to unpack my new office. Millicent Long Broderick and some other folks also contributed typing. Today, authors pay many of publishing's costs. I didn't have even a "shoestring" to budget on. But people who purchased my art, intentionally to help cover author expenses, are true champions of indie-culture. My readers and students are fellow travelers beside me as we explore life's spiritual trails; I don't know what I would do without them. Steve Foster and Doric T. Jemison-Ball at BBS-LA (http://bbs-la.com) as well as Dawn Walker and Kathi Somers provide an immense amount of Internet and computer support. The Pink Bunny Tribe keeps me *literally* alive by doing dishes, running grocery trips, etc., since my physical disabilities are so extreme. Throughout the ages, tricksters were often hermaphrodites or otherwise outside the "norm;" many were nightmarishly harassed and misunderstood, including being wrongly diagnosed as mentally ill or actually *driven* insane. I am indebted beyond compare; tricksters of times past are the spiritual and biological ancestors of all present-day tricksters; may this book bless and feed them. The folks in the "fellowship" give me the chance for a real life. My Divine Mother and Father love me via every atom of the cosmos, and ultimately give me everything I'm acknowledging in these acknowledgements.

About the Author

Francesca De Grandis AKA Outlaw Bunny is multi-purpose: humorist, mystic, semi-recluse, public figure, Yule elf, bard, painter, mega-upcycler, spiritual innovator. Busy busy rabbit. She adds, "I don't try to be everything to everybody. I *do* help a *lot* of people find *their* everything—the huge world inside them and around them." Peter Coyote said, "Like all good humorists, Francesca De Grandis has a radical and subversive agenda." For 20+ years, she's been a grassroots minister and spiritual healer who helps people of all faiths—and those who are just fine without one—through pastoral counseling and classes. Her goal in this is to help others find both personal fulfillment and the power to make a difference in the world.

A one-woman interfaith community, she practices Goddess Spirituality and Chi Gung, is a long-time student of Taoism, and hangs out with Christ. She's also been told she's somewhat of a Buddhist. She's secretly a Druid. Francesca struggles spiritually because she's a brat, but she does her best and *tries* to stay tight with God.

Kidnapped by faeries when she was working as a musician and comedian, she completed a rigorous seven-year training to become a traditional spiritual healer. She created The Third Road, a Goddess Spirituality curriculum of transformative, sanity-sustaining, shamanic exercises taught globally through oral tradition, written text, and the Web. Her books *Be a Goddess!* (HarperSanFrancisco), *Goddess Initiation* (HarperSanFrancisco), and *Be a Teen Goddess!* are part of Third Road.

She crafted Another Step, an empowering curriculum for people of all faiths as well as those who are perfectly happy without one. Another Step, which Crazy Sage wisdom is part of, is practiced worldwide. Outlaw Bunny starts major international underground movements, often unintentionally.

She's a Renaissance woman. She's obviously an eccentric. She's effective: First as a shaman-poet who passed on her work orally, then as a published author, she's been a seminal influence on the literary and spiritual culture of earth-based spirituality, alternative thought, and self-help. Many of her poems—prayers, rituals, liturgy, meditations, and lectures (often presented as prose)—anonymously entered the oral and written literature of earth-centered and "new" spirituality. So have her innovative techniques. More important, people get *real* help from her, and long-lasting results.

De Grandis avoids formulaic approaches. Her groundbreaking material, in different mediums and genres, draws imitators and starts trends. That's not her intent. She doesn't even stick around to cash in. (Silly, silly rabbit.) She moves on to her next innovation. A lot of it happens solely within oral tradition, because it can only be conveyed orally. **"Resources for Illuminated Lunatics" explains more and shows the doorway into her oral teachings.**

After leaving the music business for a contemplative life as a mystic, she realized music is part of her spirituality. "Resources for Illuminated Lunatics" has more info.

De Grandis teaches both Third Road and Another Step through international teleseminars—classes through group phone calls. In addition, clients living everywhere from Boston to Canada to Arabia call her for professional pastoral counseling by phone.

After 25 years in San Francisco, she was kidnapped by faeries, *again*, and relocated to northwestern rural Pennsylvania, where she lives amidst trees and sylphs, tries unsuccessfully to avoid deep thoughts, and juggles a large number of projects. **"Resources for Illuminated Lunatics" has more about her work and contact info.**

CPSIA information can be obtained at www.ICGtesting.com
Printed in the USA
BVOW011800150911

271343BV00001B/7/P